Competition Law in Croatia

Competition Law in Croatia

Second Edition

Jasminka Pecotić Kaufman
Vlatka Butorac Malnar
Dubravka Akšamović

This book was originally published as a monograph in the International Encyclopaedia of Laws/Competition Law.

Founding Editor: Roger Blanpain
General Editor: Frank Hendrickx
Volume Editors: Francesco Denozza & Alberto Toffoletto

Wolters Kluwer

Published by:
Kluwer Law International B.V.
PO Box 316
2400 AH Alphen aan den Rijn
The Netherlands
E-mail: lrs-sales@wolterskluwer.com
Website: www.wolterskluwer.com/en/solutions/kluwerlawinternational

Sold and distributed by:
Wolters Kluwer Legal & Regulatory U.S.
7201 McKinney Circle
Frederick, MD 21704
United States of America
E-mail: customer.service@wolterskluwer.com

ISBN 978-94-035-1626-4

e-Book: ISBN 978-94-035-1106-1
web-PDF: ISBN 978-94-035-1106-1

The Authors

Jasminka Pecotić Kaufman is Professor of Law at the University of Zagreb (Department of Law, Faculty of Economics and Business), where she teaches Competition Law, and Commercial and Company Law. She is President of the Croatian Competition Law and Policy Association (HDPPTN), Co-Director of ASCOLA (Academic Society for Competition Law) South-East Europe Chapter, Member of the Editorial Board of the Yearbook of Antitrust and Regulatory Studies (YARS), Member of the International Advisory Board of the Institute for Consumer Antitrust Studies (Loyola University Chicago), and Non-Governmental Advisor (NGA) for the International Competition Network (ICN). Her recent research has focused on the challenges of enforcing competition rules in European post-socialist countries. Professor Pecotić Kaufman's work has appeared in the *Journal of Antitrust Enforcement*, the *World Competition Law and Economics Review*, and the *Yearbook of Antitrust and Regulatory Studies*, among other journals. She co-authored several books on competition law, including *Competition Law and State Aid Law* (in Croatian, University of Zagreb Faculty of Law, 2021).

Vlatka Butorac Malnar is Associate Professor at the Faculty of Law, University of Rijeka, where she teaches Competition Law and European Private Law to both undergraduate and postgraduate students. She is Vice President of the Croatian Association of Competition Law and Policy, a non-governmental advisor for the ICN, a member of ICC and of the scientific board of the Yearbook of Antitrust and Regulatory Studies, and a member of the International Advisory Board of the Legal Yearbook IPP-PF. She holds LLM and SJD degrees from the Central European University, Budapest, Hungary. Over the years, she has researched in a number of academic institutions (Cornell Law School, NY, USA; Max-Planck Institute for Comparative and International Private Law, Hamburg, Germany; the European University Institute, Florence, Italy). She writes mostly on competition law and is the co-author of the Croatian textbook *Competition Law and State Aid*

The Authors

Law published by the University of Zagreb Faculty of Law in 2021. She is engaged in educational activities for legal practitioners and national and EU judges.

Dubravka Akšamović (LLM, PhD) is Professor of Law at the Faculty of Law, Osijek, Croatia. She is also a director of Master's programme in Business Law at Faculty of Law in Osijek. She obtained her bachelor's degree at the Faculty of Law in Osijek. In 2003, she passed the Bar exam. In 2008, she defended her PhD in Competition Law. She regularly teaches the following courses in undergraduate and postgraduate studies: Contract Law, Company Law, Competition Law, and Insolvency Law. She is the head of the clinical programme at the Faculty of Law in Osijek and one of the founders of the Croatian Association for Competition Law and Policy. From 2018 to 2021 she held a Jean Monnet Module in EU Competition Law at the Faculty of Economics in Osijek. Since 2022 she holds Jean Monnet Center of Excellence in EU Competition Law. She regularly participates in international conferences in Croatia and abroad. She has participated as a speaker at conferences in some of the most prominent universities, including Stanford University, Columbia University, City School of London, Humboldt University, and ELTE Hungary. She has published numerous articles, essays, and chapters in books devoted to different fields of law. She is a member of several domestic and international associations, including the Croatian Academy of Legal Science, GAJE, and ENCLE.

Table of Contents

The Authors 3

List of Abbreviations 11

General Introduction 13

§1. General Background of the Country 13
I. Geography and Climate 13
II. Population and Values 14
III. Political System and Territorial-Administrative Structure 15

§2. Economic System 18

§3. Legal System 19

§4. Historical Background of Antitrust Law 20

Part I. Structure of Antitrust Law and Its Enforcement 25

Chapter 1. Sources of Antitrust Law 25

§1. National Sources 25
I. The Constitution 25
II. The Competition Act 26
III. Procedural Rules 26
IV. Private Enforcement of Competition Rules 26

§2. International Sources 27
I. EU Law 27
II. International Agreements 27

§3. Secondary Sources 28
I. Regulations 28
A. EU Regulations 28
B. Croatian Regulations 28
II. Guidelines 29

§4. Relation and Hierarchy of Sources 29

§5. Role and Authority of Precedents 30

Chapter 2. Scope of Application 31

§1. Territorial Reach 31

§2. Special Sectors 33

§3. State-Owned Enterprises and Public Utilities 35

§4. Sensible Effect and *De Minimis* 37

Chapter 3. Overview of Substantive Provisions 41

§1. Restrictive Agreements 41

§2. Dominant Undertakings 42

§3. Concentrations 45

§4. Other Prohibitions 51

§5. Tests of Illegality 51
I. Per Se Prohibitions and Naked Restraints 51
II. Balancing Tests 51
III. Merger Tests 52

Chapter 4. Overview of Main Notions 56

§1. Undertaking 56

§2. Relevant Market 62
I. Relevant Product Market 63
II. Relevant Geographic Market 66
III. Temporal Markets 66

§3. Market Power/Dominant Position 67

§4. Agreements and Concerted Practices 69

§5. Restriction of Competition 70

§6. Monopolization and Abuse of Dominance 72

§7. Concentrations 73

§8. Joint Ventures 75

Chapter 5. Consequences of Violations and Enforcement Institutions 77

§1. Administrative Enforcement 77
I. Antitrust Authorities 77
A. Formation, Composition 77
B. Investigating Powers 80
C. Adjudicating Powers (Ascertaining and Sanctioning) 80
1. Finding and Bringing to an End an Infringement of Competition Rules 81
2. Commitment Decisions 83
3. Fining 85
D. Other Institutional Tasks (Consultancy to Parliament/ Government) 85
II. Government Direct Enforcement Activities 86
III. Other Administrative Agencies Applying Antitrust Rules 86
IV. Administrative Fines 86
A. Introduction 86
B. Amount of Fines 87
C. Calculating Fines 88
D. Enforcement of Fines 90
E. Fines Within the Leniency Programme 92
F. Daily Penalties 94
G. Settlement in Cartel Proceedings 95
V. Administrative Injunctions and Other Restrictive Orders 95
VI. Interim Measures 97

§2. Civil Enforcement 98
I. Competent Civil Courts 98
II. Sanctions 99
A. Nullity 99
B. Damages 100
1. Scope of Application 101
2. Substantive Law Issues 102
3. Procedural Issues 108
4. Consensual Dispute Resolution 114
C. Interim Measures 115

§3. Criminal Enforcement 117
I. Criminal Sanctions for Antitrust Violations 117
II. Other Applications of Criminal Law to Relevant Conduct 119
III. Role of Prosecutors 120
IV. Competent Criminal Courts 120

Part II. Application of Prohibitions 121

Chapter 1. Restrictive Agreements 121

§1. Horizontal Agreements 121
I. Cartels 121
A. Price-fixing 123
B. Market/Client Allocation 133
C. Production/Innovation Limitation 135
D. Group Boycott 135
E. Collusion on Other Objects 135
II. Information Exchange Practices 137
III. Cooperation Agreements 139
A. Research and Development 139
B. Specialization 140
C. Standardization 140
D. Joint Production 140
E. Joint Purchasing 140
F. Joint Selling 140

§2. Vertical Agreements 141
I. Distribution 145
A. Exclusive Distributorship 145
B. Exclusive Dealing 146
C. Selective Distribution 147
D. Franchising 153
II. Technology Licensing 153
A. Patent Licensing 153
B. Trademark Licensing 153
C. Know-How and Trade Secret Licensing 153

Chapter 2. Prohibited Practices of Dominant Undertakings 155

§1. Exploitative Practices 155
I. Excessive/Unfair Pricing 155
II. Discrimination 159

§2. Exclusionary Practices 163
I. Predation 163
II. Tying 166
III. Rebates 169
IV. Refusal to Deal 173
V. Price Squeeze 175

Chapter 3. Concentrations 177

§1. Horizontal Mergers 178

§2. Vertical Mergers 179

§3. Market/Product Extension Mergers 181

§4. Pure Conglomerate Mergers 182

§5. Joint Ventures 182

Part III. Administrative Procedure 185

Chapter 1. Administrative Investigations Before the Antitrust Authority 185

§1. Initiative 185
I. General Sector Inquiries 185
II. Ex Officio Investigations 186
III. Complaints 187

§2. Powers 188
I. Requests for Information 188
II. Investigating and Search Powers 190
III. Cooperation with Other State Institutions 194

§3. Right of Defence 194
I. Content and Notification of Opening Decisions 195
II. Proceedings: Hearings, Access to File, Briefs 195
III. Statement of Objections 197
IV. Final Hearing and Decision 198

Chapter 2. Voluntary Notifications and Clearance Decision & Merger Control 200

§1. Preliminary Filing Obligations 200
I. Criteria and Thresholds 203
II. Turnover Calculation 204
III. Market Share Calculation 206
IV. Other Relevant Notions 207

§2. Structure of Proceedings 208
I. Preliminary Assessment and Full Investigation 208
A. Initial Investigation: Phase I 208
B. In-Depth Investigation: Phase II 210

II. Time Framework 211
III. Right of Defence 211

§3. Clearance and Conditional Clearance 212
I. Conditions and Undertakings 212
A. Content 212
B. Timing 217

§4. Relations with Other Merger Control Authorities 217
I. Other Authorities Within Local Jurisdiction 217
II. International Coordination 218

Chapter 3. Challenging of the Administrative Decision 219

§1. Competent Courts 219
I. Constitutional Court 223
II. Commercial Courts 225

§2. Time Limits 226

§3. Scope of Judicial Review 226

Selected Bibliography 229

Index 235

List of Abbreviations

AEM	Agency for Electronic Media
BER	Block Exemption Regulation
CA	Competition Act
CCA	Croatian Competition Agency
CCC	Croatian Chamber of Commerce
CMO	Common Organization of the Markets of Fishery and Aquaculture Products
CPA	Civil Procedure Act
EA	Enforcement Act
EC	European Communities
ECJ	European Court of Justice
ECN	European Competition Network
EEC	European Economic Community
EU	European Union
GDP	Gross Domestic Product
HAKOM	Croatian Regulatory Authority for Network Industries
HANFA	Croatian Financial Services Supervisory Agency
HERA	Croatian Energy Regulatory Agency
HHI	Herfindahl-Hirschman Index
HRK	Croatian Kuna
IA	Interim Agreement on Trade and Trade-related Matters
ICN	International Competition Network
NATO	North Atlantic Treaty Organization
NCA	National Competition Authority
OA	Obligations Act
OECD	Organization of Economic Cooperation and Development
RPM	Resale Price Maintenance
SAA	Stabilization and Association Agreement
SFRY	Socialist Federative Republic of Yugoslavia
SME	Small and Medium Enterprise
TFEU	Treaty on the Functioning of the European Union

List of Abbreviations

UN	United Nations
UNCTAD	United Nations Conference on Trade and Development
WTO	World Trade Organization

General Introduction

§1. GENERAL BACKGROUND OF THE COUNTRY

I. Geography and Climate

1. The Republic of Croatia is a democratic parliamentary republic situated in southeastern Europe.[1] It extends over an area of 56,594 km^2, surrounded by the Alps in the west, the Sava and Drava rivers in the north and east, and the Adriatic Sea in the south. It has 1,244 islands, fifty of which are permanently inhabited. Croatia borders with Slovenia, Hungary, Serbia, Bosnia and Herzegovina, Montenegro, and Italy. The most southern part of Croatian territory – the area surrounding Dubrovnik – is a practical exclave (pene-exclave) separated from the rest of the mainland by a short coastline of Bosnia and Herzegovina, but connected with the rest of the country by the territorial waters of the Adriatic Sea. The capital city of Croatia is Zagreb, and the official language is Croatian, a Slavic language of the Indo-European family. The official currency is the Kuna, where one kuna is divided into 100 lipa. As of 1 January 2023, the Croatian official currency will be the EURO.

2. Croatia has a geographically very diverse terrain comprising plains, low mountains, and highlands. Consequently, different regions are characterized by different climates. Northern Croatia has a continental climate, Central Croatia a mountainous climate, and the Adriatic coast a Mediterranean climate. The sunniest parts of the Republic of Croatia are the outer islands of the middle Adriatic (Vis, Lastovo, Biševo, and Svetac) and the western shores of the islands of Hvar and Korčula, with more than 2,700 sunshine hours yearly. Its beautiful coastline and climate make Croatia a popular tourist destination.

3. Croatia is very rich in terms of biodiversity which is safeguarded by the Nature Protection Act.[2] Currently, there are 419 protected areas in the Republic of Croatia accounting for 8.19% of the total national territory. Protected areas include strict reserves, national parks, special reserves, regional parks, park forests, nature monuments, significant landscapes, and nature parks, which account for the largest

1. Figures and data used in this section are sourced from the Croatian Bureau of Statistics, *Census 2011*, *Statistical Information 2013*, *Statistical Yearbook 2016*, *Croatia in Figures 2015* and *A Statistical Portrait of Croatia in the European Union 2013*, all available at http://www.dzs.hr/default_e.htm (accessed 4 Oct. 2017).
2. Official Gazette no. 08/13.

share of all protected areas (4.79% of the total national territory). Some of the protected areas have been recognized as areas of international importance. Plitvice Lakes are included on the UNESCO World Heritage List, Velebit Mountain is part of the international network of biosphere reserves (UNESCO's scientific programme Man and Biosphere – MaB), while five areas are included on the Ramsar List of Wetlands of International Importance – Kopački Rit, Lonjsko Polje, Neretva Delta, Crna Mlaka, and Vransko Lake.[3]

II. Population and Values

4. According to the last census conducted in 2021, the Republic of Croatia has 3,888,529 inhabitants, 769,944 of whom live in the capital city of Zagreb.[4] With seventy-eight inhabitants per km^2, Croatia is loosely populated when compared to other European Union (EU) countries that have an average of 115 inhabitants per km^2.[5]

5. The sex structure of the population shows that women slightly outnumber men (51.8% women and 48.2% men) due to their higher life expectancy. Despite a slight increase in the fertility rate over the last decade (between 1.3 and 1.5 children per woman from 2002 to 2011), Croatia is still an aging country with a negative natural change. The average age is 41.7 years, which renders the Croatian population among the oldest in Europe.[6]

6. Ethnically, Croatia is a very homogenous country. The national structure shows that 90.42% of citizens are Croats by nationality. The highest minority group is Serbs (4.36%) followed by Bosniaks (0.73%), Italians (0.42%), Albanians (0.41%), and Roma (0.40%). The same homogeneous structure may be observed in religious affiliation: 86.28% are Catholics, 4.4% Orthodox, and 1.47% Muslims. Other religious groups have a share lower than 1.00%.[7]

7. Croatia has a relatively low number of immigrants, the majority of whom are Croatian nationals. The share of foreign citizens is only 0.53%. In 2011, only about 8,500 persons immigrated into Croatia which is a substantial decrease compared to the immigration figures recorded in 2001 (by about two-thirds).

3. Data in this subsection was sourced from the State Institute for Nature Protection, Ministry of Culture (Croatia), *Protected Areas in Croatia,* http://www.dzzp.hr/eng/protected-areas/protected-areas-in-croatia-68.html (accessed 4 Nov. 2016).
4. These are the first results from the 2021 Census, available at the Croatian Bureau of Statistics https://popis2021.hr/index.html (accessed 4 Feb. 2022).
5. Because the full analysis of the 2021 Census data is still not available, the rest of the data in this subsection was sourced from *Census 2011*, available at the Croatian Bureau of Statistics https://www.dzs.hr/default_e.htm (accessed 10 Mar. 2017).
6. Croatian Bureau of Statistics, *Census of Population, Households and Dwellings 2011, Population by Sex and Age, Statistical Reports* (2013).
7. Croatian Bureau of Statistics, *Census of Population, Households and Dwellings 2011, Population by Citizenship, Ethnicity, Religion and Mother Tongue, Statistical Reports* (2013).

8. In Croatia, 80.4% of the population between 25 and 64 years of age have completed secondary or higher education. Approximately 16% of the population above 15 years of age have successfully completed some form of higher (tertiary) education. Records show that the highest proportion of students studied the social sciences, business, and law (44%), followed by engineering, manufacturing, and construction (15.3%).[8]

9. Croatia safeguards pro-European and democratic values and affords high protection to human rights and fundamental freedoms guaranteed as the highest constitutional values of the domestic legal order.[9]

III. Political System and Territorial-Administrative Structure

10. Croatia is an independent sovereign state, a democratic parliamentary republic that declared its independence from the former Socialist Federative Republic of Yugoslavia (SFRY) in June 1991 (coming into effect on 8 October 1991). Resisting Croatian independence, the Yugoslav national army and paramilitary Serbian troops attacked Croatia, instigating the Homeland War, which effectively ended in 1995 when the Croatian army regained most of the occupied territories. Croatia restored the remaining occupied territories in January 1998 pursuant to the Erdut Agreement, which was enforced within the United Nations (UN) peace activities in Croatia.[10]

11. In 1992, Croatia became a member of the UN. In 2000, it became a member of the World Trade Organization (WTO), in 2009, it joined the North Atlantic Treaty Organization (NATO), and in 2013 the EU.[11]

12. The first multiparty elections in Croatia were held in 1990. The same year, the Croatian Parliament adopted the Croatian Constitution according to which Croatia operated as a semi-presidential system. Constitutional changes in 2000 and 2001 reformed the political system towards a parliamentary democracy. The last major amendments to the Croatian Constitution were made in 2010, preparing Croatia for accession to the EU.

---

8. Croatian Bureau of Statistics, *Census of Population, Households and Dwellings 2011, Population According to Education Features, Statistical Reports* (2016).
9. 'Freedom, equal rights, national and sexual equality, peacemaking, social justice, respect for human rights, inviolability of ownership, conservation of nature and the environment, the rule of law and a democratic multiparty system are the highest values of the constitutional order of the Republic of Croatia.' Article 3 of the Constitution of the Republic of Croatia, Official Gazette no. 56/1990, 135/1997, 113/2000, 28/2001, 76/2010 5/2014.
10. For a more detailed overview and discussion, *see* S. Fabijanić Gagro & B. Vukas, *The Path of the Former Yugoslav Countries to the European Union: From Integration to Disintegration and Back*, 12 Maastricht Journal of European and Comparative Law 300 (2012).
11. For a more detailed analysis, *see* B. Vukas, *The Process of the Establishment of the Independence of the Republic of Croatia from the Perspective of International Law*, 7 Review of Croatian History 11 (2012).

13. Croatia is a unitary and indivisible democratic welfare state. Power in Croatia derives from the people and rests with the people as a community of free and equal citizens.[12] The Croatian political system is based on the separation of powers among the legislative, executive, and judiciary branches, limited by the constitutionally guaranteed right to local and regional self-government. The principle of separation of powers encompasses cooperation and reciprocal checks and balances.[13]

14. Legislative power of the Republic of Croatia rests with the Croatian Parliament (*Sabor*). Originally, the Croatian Parliament consisted of the House of Representatives (*Zastupnički dom*), and the House of Counties (*&ZCaron;upanijski dom*), the latter being abolished on 28 March 2001. Since 2001, the Croatian Parliament has been a single chamber formed of Members of Parliament representing the people and elected for a term of four years. The Croatian Parliament may have no fewer than 100 and no more than 160 members, elected on the basis of direct, universal, and equal suffrage by secret ballot for a mandate of four years.[14] Members of Parliament do not have an imperative mandate and enjoy full immunity. The Croatian Parliament has a president and one or more vice presidents.

15. According to the Constitution, the Croatian Parliament:

> decides on the enactment of and amendments to the Constitution; passes laws; adopts the budget; decides on war and peace; adopts documents expressing the policy of the Croatian Parliament; adopts the National Security Strategy and the Defence Strategy of the Republic of Croatia; exercises civil control of the armed forces and security services of the Republic of Croatia; decides on alterations of the borders of the Republic of Croatia; calls referendums, conducts elections, appointments and dismissals in conformity with the Constitution and law; supervises the work of the Government of the Republic of Croatia and other holders of public offices reporting to the Croatian Parliament, in conformity with the Constitution and law; grants amnesty for criminal offences; and conducts other affairs as specified by the Constitution.[15]

16. The executive power of the Republic of Croatia is exercised by the government, consisting of a prime minister, one or more deputy prime ministers, and ministers.[16] The prime minister is usually the leader of the political party holding the majority in parliament. The Government of the Republic of Croatia 'proposes bills and other acts to the Croatian Parliament; proposes the central budget and annual accounts; executes laws and other decisions of the Croatian Parliament; adopts decrees to implement laws; conducts foreign and domestic policy; directs and controls the operation of the civil service; tends to the economic development of the

---

12. Article 1 of the Croatian Constitution.
13. Article 4 of the Croatian Constitution.
14. Articles 72 et seq. of the Croatian Constitution.
15. Article 81 of the Croatian Constitution.
16. Articles 108 et seq. of the Croatian Constitution.

country; directs the performance and development of public services; performs other duties determined by the Constitution and law'.[17]

17. The President of the Republic of Croatia represents the country at home and abroad, takes care of the stability of state power and, as commander in chief of the Croatian armed forces, safeguards the independence and territorial integrity of the state. The president is elected for a term of five years on the basis of direct universal and equal suffrage by secret ballot with the possibility of a re-election.[18]

18. The two major political parties in Croatia are the Social Democratic Party – SDP (centre-left socialist party) and the Croatian Democratic Union – HDZ (centre-right conservative party). Traditionally, there is strong rivalry between the left-wing and right-wing parties, led by the Socialist Democratic Party and the Croatian Democratic Union, respectively. Generally, the two parties alternate from mandate to mandate, either in coalition or alone. Currently, following the 2020 parliamentary election, the Croatian Democratic Union holds the largest number of seats in parliament with 62 out of 151 seats.[19]

19. The Croatian judiciary is formed by independent and autonomous courts. Ordinary courts of law are the municipal courts (first instance courts) and county courts (second instance courts). Besides ordinary courts, the Croatian judiciary has a number of special jurisdiction courts encompassing commercial, and administrative courts and their respective second instance courts, the High Commercial Court and the High Administrative Court in addition to the High Criminal Court and the High Misdemeanour Court, also special jurisdiction courts. The highest judicial instance is the Supreme Court that ensures the uniform application of laws and equality of citizens.

20. Besides the above-mentioned courts, a very important role is exercised by the Constitutional Court, having a range of specialized powers. Most important, it is empowered to strike down laws that are unconstitutional and decide on constitutional complaints.[20] While not empowered to decide on the constitutionality of legal acts, ordinary courts are among the bodies empowered to initiate proceedings before the Constitutional Court when in doubt about the constitutionality of a particular law.

21. Finally, Croatia is administratively divided into territorial local self-government units: counties (*županije*), municipalities (*općine*), and towns (*gradovi*).

17. Article 108 of the Croatian Constitution.
18. Articles 94 et seq. of the Croatian Constitution.
19. *See* https://www.sabor.hr/en/mps/statistical-indicators-mps (accessed 04. Feb 2022.).
20. Article 129 of the Constitution of the Republic of Croatia.

§2. Economic System

22. Following the collapse of the former Yugoslavia, Croatia went through transition from a socialist economy to a market-based economy. Its transition was slow, and the country suffered severe economic damage in the 1990s due to the Homeland War.[21] The economy started improving until the global financial crisis of 2008 whose consequences were felt until 2015, marking one of the longest and deepest recessions in Europe. According to the latest European Commission Report on Croatian's economy (2020), the GDP per capita in purchasing power standard was 63% of the EU average in 2018 and the country was termed a catch-up country.[22] In the Autumn 2021 forecast, the real GDP was predicted to grow by 8.1% in 2021, followed by 5.6% and 3.4% growth in 2022 and 2023.[23]

23. Croatian industry covers mining and extraction, process manufacturing, electricity, gas, steam and air conditioning, and water supply, and according to the data available for 2014, it amounts to 21.1% of Croatian Gross Domestic Product (GDP). In 2015, industrial exports amounted to EUR 10.0 billion (94.5% of total exports). Traditional process manufacturing branches are metal processing (24.9%), chemicals, pharmaceuticals, plastics and rubber production (13.7%), computers, electrical products and equipment (9.5%), food and beverages (8.1%), petroleum production (6.8%), and the wood processing industry (4.9%).[24] The Croatian economy is trade oriented, the most important part being the retail sector: '28.1% of the total number of registered economic entities is in the sector of trade, and this sector employs about 22.1% of the total number of the employed. The contribution of distributive trade to GDP amounts to 10%'.[25] Agriculture, forestry, and fishing contribute with 3.7% of Croatian GDP. Tourism plays a central role in the Croatian economy, contributing greatly to the country's GDP and seasonal employment.[26]

---

21. For a detailed account of the Croatian transition, *see* M. Staničić, *Dugo putovanje Hrvatske u Europsku uniju* (Naklada Ljevak, 2005).
22. Commission staff working document, *Country Report Croatia 2020* with the Accompanying the document Communication from the Commission to the European Parliament, the European Council, the Council, the European Central Bank and the Eurogroup 2020 European Semester: *Assessment of progress on structural reforms, prevention and correction of macroeconomic imbalances, and results of in-depth reviews under Regulation (EU) No 1176/2011,* COM(2020) 150 final, 26.2.2020, https://eur-lex.europa.eu/legal-content/EN/TXT/?qid=1584545612721&uri=CELEX%3A52020SC0510 (accessed 04. Feb 2022).
23. *See* https://ec.europa.eu/economy_finance/forecasts/2021/autumn/ecfin_forecast_autumn_2021_hr_en.pdf (accessed 04 Feb 2022)
24. Croatian Chamber of Economy, *Croatia Your Business Partner* (2016) http://www.hgk.hr/croatia-your-business-partner-najava (accessed 11 Apr. 2017).
25. Ministry of Economy http://www.mingo.hr/en/page/kategorija/trade-and-internal-market-2 (accessed 10 Apr. 2017).
26. In 2016 tourism made up 18.9% of Croatian GDP. Source: Croatian National Bank, https://www.htz.hr/sites/default/files/2018-08/HTZ%20TUB%20HR_%202017%20FINAL.pdf (accessed 6 Sep. 2018).

§3. LEGAL SYSTEM

24. Croatia belongs to the continental, civil law family that has been strongly influenced by the Austrian legal heritage. To a lesser degree, the Croatian legal system has also been influenced by French, Swiss, and German law.[27] After gaining independence, Croatia inherited many legal acts of the former SFRY that were gradually amended and replaced so as to reflect new democratic and market values. Particular efforts were placed on areas such as corporate law, banking, competition law, intellectual property, financial law, and others.[28]

25. As a continental legal system, Croatian law relies on the application of statutory laws with a clearly defined hierarchy of legal acts and observing the principle of the rule of law. In the hierarchy of legal norms, the Constitution as the highest source of law is complemented by the Constitutional Act on the Constitutional Court and is followed by international agreements, organic laws, ordinary laws, and secondary sources of law (by-laws). The Constitutional Court is vested with the authority to safeguard the supremacy of the Constitution.

26. In 2010, major constitutional amendments prepared the Croatian legal system for Croatian membership of the EU. According to Article 145 of the Croatian Constitution, all legal acts and decisions accepted by the Republic of Croatia in EU institutions must be applied in the Republic of Croatia in accordance with the EU *acquis communautaire*. On the ground of the principle of supremacy of EU law, in the case of conflict between national and EU legal norms regulating the same issue, EU rules have precedence. However, it is important to note the jurisprudence of the Constitutional Court in regard to the relationship of EU law and the Croatian Constitution. In two decisions, the Constitutional Court expressly ruled that the Croatian Constitution retains supremacy over EU law.[29] In doing so, the court established the foundation of Croatian constitutional identity in a manner similar to the jurisprudence of the German Constitutional Court.

27. The case law of national courts does not have the consistency of application typical of common law systems based on the doctrine of *stare decisis*, since the case law in Croatia is not a formal source of law. However, the lower courts will usually follow the interpretation of statutory rules given by higher courts and the Supreme Court so as to preserve the uniformity of the application of legal norms.[30] Unlike

27. H. Ernst, *General Introduction*, in *Introduction to the Law of Croatia* 4 (T. Josipović ed., Wolters Kluwer, 2014).
28. *Ibid.*, p. 5.
29. Decision of the Constitutional Court of the Republic of Croatia of 8 April 2015, U-VIIR-1159/2015, para. 45; Decision of the Constitutional Court of the Republic of Croatia of 21 April 2015, U-VIIR-1158/2015, para. 60.
30. For a detailed analysis of the authority of court decisions in Croatia, *see* Ž. Harašić, *Autoritet i sud*, 52 Zbornik radova Pravnog fakulteta u Splitu 407 (2015).

the judgments of higher courts which influence the decisions of lower courts by argument and authority, constitutional rulings are binding and must thus be observed.[31]

28. Croatian law was fully harmonized with the *acquis communautaire* during accession negotiations on the ground of the Stabilization and Association Agreement between the EU and the Republic of Croatia (SAA)[32] signed in 2001. Pending the entry into force of the SAA (2005), the Interim Agreement on Trade and Trade-related Matters (IA)[33] was signed in 2001, incorporating several agreements annexed to the SAA and supplemented by a number of protocols and agreements relating to areas covered by the SAA.[34] State aid and competition rules were given priority of harmonization and thus Croatian competition law was fully harmonized with the provisions of ex Articles 81, 82, and 86 of the Treaty establishing the European Community long before Croatia became a full Member State of the EU.

§4. Historical Background of Antitrust Law

29. The introduction of antitrust legislation was directly linked to the transition from a socialist to a market-based economy in the 1990s. The first Competition Act (CA) was enacted in 1995,[35] by which the Croatian Competition Agency (CCA) was established and the general legal framework was put into place. The first CA was rather general with many legal gaps that were filled even at that time by reference to the legislative solutions of the European Communities (EC).

30. The obligation to fully harmonize national competition law arose with the signing of the SAA, by virtue of its Article 69, whereby Croatia undertook to gradually make its existing laws and future legislation compatible with the EC *acquis*. In addition, by virtue of Article 70 SAA, Croatia was obliged to create a fully independent and operational public body entrusted with the enforcement of competition rules. This obligation resulted in a more comprehensive second CA adopted in 2003[36] accompanied by a number of secondary legislation acts.[37]

---

31. Article 31 of the Constitutional Act on the Constitutional Court of the Republic of Croatia, Official Gazette no. 49/02. For more on legal nature of court decision, *see* Part I, Ch. 1, §5, Role and Authority of Precedents, *infra*.
32. Stabilization and Association Agreement between the European Communities and their Member States, of the one part, and the Republic of Croatia, of the other part, Official Gazette, International Agreements, nos 14/2001, 14/2002, 7/2005, 11/2006, 10/2008, 10/2011.
33. Interim Agreement on trade and trade-related matters between the European Community, of the one part, and the Republic of Croatia, of the other part, Official Gazette, International Agreements, no. 15/2001 (IA).
34. Summary of Treaty, available at http://ec.europa.eu/world/agreements/prepareCreateTreatiesWorkspace/treatiesGeneralData.do?step=0&redirect=true&treatyId=140 (accessed 19 Apr. 2017).
35. Official Gazette nos 48/1995, 52/1997, 89/1998.
36. Official Gazette no. 122/2003.
37. *See* para. 38, *infra*.

31. For the most part, the 2003 CA was aligned with the community legislation, and new rules on the composition and authorities of the Competition Agency were introduced. A major problem arose from the Competition Agency's application of EU legislative solutions in the assessment of cases before it. Extensive reference to EU competition law in the Competition Agency's practice was justified on the ground of Article 70(2) SAA and the corresponding Article 35(2) IA. Those articles prescribed the obligation of Croatian authorities to apply to restrictive agreements, to the abuse of a dominant position, and to illegal state aid, the criteria arising from the application of community competition rules and the interpretative instruments adopted by community institutions, provided there was an effect on trade between Croatia and the community. Since Croatia at the time was still not a member of the EU, and the Competition Agency applied EU rules even in a purely domestic context, such a practice of the Competition Agency was challenged before the Constitutional Court. In a seminal *P.Z. Auto* judgment, the Constitutional Court proclaimed that it is both the right and obligation of the Competition Agency and review courts when applying national rules also to take account of relevant EU law.[38] The Constitutional Court argued that:

> the criteria, standards and interpretative instruments of the European Communities are not applied as the primary source of law, but only as an auxiliary instrument of interpretation. The provisions of Article 70/2 SAA and Article 35/2 of the Interim Agreement should be seen in the context of the obligation of the Republic of Croatia to harmonise its legislation, also that related to market competition, with the acquis communautaire of the European Union. When applying such harmonised legislation, government institutions are obliged to apply it in the same way as the European Communities, that is in the sense and spirit of the legislation pursuant to which the harmonisation was carried out.[39]

32. This judgment paved the way for the full alignment of Croatian substantive competition rules with EU competition rules, and enabled the Competition Agency to continue considering EU competition law as a point of reference even in the assessment of purely domestic cases, with beneficial results on the convergence of competition law enforcement and the quality of decisions.[40]

33. Although almost fully harmonized in substance, the 2003 CA had one important shortcoming – the inefficient institutional setting which undermined the effectiveness of competition law enforcement, eventually leading to the adoption of a third CA in 2009. The major enforcement obstacle resulted from the fact that under the 2003 CA the Competition Agency was not vested with the power to sanction

38. Decision of the Constitutional Court of Croatia of 13 February 2008, U-III-1410/2007, available in English at https://sljeme.usud.hr/usud/prakswen.nsf/Praksa/1A9EF887CC850D54C1257E5F003E1F57?OpenDocument (accessed 19 Apr. 2017).
39. Decision of the Constitutional Court of Croatia of 13 February 2008, U-III-1410/2007, 7
40. For a detailed analysis of the Croatian historical background of antitrust law in the EU context, *see* J. Pecotić Kaufman & V. Butorac Malnar, *The Interaction Between EU Regulatory Implants and the Existing Croatian Legal Order in Competition Law*, in *Economic Evidence in EU Competition Law* (M. Kovač, A. Vandenberghe, eds., Cambridge-Antwerp- Portland, Intersentia, 2016).

infringing undertakings. Since at the time competition infringements were characterized as misdemeanour offences, pursuant to the Misdemeanour Act, the sanctioning of the infringing undertakings was under the authority of misdemeanour courts. Consequently, once the Competition Agency found a competition law infringement, it would initiate misdemeanour proceedings before the competent misdemeanour court against the undertaking concerned and the responsible person.[41] Misdemeanour courts, however, were very reluctant to impose fines which is evidenced by the fact that even though between 2004 and 2008 the Competition Agency found over 100 competition law infringements,[42] in the same period misdemeanour courts imposed overall fines of only HRK 1 million (approx. EUR 130,000).[43] Obviously, such a deficiency in sanctioning mechanisms did not act as a deterrent and resulted in undertakings disregarding competition law rules.

34. This institutional deficiency was resolved by the 2009 CA[44] whereby the Competition Agency was granted full authority to impose fines on infringing undertakings. In addition, the 2009 CA introduced the Leniency Programme, which, however, remained unused by cartelists for many years. Following the entry into force of the 2009 CA, in 2011 many new accompanying regulations replaced the old ones, creating an efficient, modern, and detailed legislative competition law framework.

35. The amendments to the 2009 CA were made in 2013[45] to reflect the obligations arising out of the full membership of Croatia in the EU. The amendments restated some of the main obligations of Regulation 1/2003.[46] In particular, the current rules reiterate the authority and obligation of the Competition Agency to apply directly Articles 101 and 102 Treaty on the Functioning of the European Union (TFEU) in addition to national competition rules in cases affecting trade between the Member States. These revisions mostly served the purpose of having a comprehensive set of EU and Croatian rules reflecting the parallel competence of the EU Commission and the national enforcers in cases affecting trade between Member States and the parallel application of EU and national competition law provisions in these situations. Another novelty of the 2013 amendments was the introduction of a provision dealing with antitrust actions for damages, whereby commercial courts were given the competence to deal with such claims.

41. Pecotić Kaufman, Butorac Malnar, *supra* n. 41, at 340.
42. Croatian Parliament, Competition Bill – Preparatory notes (*Prijedlog zakona zaštiti tržišnog natjecanja, s konačnim prijedlogom zakona*), https://infodok.sabor.hr (accessed 18 Jun. 2013).
43. Pecotić Kaufman, Butorac Malnar, *supra* n. 41, at 340.
44. Competition Act, Official Gazette no. 79/2009.
45. The Act on Amendments to the Competition Act, Official Gazette no. 80/2013.
46. Council Regulation 1/2003/EC of 16 December 2002 on the implementation of the rules on competition laid down in Arts 81 and 82 of the Treaty, OJ L 1/1, 4.1.2003, amended by Council Regulation 411/2004/EC of 26 February 2004, OJ L 68/1, 6.3.2004, and Council Regulation 1419/2006/EC of 25 September 2006, OJ L 269/1, 28.9.2006 – Consolidated version of 18 October 2006.

36. The latest amendments to the CA were made in 2021[47] as a result of the transposition of the EU Directive 2019/1[48](ECN+ Directive) into the national legal system aimed at empowering the national competition authorities. This opportunity was taken to make other changes to the CA as well, such as the introduction of the settlement procedure and corrections of some provisions of the previous CA. With these, rather vast amendments to the Croatian legislative framework, national rules continue to be fully aligned with the EU law.

37. Finally, another legislative development in the area of competition law relates to the Act on Antitrust Damages actions,[49] adopted by the Parliament in 2017, as a result of the obligation to transpose into national legislation EU Directive 2014/104 on antitrust damages.[50]

47. The Act on Amendments to the Competition Act, Official Gazette no. 41/21.
48. Directive 2019/1/EU of the European Parliament and of the Council of 11 December 2018 to empower the competition authorities of the Member States to be more effective enforcers and to ensure the proper functioning of the internal market OJ L 11/3, 14.1.2019 (ECN+ Directive).
49. Act on Actions for Damages Arising out of Antitrust Infringements, Official Gazette no. 69/17.
50. Directive 2014/104/EU of the European Parliament and of the Council of 26 November 2014 on certain rules governing actions for damages under national law for infringements of the competition law provisions of the Member States and of the European Union Text with EEA relevance, OJ L 349/1, 5.12.2014.

Part I. Structure of Antitrust Law and Its Enforcement

Chapter 1. Sources of Antitrust Law

§1. National Sources

I. The Constitution

38. The highest source of competition law in Croatia is the Croatian Constitution, which proclaims in its Article 49(1) that free enterprise and free markets shall form the foundation of the economic system of the Republic of Croatia. In addition, Article 49(2) of the Constitution ensures all entrepreneurs equal legal status on the market, and that the abuse of monopolies, as defined by law, is forbidden. These rules are part of larger guarantees of entrepreneurial freedom in Croatia whereby the state is entrusted with the duty to stimulate economic progress and social welfare and guarantee the right of ownership and the free transfer and repatriation of profits and capital invested.[51] These economic rights are the cornerstones of the preservation and growth of a market economy and represent the legal basis for the introduction of competition law rules in Croatia. On several occasions, the Constitutional Court of Croatia has stated that entrepreneurial and market freedoms are achieved through the application of the CA. In the opinion of the Constitutional Court:

> Regulations on the protection of market competition are by their very nature public, because they protect the common good (free market competition) and they serve to achieve the implementation of important entrepreneurial and market freedoms as they prevent, inter alia, entrepreneurs from disrespecting market and entrepreneurial freedoms of other entrepreneurs and consumers. Protection of the free market can be ensured only by restricting the operation of entrepreneurs who undermine free enterprise.[52]

51. Croatian Constitution, Arts 48(1) and 49(3) and (4).
52. Decision of the Constitutional Court of Croatia of 17 February 2011, U-III-4082/2010, https://sljeme.usud.hr/usud/prakswen.nsf/Praksa/3C7710399865A4F1C1257D41002D1827?OpenDocument (accessed 25 Sep. 2018).

II. The Competition Act

39. Detailed competition law rules are contained in the CA[53] which is the main legislative act laying down substantive competition rules on prohibited agreements, abuse of a dominant position and concentrations of undertakings, and regulating the powers, duties, internal organization, and proceedings carried out by the Competition Agency.[54] The CA is modelled on the relevant EU competition rules, it is applicable to all sectors irrespectively of the possible existence of *ex ante* regulation in a particular sector, and it has extraterritorial reach.[55] Where particular market behaviour has an effect on trade between Member States, by virtue of the obligations arising from TFEU, parallel to the CA, EU competition rules apply.[56] In addition to legislative acts, Croatian competition law encompasses a number of by-laws adopted on the grounds of the CA, which are of a binding nature.

III. Procedural Rules

40. The procedural aspects of competition law proceedings are regulated by the CA as *lex specialis* and the General Administrative Procedure Act[57] as *lex generalis*.

IV. Private Enforcement of Competition Rules

41. Private enforcement of competition rules falls outside the scope of the CA. The Directive on antitrust damages has been transposed via a special new Act on Actions for Damages Arising from Antitrust Infringements (hereinafter: Act on Antitrust Damages)[58] which is a *lex specialis* in relation to the general provision of the Civil Procedure Act (CPA)[59] and the Obligations Act (OA).[60] Other types of private enforcement mechanisms, such as injunctive or declaratory relief, are regulated by the general provisions of the CPA.[61]

53. Official Gazette nos 79/2009, 80/2013, 41/2021.
54. Article 1 CA.
55. Article 2 CA.
56. *See* Part I, Ch. 1, §2, *infra*.
57. General Administrative Procedure Act, Official Gazette nos 47/2009, 110/21.
58. Act on Actions for Damages Arising out of Antitrust Infringements, Official Gazette no. 69/17.
59. Civil Procedure Act, Official Gazette nos 53/91, 91/92, 58/93, 112/99, 88/01, 117/03, 88/05, 02/07, 84/08, 123/08, 57/11, 148/11, 25/13, 89/14, 70/19, 80/22.
60. Obligations Act, Official Gazette nos 35/05, 41/08, 125/11, 78/15, 29/18, 126/21.
61. For more on private enforcement of competition rules, *see* Part I, Ch. 5, §2, Civil Enforcement.

§2. INTERNATIONAL SOURCES

I. EU Law

42. In 2013, when Croatia became a Member State of the EU, the 2010 Amendments to the Constitution entered into force, whereby EU sources of law became an integral part of the national legal system, with supremacy of application over national laws. Accordingly, as in other Member States, national and EU competition regimes have parallel application. Articles 101 and 102 TFEU apply directly to all cases affecting trade between EU Member States, while the national competition rules are applicable to purely domestic cases (having effect on the Croatian territory only). Detailed rules on the relationship between Articles 101 and 102 TFEU and the corresponding national competition rules are laid down by EU Regulation 1/2003, which, together with other EU regulations (EU block exemption regulations (BERs) and the Merger Control Regulation), apply directly in the Croatian national legal order without the need for legislative intervention.[62] By virtue of Article 74 of the CA, the application of EU competition law is further extended to cases of legal gaps or uncertainties relating to the interpretation of national competition law rules.[63] This legislative solution empowers national competition law enforcers to take into consideration the entirety of EU competition law, including non-binding sources of law, such as EU notices and guidelines, in all competition cases (whether or not they affect trade between Member States)

II. International Agreements

43. Although there are no binding international sources of law applicable in the assessment of competition law cases, there are a number of bilateral and multilateral agreements of cooperation between the Competition Agency and foreign antitrust enforcers. At the bilateral level, the Competition Agency has entered into Agreements of Cooperation with competition agencies from Austria, Kosovo, Macedonia, Bulgaria, Hungary, and Bosnia and Herzegovina.[64] At the multilateral level, cooperation is achieved through the membership of the Competition Agency in the European Competition Network (ECN) and in the International Competition Network (ICN). In addition, Croatia participates in activities related to competition law within the framework of the WTO, the Organization of Economic Cooperation and Development (OECD), and the United Nations Conference on Trade and Development (UNCTAD).[65]

---

62. *See* Part I, Ch. 1, §4. Relation and Hierarchy of Sources, *infra*.

63. Article 74 CA.

64. *See* http://www.aztn.hr/trzisno-natjecanje/nadleznosti/medunarodna-i-europska-suradnja/bilateralni-odnosi/ (accessed 6 Apr. 2018).

65. *See* http://www.aztn.hr/trzisno-natjecanje/nadleznosti/medunarodna-i-europska-suradnja/ (accessed 6 Apr. 2018).

§3. Secondary Sources

I. Regulations

A. EU Regulations

44. Because EU competition law is an integral part of the national legal order, all EU regulations apply directly to cases affecting trade between Member States. This in particular relates to Regulation 1/2003,[66] all BERs, and the Merger Control Regulation.[67]

B. Croatian Regulations

45. On the grounds of the CA, many binding by-laws in the form of regulations have been adopted to tackle specific issues pertinent to competition law enforcement. The regulations are adopted by the government upon the proposal of the Competition Agency and are modelled on the corresponding EU regulations. The following are currently in force:

- Regulation on block exemption granted to agreements in the transport sector.[68]
- Regulation on block exemption granted to certain categories of horizontal agreements.[69]
- Regulation on block exemption granted to certain categories of vertical agreements.[70]
- Regulation on block exemption granted to agreements on distribution and servicing of motor vehicles.[71]
- Regulation on block exemption granted to certain categories of technology transfer agreements.[72]
- Regulation on agreements of minor importance.[73]
- Regulation on the definition of relevant market.[74]
- Regulation on the method of setting fines.[75]
- Regulation on immunity from fines and reduction of fines.[76]

66. Council Regulation (EC) no. 1/2003 of 16 December 2002 on the implementation of the rules on competition laid down in Articles 81 and 82 of the Treaty (Text with EEA relevance), OJ L 1, 4.1.2003, 1–25.
67. Council Regulation (EC) no. 139/2004 of 20 January 2004 on the control of concentrations between undertakings (the EC Merger Regulation) (Text with EEA relevance), OJ L 24, 29.1.2004, 1–22.
68. Official Gazette no. 78/2011.
69. Official Gazette no. 72/2011.
70. Official Gazette no. 37/2011.
71. *Ibid.*
72. Official Gazette no. 9/2011.
73. *Ibid.*
74. *Ibid.*
75. Official Gazette nos 129/2010, 23/2015.
76. Official Gazette nos 129/2010, 96/2017.

- Regulation on revised tariffs on administrative fees under the Administrative Fees Act.[77]
- Regulation on notification and assessment of concentrations.[78]

II. Guidelines

46. Croatia does not have any rules in the form of guidelines but instead applies EU guidelines as a source of interpretation of the CA and EU competition rules.[79]

§4. Relation and Hierarchy of Sources

47. The highest source of competition law is the Constitution of the Republic of Croatia, hierarchically followed by EU law, national legislative acts, and national by-laws. Accordingly, by virtue of obligations arising out of the TFEU, primary sources of EU competition law, Articles 101 and 102 TFEU, the practice of EU courts, and all other generally binding EU competition rules must be applied in cases affecting trade between Member States of the EU.

48. Article 3 of Regulation 1/2003 defines in more detail the relationship between Articles 101 and 102 TFEU and national competition laws. Essentially, when national competition law is applied to prohibited agreements or abuse of a dominant position, which may affect trade between Croatia and other Member States of the EU, the Competition Agency and national courts have the right and the obligation to apply to such practices Articles 101 and 102 TFEU as well. In such cases, when assessing agreements, concerted practice, and decisions by associations of undertakings, the application of national laws may not lead to a prohibition decision where such behaviour would be permissible under Article 101 TFEU.[80] In essence, Regulation 1/2003 thereby provides that national provisions in relation to prohibited agreements may not be stricter than EU law, which brings about a high level of convergence in the application of national rules dealing with prohibited agreements.[81] A somewhat different situation is envisaged for the application of national rules to unilateral conduct, in which case Member States are allowed to adopt and apply on their territory stricter national laws.[82] Irrespective of this possibility granted by Regulation 1/2003, Croatian competition law does not envisage

77. Official Gazette no. 126/2011.
78. Official Gazette no. 38/2011.
79. *See* Part I, Ch. 1, §2. I EU Law.
80. Article 3(2) Regulation 1/2003.
81. K. Cseres, *Comparing Laws in the Enforcement of EU and National Competition Laws*, 3 European Journal of Legal Studies 7, 9 (2010).
82. Article 3(2) of Regulation 1/2003 reads: 'Member States shall not under this Regulation be precluded from adopting and applying on their territory stricter national laws which prohibit or sanction unilateral conduct engaged in by undertakings.'

stricter rules for unilateral behaviour. Concurrent competences and the simultaneous application of EU and national rules do not apply to the concentration of undertakings and laws pursuing a predominantly different objective.[83]

§5. Role and Authority of Precedents

49. In a purely domestic context, bodies entrusted with the application of competition rules are not legally bound by previous rulings in similar or analogous cases, which is a reflection of the continental legal system in which case law is not a formal source of law. Higher-instance rulings have only a binding *inter partes* effect. However, it would be incorrect to state that case law in general has no uniformity of application. Any legal system based on the rule of law and on guarantees of equal treatment and legal certainty has to envisage mechanisms ensuring the consistent application of law.

50. In the Croatian legal system, if there is a difference in legal positions, they are unified at sessions of court divisions and by the Supreme Court.[84] According to the Judiciary Act, in order to ensure the uniformity and transparency of court case law, the Supreme Court and Presidents of the court divisions of all county courts meet regularly to discuss problematic legal issues. The conclusions reached at such discussions are published on the website of the Supreme Court.[85] In addition, in cases of the diversified application of a particular legal rule, the courts meet at general sessions with the aim of creating a unified legal position on that particular issue.[86] Legal understandings adopted at the sessions of all judges or divisions of the Supreme Court, the High Administrative Court, the High Commercial Court, the High Misdemeanour Court or a county court are binding for all second instance chambers or single judges of that division or court.[87] However, to date, no binding legal understanding related to the application of the CA has been adopted. Nevertheless, looking at the decisions of the Competition Agency, it may be observed that for the most part the agency follows its own practice and previous High Administrative Court rulings in order to preserve the uniformity of application of competition rules, their coherence and transparency. The judgments of the EU courts and the decisions of the EU Commission are of particular importance, and these are always followed, even in a purely domestic context.

83. Article 3(3) of Regulation 1/2003. As to the relationship between different national sources of competition law, *see* §1 National Sources, *supra*.
84. Article 38 of the Judiciary Act, Official Gazette nos 28/2013, 33/2015, 82/2015, 82/2016, 67/18, 126/19, 130/20, 21/22, 60/22.
85. Article 27(3) of the Judiciary Act.
86. Article 40(1) of the Judiciary Act.
87. Article 40(2) of the Judiciary Act.

Chapter 2. Scope of Application

§1. Territorial Reach

51. Croatian competition law has extraterritorial application, specifically proclaimed in Article 2 of the CA, according to which competition rules 'apply to all forms of prevention, restriction or distortion of competition by undertakings, within the Croatian territory or outside its territory, if such practices take effect in the Croatian territory'.[88] This rule is a clear expression of the effects doctrine according to which '[…] domestic competition laws are applicable to foreign firms – but also to domestic firms located outside the state's territory, when their behaviour or transactions produce an "effect" within the domestic territory'.[89] The irrelevance of the nationality of the undertakings involved for the application of Croatian competition rules is expressly acknowledged by Article 3(2) of the CA, whereby it is stated that the place of establishment or residence in Croatia or abroad is of no significance in defining an undertaking.[90]

52. In Croatia, the first CA in 1995 already contained a provision on extraterritoriality based on the effects principle; however, this rule has remained dormant to date. Given the fact that there have been no cases decided by the extraterritorial application of national competition rules, it is impossible to draw a clear conclusion on the exact kind of effects required for its establishment. Although extraterritoriality is justified under the rules of public international law and is applicable in the field of competition law across the countries, there are no universally accepted criteria for its establishment. Therefore, should the opportunity arise, the enforcers of Croatian competition law are likely to rely on EU jurisprudence in this regard and embrace the 'qualified effects' theory, confirmed recently by the EU Court in the *Intel* [91] case. If indeed embraced by the Competition Agency, extraterritorial jurisdiction would be established in cases of 'substantial, immediate, and foreseeable'[92] effects of anticompetitive practices on the Croatian territory. Such an effect on the Croatian market would cover both actual and potential effects and would be established on a case-by-case basis, depending on the particular circumstances of each individual case.

88. Article 2 CA.
89. Glossary of competition terms, https://www.concurrences.com/en/droit-de-la-concurrence/glossary-of-competition-terms/Effects-doctrine?lang=en (accessed 3 Mar. 2018).
90. Article 3(2) CA.
91. Judgment of 12 June 2014, Case T-286/09 *Intel v. Commission* ECLI:EU:T:2014:547; Judgment of 6 September 2017, Case C-413/14 P *Intel* ECLI:EU:C:2017:632.
92. For a short overview on the current state of development of the extraterritorial reach of EU competition rules, *see* V. Butorac Malnar & I. Kunda, *EU Competition Law in the Digital Era: What to Tell About* Intel 31, in *EU Law in Context: Adjustment to Membership and Challenges of Enlargement* Vol. 2 (D. Duić, T. Petrašević, eds., Faculty of Law Josip Juraj Strossmayer University of Osijek, 2018); P. Behrens, *The Extraterritorial Reach of EU Competition Law Revisited: The 'Effects Doctrine' Before the ECJ*, Discussion Paper 3(16) (Europa-Kolleg Hamburg, Institute for European Integration, 2016).

53. While no decisions exist where Croatian competition rules have been applied extraterritorially, there have been a few decisions discussing the limits of their territorial reach. The most illustrative example was two decisions regarding vertical agreements between a Croatian sugar producer and Croatian buyers and retailers containing clauses restricting the export of sugar.[93] The Competition Agency regarded the clause to be non-distortive in relation to export to EU countries on the grounds of special EU and domestic legislation fixing the export quotas with preferential treatment and granting export only to registered sugar producers. Considering that the buyer was not a registered sugar producer, a clause restricting its export activities could not have had any effect on the market because special legislation anyhow prevented it from exporting sugar. In addition, the Competition Agency found that the purpose of the clause was not to distort competition but instead to prevent fraud with sugar imports.

54. Regarding the territorial reach of competition law, an interesting part of the decisions was related to the export ban to non-EU countries where no special legislative treatment comparable to that with EU countries existed and thus such a clause would have been contrary to Croatian competition rules had they been applicable to the case. However, the Competition Agency held that export to non-EU countries does not affect competition on the territory of Croatia or the EU. The list of hardcore restraints is applicable only to vertical agreements affecting trade on the territory of Croatia or affecting trade between Croatia and the EU Member States. Since that was not the case, Croatian competition rules were not applicable here. The Competition Agency reached the decision by invoking the decision *Javico v. Yves Saint Laurent* [94] where the EU Court concluded that:

> A distribution agreement intended to apply in a territory outside the Community […] cannot be regarded as having the object of appreciably restricting competition within the common market or as being capable of affecting, as such, trade between Member States and cannot therefore be contrary, by its very nature, to Article 85(1) of the Treaty.[95]

55. The Competition Agency decisions unequivocally affirm the basic principle of the effects doctrine – the nationality of the undertakings involved neither matters for the application of Croatian competition rules, nor the fact that the agreement was concluded and implemented in Croatia. Instead, the actual effect on the Croatian market triggers their application. Therefore, the effects doctrine works in both directions – as a justification of the extraterritorial application of national competition rules where the national market is affected, or the denial of their application in cases involving Croatian undertakings operating on the Croatian market if the latter is unaffected.

93. Decision of the Croatian Competition Agency of 12 June 2014, *Competition Agency v. Viro tvornica šećera d.d., Virovitica and Konzum d.d., Zagreb,* UP/I-034-03/2013-01/019; Decision of the Croatian Competition Agency of 12 June 2014, *Competition Agency v. Viro tvornica šećera d.d., Virovitica and Stridon-promet d.o.o., Dugo Selo*, UP/I-034-03/2013-01/020.
94. Judgment of 28 April 1998, Case C-306/96 *Javico v. Yves Saint Laurent* ECLI:EU:C:1998:173.
95. *Ibid.*

56. When it comes to merger control rules, already with the 2009 CA the Croatian legislator limited their extraterritorial reach, most likely in order to ease the burden of the Competition Agency facing an increase of 'foreign' notifications anticipated to be made on accession to the EU. According to Article 17 of the CA, the parties to the concentration are obliged to notify any proposed concentration to the Competition Agency where, in addition to meeting the defined turnover thresholds, at least one of the parties to the concentration has its seat and/or branch in the Republic of Croatia. Therefore, unlike in cases of anticompetitive agreements or abuse of dominant position, in cases of merger control, a clear territorial link of at least one of the parties to the concentration has to exist in order to give rise to Croatian jurisdiction over such a concentration.

§2. Special Sectors

57. The Croatian CA is applicable to all sectors. Historically, some of the competences of the Competition Agency were previously under the competence of sector-specific regulators. An interesting example of the historical transfer of competences from the Croatian National Bank to the competence of the Competition Agency is most certainly the *Competition Agency v. Société Générale – Splitska banka d.d.* case.[96] The case was originally brought by the Croatian National Bank, which had jurisdiction to decide in competition cases where perpetrators were financial institutions. After 1 July 2013, when Croatia acceded to the EU, the case was transferred to the Competition Agency which then had exclusive competence to apply competition rules to all sectors. In this case, the Competition Agency did not investigate if there was an abuse since within those proceedings Société Générale had already submitted a commitments proposal. Thus, the Competition Agency in the proceedings merely looked at the proposed commitments, and found them adequate to eliminate the negative effects of its conduct on the market. There would be nothing particularly interesting about this case had it not been for another one conducted at the same time and dealing with the same issue – *Competition Agency v. Zagrebačka banka d.d.* [97] This was essentially the same case – it related to the same facts and was also originally brought by the Croatian National Bank. However, unlike in the previous example, the parties to these proceedings did not propose any commitments and consequently the Competition Agency had to perform a full competition law assessment. However, it decided it would not and instead it terminated proceedings, finding no legal grounds to continue. The Competition Agency considered that for the purposes of competition law there could be no such thing as a relevant market of issuing and enforcing debit notes on which the undertaking concerned had allegedly abused its dominant position. Essentially this meant that the same circumstances and facts had been assessed differently in the two cases. Interestingly, the Croatian National Bank filed an unsuccessful appeal before the

96. Decision of the Competition Agency of 1 August 2013, *Competition Agency v. Société Générale – Splitska banka d.d.* UP/I-034-03/2013-01/029.
97. Decision of the Competition Agency of 3 June 2014, *Competition Agency v. Zagrebačka banka d.d.*, UP/I-034-03/2013-02/028.

High Administrative Court of the Republic of Croatia against the decision of the Competition Agency to terminate proceedings against Zagrebačka Banka.[98]

58. Some industries, most notably electronic communications, media, financial services, and energy, are additionally regulated by special legislative acts.[99] These acts grant authority to sector-specific regulators to operate *ex ante* in the markets concerned. Sector-specific regulators are the Croatian Financial Services Supervisory Agency (HANFA), the Croatian Regulatory Authority for Network Industries (HAKOM), the Croatian Energy Regulatory Agency (HERA), and the Agency for Electronic Media (AEM). Unlike these regulators whose jurisdiction for *ex ante* control is limited to the relevant sector, the Competition Agency has the sole authority to carry out *ex post* antitrust proceedings in 'all the sectors regardless of the fact whether there is a specific regulator in the market concerned or not'.[100] That being said, under Article 66 of the CA, the Competition Agency is obliged to cooperate with sector-specific regulators and judicial and other authorities in cases affecting competition on Croatian territory. The Competition Agency carries out such an obligation in the form of requests to the relevant agencies to deliver opinions, expert assistance, and information of relevance for the assessment of cases before it. The Competition Agency usually takes into careful consideration the input given by sector-specific regulators, rarely departing from their expert view. Finally, it should be stressed that cooperation between the Competition Agency and sector-specific regulators is reciprocal; therefore, very often upon the request of a specific regulator the Competition Agency delivers opinions relevant for *ex ante* control.

59. As for derogations to the applicability of competition rules, the Croatian competition law regime does not recognize any sectors where derogations would be applicable, save the one stemming directly from EU law. Relevant in this regard is the agriculture sector which, although captured by EU competition rules, is subject to a number of derogations and exemptions provided by Regulation 1308/2013[101] (the CMO Regulation) as amended in 2018 by the Regulation 2017/2393 (the Ominbus Regulation)[102] and the fisheries sector covered by

---

98. *See* Judgment of the High Administrative Court of the Republic of Croatia of 27 August 2015, UP/I-034-03/2013-01/028; UsII-43/14-10.

99. Electronic Communications Act, Official Gazette no 73/2008, 90/2011, 133/2012, 80/2013, 71/2014, 72/2017; Media Act, Official Gazette no 59/04, 84/11, 81/13; Electronic Media Act, Official Gazette no 111/2021.

100. *Summary Annual Report of the Croatian Competition Agency for 2015*, available at http://www.aztn.hr/ea/wp-content/uploads/2015/05/Summary-GI-2015-ENG.pdf (accessed 26 Apr. 2017).

101. Regulation (EU) no. 1308/2013 of the European Parliament and of the Council of 17 December 2013 establishing a common organization of the markets in agricultural products and repealing Council Regulations (EEC) no. 922/72, (EEC) no. 234/79, (EC) no. 1037/2001 and (EC) no. 1234/2007 (CMO Regulation).

102. Regulation (EU) 2017/2393 of the European Parliament and of the Council of 13 December 2017 amending Regulations (EU) No 1305/2013 in support for rural development by the European Agricultural Fund for Rural Development (EAFRD), (EU) No 1306/2013 on the financing, management, and monitoring of the common agricultural policy, (EU) No 1307/2013 establishing rules for direct payments to farmers under support schemes within the framework of the common agricultural policy, (EU) No 1308/2013 establishing a common organization of the markets in agricultural

Regulation 1379/2013.[103] Given the special treatment prescribed by the CMO Regulation in November 2015, the Commission issued guidelines concerning the implementation of the new rules regarding joint sales by producers of olive oil, beef and veal, and arable crops.[104]

§3. State-Owned Enterprises and Public Utilities

60. State-owned enterprises and public utilities are included in the application of Croatian Competition rules. This is of no surprise given that the Croatian CA is modelled on EU competition rules including Article 106 TFEU. However, unlike Article 106 TFEU, the Croatian CA does not explicitly mention public undertakings as addressees of competition rules. This omission should not be understood as a limit to the application of the general and functional definition of an undertaking whereby any person performing an economic activity is considered to be an undertaking irrespective of its legal form, means of financing, intention to make a profit, and the like. Consequently, in defining an undertaking, the ownership structure is of no relevance either.

61. The CA explicitly includes state bodies, local and regional self-government bodies, and state institutions in the definition of an undertaking, where such bodies directly or indirectly act in the market.[105] Accordingly, while the state itself is considered an undertaking within the meaning of the CA, this applies even more to state-owned enterprises performing an economic activity on the market. This understanding of the notion of an undertaking has been confirmed many times by the Competition Agency, as it has conducted many proceedings against state-owned enterprises defined as undertakings within the meaning of the CA. These examples include a waste-management company, wholly owned by local and regional self-government bodies, found to have abused its dominant position on the market;[106] a national oil company, partially owned by the state, also found to have abused a dominant position on the market;[107] a national enterprise responsible for managing

---

products and (EU) No 652/2014 laying down provisions for the management of expenditure relating to the food chain, animal health, and animal welfare, and relating to plant health and plant reproductive material, OJ L 350/15, 29.12.2017

103. Regulation (EU) no. 1379/2013 of the European Parliament and of the Council of 11 December 2013 on the common organization of the markets in fishery and aquaculture products, amending Council Regulations (EC) no. 1184/2006 and (EC) no. 1224/2009 and repealing Council Regulation (EC) no. 104/2000.

104. Commission Notice – Guidelines on the application of the specific rules set out in Arts 169, 170 and 171 of the CMO Regulation for the olive oil, beef and veal and arable crops sectors, OJ C 431 of 22.12.2015.

105. Article 3(1) CA.

106. Decision of the Croatian Competition Agency of 12 April 2006, *Competition Agency v. Čistoća d.o.o. Zadar*, UP/-030-02/2001-01/98. It is interesting to note that in another decision in 2014, the Competition Agency found that derogations from Art. 3(3) of the Competition Act applied to the same undertaking. *See* Decision of the Competition Agency of 10 April 2014, *Competition Agency v. Čistoća d.o.o., Zadar*, UP/I-034-03/2014-01/006.

107. Decision of the Croatian Competition Agency of 19 May 2011, *Competition Agency v. INA d.o.o.*, UP/I-030-02/2009-01/035.

woods and all related activities, wholly owned by the state which, although not found to have infringed competition rules, was a party to infringement proceedings;[108] a state-owned company responsible for managing water-related activities, against which the Competition Agency imposed several interim measures during infringement proceedings for the abuse of a dominant position, eventually leading to a commitment decision,[109] and others.[110]

62. Limited derogation from the application of competition rules are provided for by Article 3(3) of the CA in relation to undertakings entrusted with the operation of services of general economic interest, undertakings having the character of a revenue-producing monopoly, and undertakings granted special or exclusive rights to perform certain economic activities. As a rule, these undertakings are subject to competition rules. However, where the application of competition rules obstructs 'in law or in fact, the performance of the particular tasks assigned to them by separate rules or measures and for the performance of which they have been established',[111] competition rules may be derogated from. This carve-out stems from Article 106(2) TFEU whose purpose is to reconcile the public interests of the Member States with the Union's interest to ensure undistorted competition and the unity of the internal market.[112]

63. The problem arising in the context of this exception is the lack of a clear definition of which activities constitute services of general economic interest. Here, it is important to stress that Croatia in general exhibits an inconsistent and fragmented approach to such services, lacking a coherent legal framework[113] that would be helpful for the purposes of analysing competition law. Due to the conceptual and terminological ambiguities related to such services, the practice of the CCA is of utmost importance. To date, several services have been labelled services of general economic interest covered by the derogations of Article 3(3) CA. One of the most illustrative examples of the application of Article 3 CA is a decision of the CCA regarding the waste collection company 'Čistoća' owned by the City of Zadar.[114] The Competition Agency argued that this state-owned undertaking, although an

108. Decision of the Croatian Competition Agency of 21 May 2015, *Competition Agency v. Hrvatske šume d.o.o.*, UP/I-034-03/2014-01/009.

109. Decision of the Croatian Competition Agency of 6 March 2014, *Competition Agency v. Vodoopskrba i odvodnja d.o.o.*, UP/I-034-03/2013-01/037; Decision of the Croatian Competition Agency of 28 October 2014, *Competition Agency v. Vodoopskrba i odvodnja d.o.o.*, UP/I-034-03/2013-01/037.

110. For more on the notion of an undertaking, *see* Part I, Ch. 4, §1, *infra*.

111. Article 3(3) CA.

112. Case C-202/88 *France v. Commission* ECLI:EU:C:1990:64, para. 12 and the subsequent case law of the ECJ.

113. For more detail on services of general economic interest in Croatia, *see* Marijana List, V. Butorac Malnar, *SGEI in Croatia: The Legal Framework for Economic Necessity*, 15 European State Aid Law Quarterly 622 (2016).

114. Decision of the Competition Agency of 10 April 2014, *Competition Agency v. Cistoca d.o.o., Zadar*, UP/I-034-03/2014-01/006.

undertaking, in the circumstances of the case, should be regarded as an entity providing services of general economic interest under separate rules, and the application of competition rules would prevent it from performing such services, and thus the derogation of Article 3(3) applied.

§4. SENSIBLE EFFECT AND *DE MINIMIS*

64. Article 8(1) of the Croatian CA sets out the prohibition of agreements, concerted practice, and decisions by associations of undertakings having as their object or effect the distortion of competition in the relevant market. As a rule, agreements that have as their object the restriction of competition on the relevant market are presumed to be anticompetitive. Accordingly, in such situations the Competition Agency does not have the obligation to prove the actual negative effects of the behaviour on the relevant market. This rule has been confirmed many times in the practice of the Competition Agency. For example, building upon the guidelines for the application of Article 81(3),[115] in the case *Presečki grupa,* the Competition Agency concluded:

> As this was an agreement prohibited by its object, it was not necessary to examine its effects. In other words, since such arrangements by their nature have as their aim the distortion of competition, there was no need in the concrete case to prove any anticompetitive effects of such conduct. Therefore, no concrete detrimental effects regarding the market, in particular consumer interests, arising from the conclusion of the prohibited agreement were neither analyzed nor established.[116]

65. When an agreement does not contain restrictions by object, actual or potential anticompetitive effects on the market have to be established. However, in order to be captured by the prohibition, such effects must be significant enough to be capable of distorting competition. Article 8 does not specify the exact degree of restraint to competition necessary to be captured by the prohibition. Given the fact that Croatian competition law is modelled on EU competition rules, it applies the corresponding benchmark of the *appreciable* negative impact on competition as developed by the EU Commission and courts under Article 101 TFEU and summarized in the EU Horizontal Cooperation Guidelines and Vertical Restraints Guidelines that are used regularly by the Competition Agency.

66. Due to the requirement of significant negative effect on the market, when an agreement between undertakings has only negligible effect on the market, it is not prohibited. This is the rule on agreements of minor importance, explicitly recognized by Article 11 of the CA and equally applicable to restrictions by object and

115. Communication from the Commission – Notice – Guidelines on the application of Art. 81(3) of the Treaty (Text with EEA relevance) OJ C 101, 27.4.2004, 97–118.

116. Decision of the Croatian Competition Agency of 27 December 2012, *Competition Agency v. Presečki grupa d.o.o. et al.*, UP/I-030-02/2011-01/024.

effect (actual or potential). More detailed guidance on the appreciability threshold is provided in the regulation on agreements of minor importance[117] (hereinafter: *de minimis* Regulation), according to which the significance of an agreement to competition is directly linked to the level of market shares of the undertakings involved. Where the joint market share of the parties to an agreement is low, there is a presumption that the agreement concluded between them is incapable of distorting competition, unless it contains hardcore restraints, in which case actual or potential distortion of competition is likely and thus such agreements cannot benefit from the *de minimis* rule. This approach basically quantifies through market share thresholds what should not be considered an appreciable effect on competition.

67. According to Article 3 of the *de minimis* Regulation, a horizontal agreement between actual or potential competitors is negligible where the 'total market share held by the parties to the agreement and their controlled undertakings do not exceed 10% on any of the relevant markets affected by the agreement'.[118] Being less distortive, vertical agreements are considered negligible where the joint market share of all undertakings involved (and their controlled undertakings) does not exceed 15% of the relevant market affected.[119] In situations where it is difficult to classify an agreement as horizontal or vertical, the lower market share of 10% applies.[120]

68. The lowest market share threshold applies where the relevant market is characterized by parallel networks agreements. This situation occurs when competition is restricted by the cumulative effect of agreements entered into by different suppliers or distributors (and their controlled undertakings) having similar effects on the market. Such an effect is likely to exist if 30% or more of the market is characterized by such networks of agreements. Where this is the case, the individual market share threshold may not exceed 5% for both horizontal and vertical agreements in order to benefit from the presumption of negligible contribution to the cumulative foreclosure effect.[121] In any event, it is considered that an agreement has negligible effect on the market so long as market shares do not exceed the thresholds by more than 2% during two successive calendar years.[122]

69. One typical example of the application of the *de minimis* rule is a recent decision by the Competition Agency in the case *Peugeot*,[123] involving a selective distribution agreement on motor vehicles. The Competition Agency decided to terminate proceedings because the market share of the undertaking *Peugeot Hrvatska* was lower than 10%, and the disputed agreement did not contain any hardcore restrictions. In addition, the Competition Agency argued its decision on the grounds of the criteria set in the BER on vertical agreements. This case clearly shows that

117. Official Gazette no 9/2011.
118. Article 3(2)(a) of the *de minimis* Regulation.
119. Article 3(2)(b) of the *de minimis* Regulation.
120. Article 3(2)(c) of the *de minimis* Regulation.
121. Article 4 of the *de minimis* Regulation.
122. Article 5 of the *de minimis* Regulation.
123. Decision of the Croatian Competition Agency of 16 June 2015, *Competition Agency v. Peugeot Hrvatska d.o.o., Zagreb*, UP/I-034-03/2014-01/019.

when market share thresholds are met and the disputed agreement does not contain hardcore restraints, the Competition Agency is unlikely to formally open infringement proceedings due to the lack of public interest to do so.

70. As already mentioned, where an agreement contains hardcore restraints, despite the inappreciable market share of the parties involved, it will not be considered an agreement of minor importance and will consequently deprive the parties of the benefit of *de minimis* exemption to the prohibition set out in Article 8 of the CA. Hardcore restrictions are restrictions by object that seriously prevent, distort, or restrict competition on the relevant market. When it comes to horizontal agreements, typical hardcore restraints are price-fixing clauses, limitations of output sales, and market or customer allocation. Vertical hardcore restraints include minimum resale price maintenance (RPM), agreements providing absolute territorial protection, export restrictions, and market partitioning.[124]

71. It should be stressed that the *de minimis* Regulation negatively defines appreciability. However, this does not imply that agreements between undertakings, whose market share exceeds the set thresholds, automatically restrict competition in an appreciable manner. Such agreements may still fall outside the prohibition of Article 8 on the grounds of an insignificant effect on competition. Such an approach clearly shows that the assessment of appreciability is not limited to market share thresholds.

72. On several occasions, without invoking *de minimis* market share thresholds, the Competition Agency held that allegedly anticompetitive behaviour was not a prohibited agreement under Article 8 of the CA because it lacked appreciable negative effect on competition. The first two decisions involved a 'no-discrimination rule' inserted in the American Express Card acceptance agreement concluded between PBZ Card d.o.o. and merchants.[125] The named rule basically prohibited merchants from adding charges to cardholders who pay with an American Express Card. Payment by card was not to be discriminated against cash payment, as in both cases the merchants undertook the obligation to treat equally card and cash payments. After having analysed the relevant market, the Competition Agency held that the PBZ card did not have a dominant position, dismissing thus the claim on the ground of abuse of dominance. Likewise, after having analysed the disputed contract clause, the Competition Agency held that the agreement had a negligible effect on competition, and thus it was not prohibited under Article 8 of the CA either. The Competition Agency invoked a decision by the EU Commission in the case *Visa*

124. *See* Arts 6–10 of the *de minimis* Regulation.
125. Decision of the Croatian Competition Agency of 27 February 2012, *Competition Agency v. PBZ Card d.o.o.*, UP/I-030-02/11-01/049; Decision of the Croatian Competition Agency of 27 February 2012, *Competition Agency v. PBZ Card d.o.o.*, UP/I-034-03/12-01/004.

International, [126] where it was held that a similar non-discrimination clause did not have an appreciable negative effect on the market and thus was not prohibited under Article 101 TFEU.[127]

73. Another case where the Competition Agency dismissed a claim on the ground of lack of appreciable effect on the market without invoking the *de minimis* rule was in *Tikveš and Orbico*[128] in 2013. At issue was a distribution agreement containing potentially restrictive clauses related to the freedom of establishing wholesale prices. However, the Competition Agency dismissed the claim because the disputed agreement had been in force for not more than a year, restrictive clauses were not applied in practice, and they were no longer part of the agreement at the moment the Competition Agency started the investigation. On these grounds, the Competition Agency found that the agreement had a negligible effect on the market and thus was not prohibited under Article 8 of the CA.

126. Decision of the EU Commission of 9 August 2001, no. COMP/29.373, *Visa International,* para. 58.
127. *Competition Agency v. PBZ Card d.o.o*, UP/I-030-02/11-01/049, 2012, *supra* n. 124, at 5.
128. Decision of the Croatian Competition Agency of 9 May 2013, *Competition Agency v. VV Tikveš and* Skopje, *Republic of Macedonia and Orbico d.o.o., Zagreb,* UP/I-034-03/2013-01/014.

Chapter 3. Overview of Substantive Provisions

§1. Restrictive Agreements

74. The provision on prohibited agreements in the Croatian CA mirrors Article 101 TFEU.[129] Agreements, concerted practice, and decisions by associations of undertakings, which have as their object or effect the restriction of competition in the relevant market, are prohibited.[130] If the object or effect of the agreement is to restrict competition, an exemption is available if the agreement meets certain cumulative criteria: (a) the agreement has to contribute to improving the production or distribution of goods or to promoting technical or economic progress; (b) while allowing consumers a fair share of the resulting benefit; and (c) not imposing on the undertakings concerned restrictions which are not indispensable to the attainment of these objectives; and (d) not affording such undertakings the possibility of eliminating competition in respect of a substantial part of the products in question.[131] The burden of proof is on the parties to the agreement to prove that the conditions listed above are met.[132] A restrictive agreement is *ex lege* null and void.[133]

75. Six BERs were adopted on the basis of Article 10 of the CA:

(1) BER on horizontal agreements.[134]
(2) BER on vertical agreements.[135]
(3) BER on technology transfer agreements.[136]
(4) BER on motor vehicles distribution and servicing.[137]
(5) BER on agreements in the area of transport.[138]
(6) BER on insurance agreements.[139]

76. Block exemption is also available for agreements which have an effect on the trade between Croatia and the EU, provided they meet the conditions set out in Article 101(3) TFEU and relevant EU regulations.[140]

---

129. Article 8 CA.
130. Article 8(1) CA.
131. Article 8(3) CA.
132. Article 8(5) CA.
133. Article 8(4) CA.
134. Uredba o skupnom izuzeću horizontalnih sporazuma između poduzetnika, Official Gazette no. 72/2011.
135. Official Gazette no. 37/2011, Uredba o skupnom izuzeću vertikalnih sporazuma između poduzetnika, Official Gazette no. 37/2011.
136. Uredba o skupnom izuzeću sporazuma o prijenosu tehnologije, Official Gazette no. 9/2011.
137. Uredba o skupnom izuzeću sporazuma o distribuciji i servisiranju motornih vozila, Official Gazette no. 37/2011.
138. Uredba o skupnom izuzeću sporazuma u sektoru prometa, Official Gazette no. 78/2011.
139. Uredba o skupnom izuzeću sporazuma o osiguranju, Official Gazette no. 78/2011. Out of force as of 24 April 2021, see Article 48 Amendments to the Competition Act, Official Gazette no. 41/2021.
140. Article 10.a CA.

77. The general prohibition set out in Article 8(1) of the CA is not applicable to *de minimis* agreements, which are defined as agreements where the joint market share of the parties (including undertakings under their control) is negligible, provided they contain no hardcore restrictions, which result in distortion of competition despite the fact that the parties' market share is negligible. [141] The Regulation on *de minimis* agreements provides more detailed provisions.[142]

78. In its decisions, the Competition Agency regularly finds that restrictive agreements containing hardcore restraints are not eligible for the application of the *de minimis* rule. On the contrary, it ruled that a vertical agreement was *de minimis*, where the market share of the undertaking was lower than 10%, and no hardcore restrictions were present.[143] Similarly, the Competition Agency regularly finds that agreements with hardcore restraints are not eligible for block exemption.

§2. Dominant Undertakings

79. As already mentioned, rules on unilateral conduct in Croatian competition law are inspired by and modelled on EU competition law. Dominant undertakings must ensure they do not abuse their market power. There is a legal presumption of dominance which is linked to the notion of market power. It is presumed that an undertaking is in a dominant position if, due to its market power, it can act in the relevant market to a significant extent independently of its actual or potential competitors, consumers, buyers or suppliers.[144] In particular, and this is by no means a *numerus clausus*, an undertaking is dominant if it has no significant competitors in the relevant market, and/or it has significant market power in the relevant market in relation to its actual or potential competitors due to its market power, financial power, access to sources of supply or markets, links with other undertakings, legal or factual market barriers, its capability to dictate market conditions considering its supply or demand, or its ability to foreclose competitors from the market by redirecting to other undertakings.[145]

80. There is, however, a benchmark for dominance in the CA. If the market share in the relevant market is higher than 40%, the undertaking 'may' be in a dominant position.[146]

141. Article 11 CA.
142. Uredba o sporazumima male vrijednosti, Official Gazette no. 9/2011. *See* more Part I, Ch. 2, §4, *supra*.
143. *Peugeot*, UP/I-034-03/2014-01/019, 2015, *supra* n. 124.
144. Article 12 CA.
145. *Id.*
146. Article 12(2) CA.

81. The market share is not deemed as decisive as other factors need also be taken into account when deciding if a firm has a dominant position, for example competitors' market shares, market trends, etc.[147]

82. In a dynamic market, the fact that the firm managed to achieve market share above 40% in the last year of the period under assessment is not sufficient to hold that it has a dominant position in the relevant market.[148]

83. The stability of market share is necessary to find that an undertaking is in dominant position. No dominance was found in a situation where, in the period from 2007 to 2009, the company's market share was below 40%, reaching that benchmark in 2009, and that this period was not long enough to indicate stable market shares.[149] The Competition Agency also looks at the position and market shares of competitors, the nature of the market (in the specific case it was fast growing and dynamic), and market trends.

84. If the undertaking is going through bankruptcy proceedings, it cannot be deemed dominant.[150] An undertaking with a market share above 40% may be in a dominant position, provided it has such market power to allow it to act to a significant extent independently of its actual or potential competitors, consumers, buyers, or suppliers in the market.[151]

85. According to the CA, two or more legally independent undertakings may be in a joint dominant position if they act together in a specific market in relation to their competitors, suppliers, or consumers.[152] Furthermore, joint dominance exists where companies are able to act independently of their competitors due to their market position and their financial strength.[153] For the finding of joint dominance in the *Media-ideja v. Tisak and Distri-Press* case, the Competition Agency relied on several features of the market: a high market share of the two companies in an oligopolistic market (joint market share of 60%–70% in 2004, and growing, reaching 80%–90% in 2006); a small number of competitors (the next biggest competitor had a market share of only 10%–20% in 2004); regional significance; stable market/

147. *See* Decision of the Croatian Competition Agency of 17 September 2020, *FlixBus CEE South d.o.o.*, UP/I-034-03/20-01/001. In this case, the Competition Agency found that FlixBus was exposed to strong competitive pressure during the relevant period so it could not have acted independently of its competitors and consumers.
148. *Ibid.*
149. Decision of the Croatian Competition Agency of 31 August 2010, *B.net Hrvatska v. Hrvatski telekom d.d.*, UP/I-030-02/2008-01/45, Official Gazette no. 115/2010.
150. Decision of the Croatian Competition Agency of 6 May 2011, *Competition Agency v. Croatia bus d.d. u stečaju (Promet d.d.)* UP/I-030-02/2011-01/017.
151. *Ibid.*
152. Article 12(3) CA.
153. Decision of the Croatian Competition Agency of 15 October 2007, *Media ideja d.o.o. v. Tisak d.d. and Distri Press d.o.o.*, UP/I-030-02/2005-01/43; confirmed: Constitutional Court of the Republic of Croatia of 17 February 2011, *Tisak d.d.*, U-III-4082/2010.

stable demand; the two companies were the only ones operating a nationwide distribution network, so they were indispensable partners for any publisher who wanted to reach end customers nationwide; in terms of entry/exit from the market, it was a relatively stable market.[154]

86. A precondition for finding if an undertaking has a dominant position is to define the relevant product and geographic market.[155]

87. If there is no dominance, there is no abuse.[156]

88. The Competition Agency regularly finds that dominant undertakings have special responsibility in the market not to restrict competition. In the *Dubrovnik Airline v. INA* case, the Competition Agency held that a dominant position is not illegal in itself, but that the dominant undertaking bears special responsibility to prevent its conduct from distorting existing effective competition in neighbouring markets.[157] Similarly, in the *VIPnet v. HT and T-Mobile Hrvatska* case, the Competition Agency held that, although a dominant position is not prohibited per se, by concluding the contracts in question, the dominant firms did not behave with special responsibility to preserve effective competition which is a level of care demanded of dominant firms.[158]

89. In another example, the *Kino Zadar Film v. Blitz and Duplicato Media* case, where the Competition Agency found no abuse of a dominant position by vertically integrated movie distribution and movie theatre companies, the Competition Agency warned the dominant firm and its subsidiaries which had dominance in the market for movie distribution in Croatia that they had a special responsibility 'to treat equally all movie theatre firms, to secure on time a sufficient number of copies of a movie title, and, if it is their assessment that the movie will not be financially profitable, to offer a minimum guarantee based exclusively on the amount of the unit cost of the additional movie copy, and not on some other unreliable criteria'.[159] In

154. *Ibid.*

155. The Regulation on relevant markets sets out detailed provisions on defining relevant markets, Official Gazette no. 9/2011.

156. *See*, for example, Decision of the Croatian Competition Agency of 6 February 2014, *Wüstenrot*, UP/I-034-03/2014-01/008, Decision of the Croatian Competition Agency of 16 January 2020, *Competition Agency v. Nike European Operation Netherlands B.V.*, UP/I-034-03/19-01/006 or Decision of the Croatian Competition Agency of 17 September 2020, *FlixBus CEE South d.o.o.*, UP/I-034-03/20-01/001. In those cases the initiative to start proceedings was dismissed due to a lack of dominance of the undertaking allegedly abusing its market position.

157. Decision of the Croatian Competition Agency of 19 May 2011, *Competition Agency v. INA d.o.o.,*, UP/I-030-02/2009-01/035, Official Gazette no. 79/2011, confirmed: Judgment of the High Administrative Court of the Republic of Croatia of 9 February 2012, *INA Industrija nafte d.d. v. Competition Agency*, Us-7153/2011-8.

158. Decision of the Croatian Competition Agency of 12 July 2007, *Competition Agency v. HT-Hrvatske telekomunikacije d.d. and T-Mobile Hrvatska d.o.o.*, UP/I-030-02/2005-01/50, Official Gazette no. 100/2007; confirmed: Judgment of the Administrative Court of the Republic of Croatia of 9 September 2010, Us-8992/2007-8.

159. Decision of the Croatian Competition Agency of 24 February 2011, *Kino Zadar Film d.d. v. Blitz d.o.o. and Duplicato Media d.o.o.*, UP/I-030-02/2008-01/080.

the *Jadranski naftovod d.d.* case, the Competition Agency held that a dominant undertaking had greater responsibility when dealing with other market participants.[160]

90. The Competition Agency held that an undertaking, such as the sole national body for collective rights management, had special responsibility not to act in a way that weakens the level of competition existing in the market, since it can significantly influence the level and development of effective competition in the relevant market.[161] Because of its status regulated by law, HDS-ZAMP was an economically stronger party since it was in a position to enforce its conditions in the relevant market. The Competition Agency held that it did not act in accordance with its particular responsibility to preserve effective competition, as expected from a dominant undertaking.

91. The finding of a dominant position becomes more solid if the dominant undertaking is an inevitable business partner. In the *Croatia Airlines v. Zračna luka Zagreb and Zračna luka Zagreb – Ugostiteljstvo* case, the Competition Agency found that, particularly because the dominant undertakings were inevitable business partners, they should not use their dominance in the relevant market to the detriment of the users of their services.[162]

92. Usually, in abuse of dominance cases related to undertakings having a very high market share in the relevant market, the Competition Agency notes that it will continue to monitor the behaviour of such undertakings and any changes in their business policy.[163]

§3. Concentrations

93. As much as in other areas of competition law, Croatian merger control rules are also modelled on EU merger rules. The main provisions governing concentrations of undertakings are contained in Articles 15 to 24 of the CA. The wording of

160. Decision of the Croatian Competition Agency of 18 July 2014, *Competition Agency v. Jadranski naftovod d.d.*, UP/I-034-03/2014-01/007.
161. Decision of the Croatian Competition Agency of 3 November 2009, *HUVEL v. HDS-ZAMP*, UP/I-030-02/2008-01/041; confirmed: Judgment of the High Administrative Court of the Republic of Croatia of 20 April 2012, *Hrvatsko društvo skladatelja v. Competition Agency*, Us-14370/2009-13.
162. Decision of the Croatian Competition Agency of 30 December 2008, *Croatia Airlines v. Zračna luka Zagreb d.o.o. and Zračna luka Zagreb – Ugostiteljstvo d.o.o.*, UP/I-030-02/2007-01/15, Official Gazette no. 66/2009; confirmed: Judgment of the Administrative Court of the Republic of Croatia of 18 October 2012, Us-4027/2009-14.
163. For example, Decision of the Croatian Competition Agency of 19 December 2006, *Branko Kunštek and Fanika Vešligaj v. Presečki grupa d.o.o.*, UP/I-030-02/2006-02/5, Official Gazette no. 142/2006, confirmed: Judgment of the Administrative Court of the Republic of Croatia of 21 January 2010, Us-13887/2006-10. In addition, Decision of the Croatian Competition Agency of 24 February 2011, *Kino Zadar Film d.d. v. Blitz d.o.o. and Duplicato Media d.o.o.*, UP/I-030-02/2008-01/080, where the Competition Agency noted that it would continue to follow closely the highly concentrated market of movie distribution and the market for public screening of movies in Croatia, since consolidation in this sector was not subject to any sector rules.

Article 15 of the CA which provides for the notion of concentration is effectively the same as that of Article 3 of Regulation 139/04. According to Article 15 of the CA, a concentration of undertakings arises in the case of permanent change of control. This change of control can be effected by a merger of two or more independent undertakings or parts of those undertakings, or by acquisition of the direct or indirect control or decisive influence of one or more undertakings over one or more other undertakings, or of a part or of parts of other undertakings, by acquiring a majority of shares or stakes, or by acquiring a majority of voting rights or in any other way in accordance with the Companies Act. A merger may also take the form of a joint venture. The CA regulates both full function joint ventures and partial function joint ventures.[164]

94. According to the CA, undertakings are obliged to notify the Competition Agency of any proposed concentration prior to its implementation if the parties of the concentration reach the threshold prescribed by the Act. A concentration which is subject to mandatory notification cannot be implemented until the issuance of a decision by the Competition Agency or the lapse of the time limit in which such a decision should have been issued.[165] The notification and assessment procedure are regulated in detail by the Regulation on the Notification and Assessment of Concentrations enacted in 2011.[166]

95. In the appraisal of concentrations, the CA provides for the application of the substantive test or so-called SIEC test according to which 'concentrations of undertakings which significantly impede effective competition shall be deemed incompatible with the competition rules and therefore prohibited'.[167] The appraisal procedure involves a detailed assessment of the proposed concentration. The Competition Agency should particularly consider: the structure of the relevant market, actual and potential competitors, the supply and demand structure in the relevant market, the market share and market position of the parties of the concentrations, their financial and market power, possible changes in business operations and business plans, distribution channels and costs, specialization in distribution, and other relevant factors.[168]

96. As in many other jurisdictions, in Croatia concentrations in some sectors are regulated by specific sectoral rules. A special legal regime is established in the following sectors: media, electronic communications, and electronic media. Such a special regime has the intention of placing under greater scrutiny consolidations in specific industries in order to prevent mergers which might adversely affect the market beyond the level of protection afforded by general competition rules.

164. Article 15(3) and (6) CA.
165. Article 22 CA and Art. 7 of the Regulation on the Notification and Assessment of Concentrations, Official Gazette no. 38/2011.
166. Regulation on the Notification and Assessment of Concentrations, Official Gazette no. 38/2011.
167. Article 16 CA.
168. Article 21 CA; Article 16 Regulation on the Notification and Assessment of Concentrations.

97. In all the above-mentioned sectors, the appraisal of concentrations lies under the competence of the Competition Agency. However, in those sectors the Competition Agency, along with the general merger rules, applies specific sector rules and/or it cooperates with sector-specific regulators when adopting a merger decision.

98. For example, in the media sector, media publishers must make a notification of the merger pursuant to the general competition rules (e.g., rules on the notion of concentration), but disregarding the filing thresholds as provided for in the CA.[169] In other words, any concentration between media publishers (media publishers within the meaning of the Media Act) must be notified to the Competition Agency, even if the filing thresholds under the CA are not met.[170] The Competition Agency then decides if the merger is compatible with the general competition rules (the SIEC test). However, in two specific markets, the market for general-information daily newspapers and the market for general-information weekly newspapers, there is a specific prohibition rule which states that any merger of undertakings in the market for publishing general-information daily newspapers, as well in the market for publishing general-information weekly newspapers, is prohibited if the post-merger market share of the parties exceeds 40% of the total circulation sold in Croatia.[171]

99. With regard to electronic media providers, Article 72 of the Electronic Media Act, prescribes that a general competition law rules apply to electronic media service providers.[172] However, Electronic Media Act regulates some aspects of concentrations between electronic media providers. So, according to the Article 62 of the Electronic Media Act all concentrations between electronic media service providers are subject to mandatory notification to the Competition Agency if the turnover threshold prescribed by the general competition law rules is met. However, Electronic Media Act also prescribes that electronic media providers must notify AEM on any change in the ownership structure, as well as on the acquisition of shares in electronic media provider if the total value of acquired shares exceeds 1% of companies' share capital. [173] The purpose of those rules is to protect the pluralism and electronic media diversity. Consequently, Article 64 of the Electronic Media Act prescribes that impermissible ownership change in media service providers (prohibited concentration as defined in previous Electronic Media Act) is considered to exist when:

- the broadcaster has a state concession and shares of more than 25% in another broadcaster of the same or lower level of concession and vice versa;

169. Article 36 of the Media Act, Official Gazette nos 59/04, 84/11, 81/13.
170. *See* Decision of the Croatian Competition Agency of 23 May 2017, *&CCaronasnik Finance d.o.o. Ljubljana, Republika Slovenija and Business Media Croatia d.o.o., Zagreb*. UP/I-034-03/17-01/005.
171. Article 37 of the Media Act.
172. Electronic Media Act, Official Gazette no 111/2021.
173. Article 61 of the Electronic Media Act.

- the broadcaster has a state concession and share in the capital of a daily newspaper publisher with a print circulation of over 3000, with share of more than 10% and vice versa;
- the broadcaster has a state concession and daily print circulation of over 3000, and vice versa;
- the broadcaster has regional or local concession and shares in another broadcaster in the same domain, or higher or lower level, with more that 30%, and vice versa; and,
- the broadcaster has concession and shares in marketing agencies with more than 10%, and vice versa.[174]

100. Furthermore, Electronic Media Act also provides specific rules with regard to the assessment procedure on proposed concentration between electronic media providers. As it is already said, electronic media providers must notify the Competition Agency on the proposed concentration in line with the mandatory notification rules of the CA. As soon as the Competition Agency receives notification on the proposed concentration, the Competition Agency will request the expert opinion from the AEM on the proposed concentration. The AEM should deliver expert opinion on the proposed concentration between electronic media providers within thirty days. If the AEM does not deliver an opinion within thirty days from the receipt of the request, the Competition Agency will deem that AEM does not oppose the proposed concentration and the proposed concentration may continue in line with the procedure prescribed by the CA.

101. Those media service providers, who fail to notify Competition Agency about proposed concentration or who fail to notify AEM about acquisition of shares or of the change in control in media providers, will lose their concession or other broadcasting rights.[175]

102. One of the most recent Competition Agencies' decision in media sector concerns concentration between the undertakings Slovenia Broadband (SBB) and Tele2.[176] In January 2020, Competition Agency approved the proposed merger after she had conducted detailed investigation on the possible impact of the concentration on the relevant market. In the course of the procedure, CA established that SBB is present in several media service markets such as the production of audiovisual content and acquisition of licensing rights of third parties' audiovisual content, wholesale of general and specialized TV channels, etc. It also established that Tele2 was not engaged in any of business activities that are carried out by SBB in Croatia and that Tele2 is not a market player with significant market power in Croatia. It also concluded that SBB and Tele2 are not present in the transmission of pay TV programmes in Croatia, so there are no overlapping activities of SBB and Tele2 in the affected relevant markets in Croatia. During the course of proceedings and prior

174. Article 64 of the Electronic Media Act.
175. Article 63 of the Electronic Media Act.
176. Decision of the Croatian Competition Agency of 23 January 2020 Slovenia Broadband, *S.a.r.l. and Tele2 društvo s ograničenom odgovornošću za telekomunikacijske usluge,* UP/I 034-03/19-02/009.

to the clearance decision, CA contacted HACOM and AEM and asked them to provide their opinion on the proposed concentration. Since none of them opposed the proposed concentration, CA found that this concentration would not raise any competition concerns in relevant market.

103. On the contrary, in another, relatively recent decision, which was assessed by the AEM, the AEM prohibited media concentration between Slovenian Broadband and Nova TV.[177] In the proposed concentration, the AEM prohibited this concentration for the reasons contained in Article 61 of the Electronic Communication Act. Article 61 prohibits concentrations between an audiovisual and/or radio programme transmission operator and/or radio broadcast operators as well as media service providers. In this case, Broadband also owned Totalna televizija and was therefore qualified as a media service operator. According to the restriction defined in Article 61 of the Electronic Communication Act, Broadband could not at the same time be a television and/or radio broadcaster, which it would have become through the acquisition of 100% of the shares of Nova TV. Therefore, the proposed concentration was declared as impermissible.[178]

104. Telecommunications are another sector regulated by sector-specific provisions. Thus, concentrations in this sector also enjoy a special legal regime. Mergers between firms in this sector ('operators') are conducted pursuant to the general competition rules, and general filing thresholds apply.[179] However, even in such a case, when deciding on a merger between operators in the sector of electronic communications, the Competition Agency must ask the regulator HAKOM for its opinion regarding the merger and its effects in the relevant market.[180] The Competition Agency will apply its general competition rules when assessing the notified merger, and when deciding on its compatibility with competition rules.[181]

105. On the contrary, when it comes to operators with significant market power as well as operators that have been granted licences to use radio frequencies, HAKOM plays a significant role. Parties to the concentration must notify HAKOM of their intention to merge in a case where no filing obligation has arisen under the general competition rules.[182] More precisely, the obligation to notify the regulator arises if there is 'any intention of a merger between the operators, and an intention

177. Decision of the Agency for Electronic Media of 16 November 2017, 612-12/14-07/0101. *See also* Decision of the Croatian Competition Agency of 23 November 2017, *Slovenia Broadband S.a.r.l. and Nova TV d.d.*, UP/I-034-03/17-02/011.
178. This concentration was approved by the Competition Agency in May 2018 after the undertakings in question removed the competition concerns identified by the Agency for Electronic Media. *See* Decision of the Croatian Competition Agency of 7 May 2018, *Slovenia Broadband S.a.r.l. and Nova TV d.d.*, UP/I-034-03/18-02/003.
179. Article 68(1) of the Electronic Communications Act, Official Gazette nos 73/2008, 90/2011,133/2012, 80/2013, 71/2014, 72/2017.
180. Article 68(3) of the Electronic Communications Act.
181. Article 68(5) of the Electronic Communications Act.
182. Article 68(2) of the Electronic Communications Act.

of any other form of joint or concerted action of operators'.[183] Following the notification, HAKOM decides on the merger, taking into account 'the regulatory principles and goals' in the Electronic Communications Act.[184] In other words, the merger will be assessed under specific sector rules, taking into account the complexity of interaction between *ex ante* regulatory rules and ex post competition rules.

106. The market for telecommunications in Croatia has for some time been showing a trend of consolidation. This started in 2006 when HT bought Iskon Internet which was at the time HT's only competitor and the second largest Internet service provider. Although it was evident that this concentration would lead to a monopolistic position of an already dominant undertaking, HT, the concentration was not subject to mandatory notification due to the fact that one of the parties, notably Iskon Internet, did not reach the threshold necessary for mandatory notification. The Electronic Communication Act was later amended to encompass all concentrations in telecommunications which can have a negative impact on the market, whether or not the parties of the concentration reach a certain threshold. However, this regulatory novelty did not have an impact on this particular problematic concentration.

107. As a result, concentrations in telecommunications are currently under the special scrutiny of national regulators. So for example, in one of the most recent 'large' merger case involving HT and Optima,[185] the Competition Agency accepted the 'failing firm defence' and thus approved the concentration by which HT, the largest Croatian telecommunications operator, acquired in pre-bankruptcy proceedings control of Optima Telekom. However, the Competition Agency imposed the fulfilment of very strict and comprehensive measures and conditions for the elimination of possible negative effects of the concentration on competition in the market of electronic communication services in fixed networks. An interesting thing worth mentioning with regard to this concentration is that in this concentration HT got only temporary management rights. The duration of concentration was limited to a period of four years. HT took over obligation to sell their stake in Optima after the expiration of four years period. However, based on the request of parties to the concentration, Competition Agency prolonged the duration of this concentration until July 2021 without possibility for further extension. Concentration between those two undertakings expired on 10 July 2021. The process of the sales of the shares of Optima started on 31 January 2020 by publication of a public invitation for submission of bids. Share purchase agreement of Optima's shares to company Telemach is closed in January 2022.

183. *Ibid.*
184. Article 68(6) of the Electronic Communications Act.
185. Decision of the Croatian Competition Agency of 19 March 2014, *Hrvatski Telekom d.d. and OT Optima Telekom d.d.,* UP/I 034-03/13-02/007; Decision of the Croatian Competition Agency of 9 June 2017, *Hrvatski Telekom d.d. and OT Optima Telekom d.d.,* UP/I 034-03/2013-02/007.

108. With regard to concentrations in the banking sector, from 2002 to 2013 they were under the control of the Croatian National Bank.[186] Following 1 July 2013, when Croatia became an EU Member State, the CCA gained full competence to control concentrations in banking sectors as well.[187] In other mentioned sectors, such as the postal service, railway traffic, or energy activities,[188] the Competition Agency is the only authority in charge of the control of concentrations. However, in the case of concentrations in any of these sectors, it closely cooperates with sector regulators based on signed agreements.[189]

§4. Other Prohibitions

109. There are no other prohibitions in Croatian competition law.

§5. Tests of Illegality

I. Per Se Prohibitions and Naked Restraints

110. For hardcore restrictions (price-fixing, market sharing, output limitations, etc.) no exemption, either individual or block, is available. As already mentioned, in the case of a *de minimis* agreement, if it contains a hardcore clause, the benefit of *de minimis* rules is revoked.[190]

111. If the object of the agreement is to restrict competition, the agreement is deemed to be prohibited. On the contrary, if the effects of the agreement are restrictive of competition, then an exemption is available provided that the cumulative conditions under Article 8(3) of the CA are met.

II. Balancing Tests

112. A balancing test is available for agreements with effects restrictive of competition. If the agreement is prohibited because of its restrictive effects pursuant to Article 8(1) of the CA, it may be exempted under Article 8(3) of the CA. As already

186. Credit Institutions Act, Official Gazette no. 117/2008.
187. Article 50(3) of the Act on the Amendments to the CA (Official Gazette no. 80/20012), states: 'On the day of the entry into force of this Act, the Croatian National Banks shall deliver all the ongoing cases covering competition issues in the banking sector and the financial services provided by credit institutions to the Competition Agency which will continue the proceedings concerned.'
188. *See*, for example, Decision of the Croatian Competition Agency of 21 March 2017, *RWE Hrvatska d.o.o., Zagreb and Koprivnica Plina- distribucija plina d.o.o.*, UP/I-034-03/17-02/002.
189. For the postal service and railway traffic, the sectoral regulator, from 2014, has been the Croatian Regulatory Authority for Network Industries (HAKOM). The sectoral regulator for energy activities is the Croatian Energy Regulatory Agency (HERA). For cooperation agreements between the Competition Agency and various institutions, *see* http://www.aztn.hr/o-nama/sektorska-suradnja (accessed 10 Apr. 2018).
190. *See* Part I, Ch. 3 §1.

mentioned in Chapter 3 §1, the conditions for exemption mirror those set out in Article 101 TFEU: (a) the agreement has to contribute to improving the production or distribution of goods or to promoting technical or economic progress; (b) while allowing consumers a fair share of the resulting benefit; (c) not imposing on the undertakings concerned restrictions which are not indispensable to the attainment of these objectives; and (d) not affording such undertakings the possibility of eliminating competition in respect of a substantial part of the products in question.[191] The balancing test is not available for object restrictions.

III. Merger Tests

113. The substantive merger test applied by the Competition Agency is the SIEC test. A concentration of undertakings, which would significantly impede effective competition, in particular where such distortion of competition results from the strengthening of an existing dominant position, or from the creation of a new dominant position of the parties to the concentration, shall be deemed incompatible with the competition rules and therefore prohibited.[192] Although the SIEC test, compared to the 'dominance test' which was applied on the basis of the CA 1995 and the CA 2003, gives a wider degree of discretion to the Competition Agency in the appraisal of concentration, the dominance test plays a significant role in the appraisal of concentration. When assessing the merger in Phase II, the Competition Agency will especially ascertain whether a new dominant position is being created by the merger or whether an existing dominant position is being strengthened.

114. For example, in *Agrokor/Roto Dinamic*,[193] the Competition Agency held that the merger would result in the increased market share of Agrokor and Roto Dinamic in the distribution of alcoholic and non-alcoholic beverages. However, it also concluded that post-merger there would be no creation of a new dominant position and no strengthening of an existing dominant position in the relevant market where the market shares of Agrokor increased to 20–30%, which was still less than the market share of Gastro Grupa, a market leader whose market share was between 30 and 40%.

115. Nevertheless, in practice, in assessing a notified concentration, the Competition Agency goes far beyond establishing only whether a new dominant position will be created or strengthened. It applies an economic-focus approach regularly applied by the Commission and other national competition authorities. On the basis of a case-by-case method, the Competition Agency selects the criteria most appropriate to analyse the effects of a particular merger. The applicable criteria are listed in Article 21(3) of the CA where it is stated that in the course of the assessment, the Competition Agency should in particular define elements such as the structure of the

191. Article 8(3) CA.
192. Article 16 CA.
193. Decision of the Croatian Competition Agency of 14 February 2012, *Agrokor d.d./ Roto Dinamic d.d.*, UP/I-030-02/2011-02/007.

relevant market, actual and potential future competitors in the relevant market, the supply and demand structure and the trends of thereof, costs, risks, and the economic, legal barriers, barriers to entry, etc. withdrawal from the market. Furthermore, it should define the market share and market position of the undertakings concerned, their economic and financial power, the general level of competitiveness of the undertakings and their possibility of changing business operations, etc. The last set of elements include the effects of the concentration on other undertakings, benefits to consumers, such as decreases in the price of goods and services, shorter distribution channels, lowering of transportation costs, technological innovation, and other benefits directly deriving from the implementation of the concentrations.

116. When assessing the impacts of a particular merger, the Competition Agency takes into consideration both the unilateral and coordinative effects of the merger and examines whether the merger will increase the likelihood of tacit collusion and whether it will lead to collective dominance or result in market foreclosure.

117. For example, in *Agrokor/Roto,* as mentioned above, the Competition Agency concluded that the post-merger concentration ratio would increase and that the market would become increasingly more oligopolistic. However, it took into consideration that after the accession of Croatia to the EU it was likely that competitive pressure would additionally increase. Relevant factors were the fact that the market was open and there were many competitors with different market power, and that no competitor expressed disagreement with the proposed concentration. In addition, the Croatian Chamber of Commerce (CCC) in its opinion on the merger held that no negative effects were likely.

118. With regard to unilateral effects, the Competition Agency held that no unilateral effects were likely, since a price increase would mean that buyers would switch to other sources of supply. There were many competitors on the market with different degrees of market power, seven competitors with larger market shares, and 100–150 local undertakings; thus, price coordination was highly improbable. Further analysis showed that the relevant market was dynamic, with one of the competitors significantly increasing its market share and that there were no legal or factual entry barriers to the relevant market. An analysis regarding the probability of a price increase post-merger showed a high degree of substitutability between the products supplied by the merger parties and the products supplied by their competitors, thus diminishing the probability of a price increase since buyers had the possibility of finding a suitable alternative source of supply.

119. When it comes to coordinative effects, the Competition Agency held that coordinative effects were more likely on highly concentrated and stable markets, i.e., static markets with fewer competitors. Here, it copied the *Airtours* criteria,[194] concluding that no coordinative effects were likely. The market was dynamic in terms of the changing market shares of the participants.

194. Judgment of the Court of First Instance of 6 June 2002 in Case T-342/99 *Airtours v. Commission* ECLI:EU:T:2002:146.

120. In this case, the Competition Agency also examined vertical foreclosure and concluded that there were no vertical foreclosure effects (closing of the market for competitors due to the vertical integration of Agrokor) on the relevant markets since Agrokor was both a producer and supplier on the mineral and spring water market. Following a detailed analysis, the Competition Agency in this case concluded that the intended transaction could be declared compatible with Croatian competition law.[195]

121. There is wide agreement that one of the aims of competition law is to promote efficiency; therefore, it is logical that efficiencies should be taken into account in the process of merger appraisal.[196] The CA which was in force from 2003 to 2010[197] explicitly endorsed the consideration of efficiency. Concentrations, that led to the creation of new or the strengthening of a dominant position could be approved if the undertakings, the parties to the concentration, were able to provide valid evidence that their concentration would bring benefits that would prevail over the negative effects of the concentration produced by the creation or strengthening of their dominant position. Such benefits include benefits resulting from innovations, technical development, cost reductions, or the like.

122. This provision was replaced when the new (and currently in force) CA was enacted in 2010. Article 16 of the current CA no longer expressly entails a provision on which efficiency claims could be based. Nonetheless, in spite of the lack of an explicit endorsement of efficiencies, the Competition Agency still has enough manoeuvring space to adopt an extensive interpretation serving the benefit of efficiencies.[198]

123. A consideration of efficiency is made possible through Article 21(3) of the CA which provides for criteria for assessment. The relevant part of Article 21(3) prescribes:

> In the course of assessment of a concentration, the Competition Agency shall in particular define the effects of the concentration on other undertakings, and especially relating to the consumer benefit such as: decrease in prices of goods and/or services, shorter distribution courses, lowering of transportation, distribution and other costs, specialization in production, technological and other benefits directly deriving from the implementation of the concentration.

---

195. *Agrokor d.d./ Roto Dinamic d.d., supra* n. 193.
196. M. Kocmut, *The Role of Efficiency Consideration Under the EU Merger Control*, Working Paper (L) 09/05, 1 (University of Oxford Centre for Competition Law and Policy, 2005), available at https://www.law.ox.ac.uk/sites/files/oxlaw/cclp_l_09-05.pdf (accessed 3 Jul. 2018).
197. CA, Official Gazette no. 122/03.
198. *See*, for example, Decision of the Croatian Competition Agency of 15 March 2007, *AGROKOR d.d. Zagreb and TISAK d.d.*, UP/I-030-2/2006-02/33 Competition Agency. *See also* Decision of the Croatian Competition Agency of 25 March 2010, *Recro Ulaganja d.o.o. and M SAN ulaganja d.o.o*, UP/I-030-02/2009-02/11.

124. Similarly, the Regulation on Notification and Assessment of Concentration prescribes that the Competition Agency shall in the appraisal of concentration take into account innovation in technology, lowering prices of goods and/or services and other benefits for undertakings, and/or consumers directly deriving from the implementation of concentration.[199]

125. The Competition Agency's practices confirm that the consideration of efficiency is not only of a declarative nature but is actually being implemented. The Competition Agency regularly examines whether positive effects on competition will outweigh potential anticompetitive effects. It conducts such an analysis both in non-problematic and problematic concentrations. For example, in the very complex and conditionally approved concentration between H1 Telekom and OT-Optima Telekom,[200] the Competition Agency first approved concentration for a limited period of time (four years), and then later it prolonged the temporary management rights for another three years since it thought that only in this way would Optima achieve its full potential, and that it would increase business efficiency and reduce costs to enable the company to survive, to keep full employment and retain its customers.

199. Article 16(3) Regulation on Notification and Assessment of Concentration.
200. Decision of the Croatian Competition Agency of 9 June 2017, *H1 Telekom d.d. and OT-Optima Telekom d.d.*, UP/I-034-03/2016-02/006.

Chapter 4. Overview of Main Notions

§1. UNDERTAKING

126. The notion of an undertaking in Croatian competition law is modelled on EU competition law. It is broadly defined to encompass any person active in the market, notwithstanding the way it is financed, its legal form or its (non-)profit-making nature.[201] Thus, undertakings are companies, sole traders, craftsmen, and other persons engaged in economic activity by participating in the production and/or circulation of goods, or the provision of services; however, state bodies, as well as local and regional self-government bodies, may also be regarded as undertakings if they directly or indirectly act in the market.[202] Furthermore, any other legal or natural persons, such as associations, sports organizations, institutions, copyright and related rights holders, are to be regarded as undertakings if they act in the market.[203]

127. The following factors are not relevant when assessing if a person is to be regarded as an undertaking: its legal form, way of financing, intention to make profit, or the fact that it makes profit, its seat or residence in Croatia or abroad, the direct or indirect performance of an activity in the market, and irrespective of whether the activity in the market is performed permanently, periodically or for one time only.[204]

128. Three other categories of undertakings are mentioned in Article 3(3) of the CA, mirroring Article 106 TFEU, to which the Act is applicable, provided the application of the Act does not obstruct, in law or in fact, the performance of the particular tasks assigned to them by separate rules or measures and for the performance of which they have been established:

- undertakings entrusted with the operation of services of special economic interest;
- undertakings having the character of a revenue-producing monopoly; and
- undertakings granted special or exclusive rights to perform a certain activity.

129. To achieve alignment with the CJEU case law on single economic entity doctrine the Croatian CA was changed in 2021.[205]

---

201. Article 3(2) CA.
202. Article 3(1) CA.
203. *Ibid.*
204. Article 3(2) CA.
205. Article 3(4) CA. After the 2021 amendments Article 4 CA remains relevant in the context of merger control only, as it describes in which cases one undertaking possesses control over the other. For the application of the single economic entity doctrine in the decisional practice of the CCA under ex-Article 4 CA, before the 2021 amendment, *see* para 148-153.

130. It is explicitly provided that the CA is neither applicable to relations between employers and employees, nor to relations regulated by collective bargaining agreements between employers and trade unions.[206]

131. In a number of cases, the Competition Agency has held that public and public-like bodies were not to be considered as undertakings, therefore making the CA not applicable in the concrete case.

132. In the *Zajednica prijevoznika na području Međimurske županije et al.* case, the Competition Agency held that neither a county (in the concrete case *Međimurska županija*) nor a regional chamber of commerce (*županijska komora*), a regional branch of the CCC, could be considered as undertakings within the meaning of the CA since in the specific case they were to be considered as the regulating bodies for the provision of transport services (pursuant to relevant transport legislation).[207] In other words, since the bidding process for transport licences was taking place before these bodies, the Competition Agency held that they were neither directly active in the market nor were they making profit.

133. The City of Zagreb was also not an undertaking within the meaning of competition rules, since control over the City of Zagreb was exercised exclusively by state bodies as regulated by the Constitution and the law.[208]

134. In another case, the Competition Agency held, invoking Article 3(3) of the CA, that although a waste collection company owned by the City of Zagreb was to be considered an undertaking, in this particular case it was providing a public service of general interest in accordance with separate laws, the provision of which service must be performed by a local self-government unit, and hence the competition rules were not applicable to its conduct.[209] The Competition Agency held that the application of competition rules would prevent, by law and by fact, the execution of tasks entrusted to these persons by separate laws. The Competition Agency held that 'Čistoća d.o.o.' did not provide its services in the open market, but that it provided a public service of general interest.

206. Article 5 CA.

207. Decision of the Croatian Competition Agency of 11 July 2013, *Competition Agency v. Zajednica prijevoznika na području Međimurske županije et al./Presečki grupa*, UP/I-034-03/2013-01/026, confirmed: Judgment of the High Administrative Court of the Republic of Croatia of 20 February 2014, *Presečki grupa d.o.o. v. Competition Agency*, Us-II-72/2013-7.

208. Decision of the Croatian Competition Agency of 30 November 2012, *Competition Agency v. Grad Zagreb*, UP/I-034-03/2012-01/018.

209. Decision of the Croatian Competition Agency of 10 April 2014, *Competition Agency v. Čistoća d.o.o. Zadar*, UP/I-034-03/2014-01/006.

135. Similarly, in another case, invoking Article 3(3) of the CA, it was held that the application of competition rules would, by law and by fact, prevent the execution of tasks entrusted to a body running a national park ('Javna ustanova NP Kornati') pursuant to special rules.[210] When charging tickets for entry into the national park, 'Javna ustanova NP Kornati' was performing its public service pursuant to separate laws, and it was founded precisely to perform that public service. If 'Javna ustanova NP Kornati' was performing other activities on the open market (e.g., the sale of food, beverages, or souvenirs), competing in that way with other undertakings, it would then be considered as an undertaking. However, the Competition Agency held that this was not the case here.[211]

136. The Croatian Ministry of Science, Education and Sports was not considered an undertaking (in a dominant position), but a body entrusted by law to ensure the provision of a certain number of services, including the service of providing student meals.[212] It was held by the Competition Agency that those services cannot be looked upon only from the perspective of competition rules, but also from the point of view of public interest for the provision of the said services.

137. In another case, it was held that certain activities performed by the Agency for Explosives were activities of interest for the Republic of Croatia, which the agency performed as a public authority, and therefore had exclusive competence to deal with them.[213] Since these activities were not performed in the open market, the Agency for Explosives was not considered as an undertaking.

138. Furthermore, it was held that the Institute for Archaeology and the Croatian Restoration Institute (Hrvatski restauratorski zavod) were not undertakings, but bodies entrusted by law to secure the protection and preservation of cultural goods, which are goods of special interest and which fall under the protection of the Republic of Croatia.[214] The Competition Agency held that the public interest aspect of performing the tasks of conservation and restoration of cultural goods cannot be looked upon only from the perspective of competition rules, but that the public interest aspect must also be taken into account.

139. In a case where the Red Cross-Town of Osijek and the Red Cross-Osječko-Baranjska County, not-for-profit legal persons, performed public activities pursuant to separate laws and regulations, but also performed 'school in nature' activities and

210. Decision of the Croatian Competition Agency of 10 September 2014, *Competition Agency v. Javna ustanova Nacionalni Park Kornati, Murter*, UP/I-034-03/2014-01/018.
211. *Ibid.*
212. Decision of the Croatian Competition Agency of 24 November 2014, *Competition Agency v. Ministarstvo znanosti, obrazovanja i sporta*, UP/I-034-03/2014-01/012.
213. Decision of the Croatian Competition Agency of 26 November 2014, *Competition Agency v. Agencija za prostore ugrožene eksplozivnom atmosferom*, UP/I-034-03/2014-01/027.
214. Decision of the Croatian Competition Agency of 11 June 2015, *Competition Agency v. Institut za arheologiju, Zagreb i Hrvatski restauratorski zavod, Zagreb*, UP/I-034-03/2014-01/030.

swimming lessons, which, pursuant to separate laws and regulations, were not considered as tourist or catering activities, irrespective of their duration, the Competition Agency held that these activities were not economic activities performed in the open market. Invoking Article 3(3) of the CA, the Competition Agency held that the application of competition rules in this case would prevent by law and by fact the performance of tasks entrusted to them by separate laws and regulations.[215]

140. On the contrary, the Competition Agency held that a collective rights management body, a legal person entrusted by law to perform tasks of collective rights management, was an undertaking within the meaning of the CA despite the fact that it made no profit (revenues, minus operating costs, were distributed to authors), since it performed an economic activity and participated in the circulation of goods and services, thereby fulfilling its economic functions in the market.[216] The Competition Agency held that the application of the CA in the specific case did not prevent the execution of its tasks within the meaning of Article 4(2) of the CA.

141. Furthermore, football clubs were deemed as undertakings in a case where the Competition Agency held that sports clubs were to be regarded as undertakings only when performing certain economic activities, such as the sale of TV rights, the sale of tickets, souvenirs, and the transfer of players in the domestic and foreign market.[217] Therefore, these clubs may be regarded as undertakings only when performing the aforementioned economic activities and only for the performance of these activities. In this case, the Competition Agency held it had exclusive competence to decide if a sports club was an undertaking, and that the opinion of the Croatian Football Association, regarding the issue whether the two clubs in question were to be regarded as a single economic entity or as two independent undertakings, was not relevant as a decision of an authority dealing with a preliminary issue.

142. In a number of cases, the Competition Agency held that the CA was applicable to trade associations. For example, the Croatian Association of Architects, an association of authorized architects, which performed economic activity and participated in the trade of goods, was found to be captured under Article 3(3) of the CA, since this would not prevent the performance of tasks entrusted to the association by separate laws and regulations for the performance of which it was established.[218]

143. In the *Bakers cartel* case, the Competition Agency held that the provisions of the CA were applicable to a trade association pursuant to Article 3 of the CA,

215. Decision of the Croatian Competition Agency of 21 May 2015, *Competition Agency v. Gradsko društvo crvenog križa Osijek i Društvo crvenog križa Osječko-baranjske županije*, UP/I-034-03/2014-01/029.
216. *HUVEL v. HDS-ZAMP*, UP/I-030-02/2008-01/041, 2009, *supra* n. 162.
217. Decision of the Croatian Competition Agency of 25 July 2013, *Competition Agency v. NK 'Lokomotiva' i GNK 'Dinamo'*, UP/I-034-03/2013-01/030.
218. Decision of the Croatian Competition Agency of 1 December 2011, *Competition Agency v. Hrvatska komora arhitekata*, UP/I-030-02/2011-01/035.

since in the specific case a prohibited agreement was reached at a meeting convened by the association at its premises, which was clear evidence that it played an active role in reaching the agreement between its members.[219]

144. In the *Marine cartel* case, the court confirmed the decision of the Competition Agency finding that the CCC, and not its subgrouping (for nautical tourism) within a local branch, was liable for participating in a cartel.[220] The court found that the CCC was an association of undertakings which was established by law as an organization of all legal persons which perform an economic activity with the goal of organizing its members with the aim of advancing their activities, and that the claim of the Chamber of Commerce that its role was merely a technical and organizational one regarding meetings of the subgroup of the local branch was not convincing, in particular due to the role given to the Chamber of Commerce by law and by its statute.[221]

145. Finally, the Competition Agency held that the CA without doubt applied to the Croatian Association of Insurance Companies (*Hrvatski ured za osiguranje-HUO*), pursuant to Article 3 of the CA, since it was an association of undertakings in the insurance industry, and since members of its management board were undertakings which provide services in the market for mandatory car insurance.[222]

146. In an odd decision, applying the CA 2003, the Competition Agency held that a trade association (*Hrvatska udruga poslodavaca-Udruga novinskih izdavača*) was not an undertaking,[223] and thus not a participant in a cartel agreement.[224] Although the proceedings were initially opened against the trade association, the Competition Agency held that the association was not to be regarded as an undertaking since it did not pursue any economic activity within the meaning of Article 3 of the CA. The Competition Agency noted that trade associations had a legitimate right to protect the interests of their members but only if this was not in breach of Croatian laws and regulations, including those which protect competition on the market.

---

219. Decision of the Croatian Competition Agency of 26 July 2012, *Competition Agency v. Pekarstvo Kadulja d.o.o., Darda (Bakers cartel) et al.*, UP/I-030-02/11-01/039.
220. Decision of the Croatian Competition Agency of 17 March 2015, *Competition Agency v. Adriatic Croatia International Club d.d. et al.*, UP/I-034-03/13-01/047; annulled: Judgment of the High Administrative Court of the Republic of Croatia of 17 March 2016, *Ilirija d.d. et al. v. Competition Agency*, UsII-39/15-10; Decision of the Croatian Competition Agency of 13 December 2016, *Competition Agency v. Adriatic Croatia International Club d.d. et al.*, UP/I-034-03/13-01/047 (Decision on the suspension of proceedings).
221. *Ibid.*
222. Decision of the Croatian Competition Agency of 17 July 2015, *Competition Agency v. Hrvatski ured za osiguranja et al.*, UP/I-034-03/13-01/046.
223. Within the meaning of Art. 3 CA (CA 2003).
224. Decision of the Croatian Competitive Agency of 25 March 2010, *Competition Agency v. Datapress d.o.o. u stečaju et al.*, UP/I-030-02/2008-01/72, confirmed: Judgment of the Administrative Court of the Republic of Croatia of 21 December 2011, *Glas Slavonije d.d. et al. v. Competition Agency*, Us-4995/2010-6, Official Gazette no. 25/12.

147. In another similar cartel case, also applying the CA 2003, the Competition Agency held on the contrary that an association of undertakings and its members had concluded a cartel agreement.[225] In this case, the association was clearly one of the addressees of the decision, and one of the participants in the cartel. No discussion was provided in the decision on the status of the association of undertakings as an undertaking.

148. As regards the issue of a single economic entity, in one case the Competition Agency held that two football clubs were not independent undertakings within the meaning of Article 8 of the CA, since one of them (NK Lokomotiva) was controlled by the other (GNK Dinamo) within the meaning of Article 4 of the CA, and that they need to be regarded as a single economic entity.[226]

149. In another case, the Competition Agency held that a mother company (Adris grupa d.d.) and a subsidiary (Ronhill d.o.o.) were a single economic entity, since they were connected undertakings within the meaning of the Croatian Company Act.[227] This had no bearing on the substantive part of the decision, since they were both found liable for abusing their dominant position.

150. In one case, the initiative to start proceedings against several undertakings, which allegedly breached Article 8 of the CA, was dismissed since the Competition Agency found that all the undertakings belonged to the same holding group.[228]

151. In a distribution agreement case, where the Competition Agency was requested to grant individual exemption for a supply agreement between a manufacturer and an exclusive importer and distributor for Croatia, and for distributor agreements between the exclusive importer for Croatia and its (exclusive and non-exclusive) authorized distributors, the single economic entity doctrine was applied.[229] Since the parties were part of the same group of companies, the Competition Agency held that if the mother company had a majority stake, its daughter companies were not able to adopt decisions autonomously, thus they were deemed as a single economic entity, and there was no need to review the request for granting an individual exemption of that agreement.

---

225. Decision of the Croatian Competition Agency of 21 July 2011, *Competition Agency v. BIRODOM d.o.o. et al.*, UP/I-030-02/2010-01/018.
226. Decision of the Croatian Competition Agency of 27 February 2013, *Competition Agency v. NK 'Lokomotiva' i GNK 'Dinamo'*, UP/I-034-03/2013-01/005, confirmed on appeal: Judgment of the High Administrative Court of the Republic of Croatia of 9 April 2015, *Udruga 'Naš Hajduk' v. Competition Agency*, UsII-118/2013-8. Note that cases discussed in paragraphs 148-153 refer to the application of the single economic entity doctrine in the decisional practice of the CCA under ex-Article 4 CA, before the 2021 amendment.
227. Decision of the Croatian Competition Agency of 28 December 2006, *Competition Agency v. Adris grupa d.d. i Ronhill d.o.o.*, UP/I-030-02/2000-01/004.
228. Decision of the Croatian Competition Agency of 4 October 2018, Erste Group Bank AG et al., UP/I 034-03/18-01/013.
229. Decision of the Croatian Competition Agency of 13 January 2006, *Piaggio Hrvatska d.o.o.*, UP/I-030-02/2005-01/002.

152. The doctrine of single economic entity was not allowed as a defence in a cartel case where some among a number of firms were connected undertakings.[230] The Competition Agency held that, although the general prohibition of restrictive agreements was not applicable to agreements between connected undertakings within the meaning of Article 5 of the CA because of the single economic entity doctrine, this was not applicable in the concrete case where the agreement was concluded not only between connected undertakings but also between other independent undertakings.

153. In a clear-cut case, the Competition Agency held that the provisions of the CA on restrictive agreements were not applicable to agreements between companies which are part of the same holding company (*koncern*), since they are presumed to be a single economic entity pursuant to Article 4 of the CA.[231] The Competition Agency held that if a mother company holds a majority share, it is presumed that its daughter companies cannot independently adopt decisions. Companies within the same group pool their resources to achieve goals which are not limited to the interests of single companies, but are reflective of the goals of the group as a whole as a single economic entity. Therefore, it is deemed that the whole economic entity enters into competition, even though its parts have legal personality when entering into a mutual commercial relationship and conclude contracts among themselves.

154. In a rare case touching on the issue of the application of the CA to agency agreements, the Competition Agency held that two companies, Eventim and Adria zabava, were not 'independent' undertakings within the meaning of Article 8(1) of the CA, although they were separate legal persons, since their actions were not autonomous due to the fact that they acted on behalf and for the account of another legal person.[232] The Competition Agency concluded that Article 8(1) of the CA was not applicable to agency contracts. Grounding its position on the EU Guidelines on Vertical Restraints, the Competition Agency held that the undertakings did not bear a financial risk in relation to their activities as agents, and that therefore no application of the provision prohibiting restrictive agreements was possible.

§2. Relevant Market

155. The notion of relevant market in Croatian competition law draws heavily on EU competition law. The CA sets out a brief outline of the concept,[233] but more elaborate provisions are found in the Regulation on Defining Relevant Market.[234]

---

230. Decision of the Croatian Competition Agency of 24 September 2007, *Competition Agency v. Autobusni promet d.d. Varaždin et al.*, UP/I-030-02/2006-1/39.
231. Decision of the Croatian Competition Agency of 17 December 2015, *Competition Agency v. Piaggio Hrvatska d.o.o.*, UP/I-034-03/2014-01/022.
232. Decision of the Croatian Competition Agency of 9 February 2012, *Competition Agency v. Eventim d.o.o. i Adria zabava d.o.o.*, UP/I-030-02/2011-01/058.
233. Article 7 CA.
234. Uredba o načinu i kriterijima utvrđivanja mjerodavnog tržišta, Official Gazette no. 9/2011.

156. Relevant market is defined as a market of certain goods and/or services which are the subject of activities performed by an undertaking in a specific geographic territory.[235] A relevant product market encompasses any goods/services which are regarded as interchangeable by consumers, by reason of their characteristics, price, or use.[236] A relevant geographic market encompasses an area in which undertakings participate in the demand or supply of goods/services.[237]

157. The court accepts the position of the Competition Agency that in cartel cases there is no need to 'strictly define the relevant market' as there is when it comes to 'other infringements' of the CA.[238] However, it has been steady practice of the Competition Agency to describe relevant markets even in cartel cases.

158. As for merger cases, the more complex the merger and the more potential antitrust harm there is, the more complex is the analysis of relevant markets provided by the Competition Agency.

I. Relevant Product Market

159. When defining relevant product markets, the Competition Agency uses several criteria: it looks at the business activities of the firms themselves, where the majority of income is achieved, and at the 'overlapping activities' of the merger parties. [239] The substitutability of demand is an important criterion and is most frequently used.[240] In some cases, the substitutability of supply has also been relevant.[241]

160. For example, in the *Agrokor/Mlinar* merger case, as in other merger cases, the Competition Agency defined relevant product markets with regard to markets on which the activities of the merging parties overlap.[242] This method of the prima facie identification of product markets is especially suitable in horizontal mergers. Each of the product markets was analysed for its structure and characteristics. One of the relevant product markets identified in this case was the grocery retail market. The Competition Agency invoked EU case law to state that in this market, as a principle, the analysis needs to focus on local markets because of consumer habits (on the demand side), and because of the sales and advertising strategies of retailers (on

---

235. Article 7(1) CA.
236. Article 7(2) CA.
237. Article 7(3) CA.
238. Judgment of the High Administrative Court of the Republic of Croatia of 17 March 2016, *Ilirija d.d. et al. v. Competition Agency*, UsII-39/15-10.
239. J. Pecotić Kaufman & S. Slijepčević, *Koncentracije poduzetnika i mjerodavno tržište: Pravni i ekonomski aspekti*, 60 Zbornik Pravnog fakulteta u Zagrebu 995 (2010).
240. *Ibid*, at 1017.
241. *Ibid*, at 1024.
242. Decision of the Croatian Competition Agency of 29 December 2009, *Agrokor d.d./Mlinar d.d.*, UP/I-030-02/2008-02/044.

the supply side). Shops were categorized according to size, and to do this the Competition Agency used outsourced methodology.[243] The Competition Agency looked at the market structure for each market segment (small stores, self-service stores, supermarkets, hypermarkets), i.e., different store formats were analysed as particular segments of the product relevant market.

161. The *Agrokor/Roto* case provides an example of the Competition Agency's elaborate effort to define relevant markets in a merger case.[244] Here the question was whether, in the market for the wholesaling of beverages, different groups of drinks (e.g., beer, wine, non-alcoholic drinks, spirits, coffee, instant drinks, tea, bottled water) had to be considered as one relevant product market or as separate markets. The Competition Agency held it was one market, since, from the point of view of substitutability on the side of demand, buyers (e.g., hotels, restaurants) purchase the whole range of drinks from one distributor; if the price increases, the buyer could switch the supplier for the whole range of products, and since, from the point of view of substitutability on the supply side, there was a high level of substitutability within a short period of time in the case of a price increase, i.e., most suppliers would be able to supply a buyer which decided to change its supplier within a short period of time.

162. The Competition Agency identified two separate distribution channels, and thus two separate distribution markets, in the market for the wholesaling of alcoholic and non-alcoholic beverages: (1) distribution in the HoReCa segment; and (2) distribution to retail shops. In this sense, consumer habits and the way the goods are purchased were relevant: in catering facilities, beverages were consumed instantly at the premises, and in-store purchase was intended for consumption at home; in catering facilities, usually only small quantities of drinks were purchased (measured in glasses, not in bottles), and in in-store purchase, the end consumer as a rule purchased bottled beverages. The price of drinks was also significantly higher in catering facilities, as compared to home use, and end consumers were less sensitive to a price increase for the purchase of beverages in catering facilities as compared with purchase for home use. This all led the Competition Agency to conclude that the HoReCa segment of the market had to be identified as a separate relevant product market.

163. Another example of using demand substitutability was the *Mosor-komerc v. Jadrolinija* case where the Competition Agency held that the maritime transport of passengers and the maritime transport of vehicles were two different product markets due to their features: the purpose of using the service, the price, and the fact that passenger ships and cargo ships have different features, and it was also deemed relevant that the allegedly abusive conduct related only to discounts granted to the maritime transport of vehicles (trucks).[245]

243. Institut für Handelsforschung, Köln, Germany.

244. *Agrokor d.d./Roto Dinamic d.d.*, *supra* n. 193.

245. Decision of the Croatian Competition Agency of 9 July 2015, *Competition Agency v. Jadrolinija*, UP/I-034-03/2015-01/024.

164. In defining the relevant market in merger cases, the Competition Agency regularly consults the past decisions of the European Commission. In printed media (newspapers) mergers, the Competition Agency found that monthly, weekly, and daily magazines were not substitutes, but also that within those categories a further division according to content needed to be made.[246] The advertising market was also seen as a separate relevant product market.[247]

165. In an interesting merger of oil producers/retailers (*INA/MOL* case), the Competition Agency held that the retail market for oil derivatives on motorways needed to be looked at separately from the same market outside motorways, since the market conditions were different (motorways were toll roads, the investment costs for motorway service stations were higher, etc.).[248] In addition, the Competition Agency looked at different motorways as separate product markets (e.g., A1: Zagreb-Split-Dubrovnik-Zagreb and A6: Zagreb-Rijeka-Zagreb), which is in compliance with the way the EU Commission approaches similar cases.[249]

166. In regulated industries, such as telecommunications, the Competition Agency pays attention to the particularities of the relevant electronic communications markets, as in the *HT/Optima* case, for example, where it looked at the market for the provision of electronic communications services in fixed networks, which are regulated *ex ante* by the sector regulator.[250] The Competition Agency here accepted the relevant markets as proposed by the merger parties, since they were almost identical to the relevant markets defined by the sector regulator for the purpose of *ex ante* regulation.

167. In an interesting abuse of dominance case, the Competition Agency held that the market for sending late payment notices by the bank to its debtors could not be defined as a separate market for the purpose of antitrust analysis.[251] Namely, the Competition Agency considered that a notice, due to its legal character, could not be considered as a product or a service: it was a legal instrument available to creditors in cases of breach of contract by the debtor. The notice itself could not be regarded as a separate product or service, in addition to the primary product (loan contract). To accept that late payment notices present a separate product market would result in an 'unattainable conclusion' that any creditor could be regarded as having a dominant position in the 'market for late payment notices'.[252]

246. For example, *see Styria et al.* (2006). More details in Pecotić Kaufman & Slijepčević, *supra* n. 247, at 1028.
247. More details in Pecotić Kaufman & Slijepčević, *supra* n. 247, at 1028.
248. Decision of the Croatian Competition Agency of 9 June 2009, *MOL/INA Industrija nafte d.d.*, UP/1 030-02/2009-02/005. More details in Pecotić Kaufman & Slijepčević, *supra* n. 247, at 1030-1031.
249. Pecotić Kaufman & Slijepčević, *supra* n. 247 at 1031.
250. Decision of the Croatian Competition Agency of 19 March 2014, *Hrvatski Telekom d.d./OT-Optima Telekom d.d.*, UP/I-034-03/2013-02/007.
251. Decision of the Croatian Competition Agency of 6 March 2014, *Competition Agency v. Zagrebačka Banka d.d.*, UP/I-034-03/2013-02/028, confirmed: Judgment of the High Administrative Court of the Republic of Croatia of 27 August 2015, *Croatian National Bank v. Competition Agency*, UsII-43/14-10.
252. *Ibid.*

168. In the *Primalab* case, the Competition Agency looked at the issue of after-markets. It held that the criteria for defining a separate after-sales market (as a market for a specific brand) were fulfilled: a high substitution cost for a primary product and no substitution spare parts for Metrohm lab equipment products.[253] The Competition Agency defined two separate after-sales markets: a separate market for the distribution of spare parts for Metrohm lab equipment, and a separate market for the servicing of Metrohm lab equipment (after the expiration of the warranty period).

II. Relevant Geographic Market

169. When defining the relevant geographic market, the agency usually looks at the national market, but occasionally also at local markets. To conclude that the specific market in question was national in scope, the Competition Agency relied on the finding that wholesale suppliers used no geographic division of buyers for their own purposes, but divided buyers according to their characteristics.[254] Although it observed that individual suppliers were active on narrower geographic markets, the Competition Agency held that in the concrete case it was not necessary to analyse narrower segments of the market because it would not make a difference for the assessment of merger effects.[255]

170. In another case, the Competition Agency found that the maritime route between the ports of Split and Ancona was the relevant geographic market.[256] The Competition Agency held that this route had no substitutes (comparable routes were seasonal and catered also for other ports of origin/destination).

171. In a typical statement, the Competition Agency held that the wholesale market as a rule needs to be looked at on the national, not local level, while the grocery retail market was typically looked at on the local level.[257]

III. Temporal Markets

172. Only exceptionally does the Competition Agency look at the temporal aspects of markets. One example is provided in the *INA/MOL* merger case, where the Competition Agency held that seasonal trends were a relevant criterion that

253. Decision of the Croatian Competition Agency of 12 July 2012, *Competition Agency v. Primalab d.o.o.*, UP/I-034-03/2012-01/003.
254. *Agrokor d.d./Roto Dinamic d.d.*, *supra* n. 193.
255. *Ibid.*
256. Decision of the Croatian Competition Agency of 9 July 2015, *Competition Agency v. Jadrolinija*, UP/I-034-03/2015-01/024.
257. Decision of the Croatian Competition Agency of 29 December 2009, *Agrokor d.d./Mlinar d.d.*, UP/I-030-02/2008-02/044. For a detailed analysis, *see* Pecotić Kaufman & Slijepčević, *supra* n. 247, at 1032-1040.

without the application of other tests and criteria, these cannot be decisive and exclusive grounds for prohibiting a merger.[269] In other words, the Competition Agency held that HHI and other tests based on market share create no legal presumption of anticompetitive effects.

179. Contrary to its previous practice, in its more recent decisions concerning restrictive agreements, such as the *Piaggio* case,[270] the Competition Agency avoided a more detailed analysis of market share in the defined relevant market, since 'this (was) not necessary for a correct determination of facts'.

§4. Agreements and Concerted Practices

180. As already noted in Chapter 3 §1 above, the notion of agreement and concerted practice in Croatian competition law mirrors EU competition law. The CA provides an illustrative list of contractual arrangements that fit the notion of an agreement, be they horizontal or vertical in nature ('contracts, specific contract clauses, oral arrangements between undertakings, written arrangements between undertakings, concerted practice which is the result of those arrangements, decisions of undertakings, decisions of associations of undertakings, general terms of agreement and other acts adopted by undertakings, other arrangements').[271]

181. The CA 2003 defined the notion of an agreement to include 'explicit and tacit agreements',[272] while the CA 2009 omits tacit agreements from the definition of an agreement.

182. Invoking EU case law, the Competition Agency held that the notions of agreement and concerted practice are complementary, and there is no need to strictly delineate these two notions.[273]

183. Invoking EU law, the Competition Agency also held that provisions on restrictive agreements were applicable also to 'informal' agreements: for a prohibited agreement to exist, it was sufficient that undertakings expressed their joint intention to act in the market in a certain manner.[274] In this case, although there was

269. *Ibid.*
270. Decision of the Croatian Competition Agency of 17 December 2015, *Competition Agency v. Piaggio Hrvatska d.o.o.*, UP/I-034-03/2014-01/022.
271. Article 8(2) CA.
272. Article 9(1) CA 2003.
273. Invoking Case C-49/92 *Commission v. Anic Partecipazioni* ECLI:EU:C:1999:356, in the case 'Private security companies cartel', Decision of the Croatian Competition Agency of 17 March 2015, *Competition Agency v. Sokol Marić d.o.o., et al.*, UP/I-034-03/2014-01/002, confirmed: Judgment of the High Administrative Court of the Republic of Croatia of 22 April 2016, *Sokol Marić d.o.o. v. Competition Agency*, UsII-40/15-10 (and other cases), annulled: Judgment of the Constitutional Court of the Republic of Croatia of 1 February 2018, *Sokol Marić d.o.o.*, U-III-2791/2016 (and other cases).
274. Decision of the Croatian Competition Agency of 24 September 2007, *Competition Agency v. Autobusni promet d.d. Varaždin et al.*, UP/I-030-02/2006-1/39.

no written agreement, there was concerted practice since the form of the agreement was not relevant, given that the identical prices of competitors and statements of the parties in the proceedings before the Competition Agency undoubtedly prove the common intent of the parties. The uniform prices by all competitors were held by the Competition Agency to be a hardcore infringement. What was important for the Competition Agency was that that the undertakings played an important role in connecting the capital, Zagreb, with Dalmatian towns and the islands, and that there was a great number of departures daily (this was before the motorway between Zagreb and Split was built). One of the cartel parties gave a statement to the Competition Agency during the proceedings in which it maintained that there were 'long years of practice of business communication, exchange of information and experience, commercial analysis and the like between the providers of transportation services of passengers in Croatia effected through mutual business contacts or institutionalized contacts through the Croatian Chamber of Commerce – Road Transportation Group'. As proof, a copy of the discussion minutes on prices between transport companies was submitted to the Competition Agency.

§5. Restriction of Competition

184. The Croatian CA is applicable to any form of restriction of competition by undertakings, in the territory of the Republic of Croatia or outside its territory, provided there is an effect on the Republic of Croatia.[275] Furthermore, restrictions of competition having an effect on trade between Member States, whereby the CCA acts on the basis of Regulation 1/2003 applying Articles 101 and 102 TFEU, are also covered.[276]

185. Agreements which restrict competition, by object or by effect, are prohibited.[277] The abuse of a dominant position is none other than conduct that restricts competition.[278] Merger control rules prohibit mergers which 'significantly restrict competition'.[279]

186. As already discussed in Part I Chapter 3 §1, general prohibition[280] is not applicable to *de minimis* agreements, which are defined as agreements where the parties' joint market share (including undertakings under their control) is negligible, provided they contain no hardcore restrictions which result in distortion of the competition despite the fact that the parties' market share is negligible.[281]

275. Article 2 CA.
276. Article 2.a CA.
277. Article 8(1) CA. *See* Part I, Ch. 3, §1, *supra.*
278. Cf. Art. 14(1)(1) CA.
279. Article 16 CA.
280. Article 8(1) CA.
281. Article 11 CA.

187. No restriction of competition can be established in situations where the Competition Agency concludes that sector rules are applicable, such as in the *Zajednica prijevoznika na području Međimurske županije et al.* case where the Competition Agency held that it had no competence to examine the alleged concerted practice, since sector-specific regulation in the area of transport was applicable.[282]

188. In another case, the Competition Agency held no cartel could be found for an agreement on the purchase of shares on the stock exchange between, *inter alia*, pension funds, since the trade of shares was regulated by specific rules and it was HANFA (the HANFA) that was in charge of ensuring the correct implementation of rules in the capital market.[283]

189. In a case concerning trade associations, the Competition Agency held that advantages offered by the association of tourist agencies to its members did not amount to a prohibited agreement; on the contrary, they were usual for any association of undertakings (enhancement of quality of services, quality control, promoting business interests of members, facilitating business contacts with other potential business partners, informing members on news regarding tourism, etc.).[284] It was relevant also that membership in the association was voluntary. The Competition Agency confirmed that all undertakings in Croatia had the right of association for pursuing and protecting their economic interests, while obeying laws and regulations, including competition rules.

190. In a group of cases on the export of sugar, the Competition Agency held that there was no restriction of competition, and that the parties were allowed to protect legitimate special interests due to special circumstances, where the producer of sugar/the supplier imposed on the buyer/retailer the obligation to obtain consent from the supplier if the buyer wanted to export the sugar bought from the supplier.[285] According to the Competition Agency, this was not hardcore restraint by object, but a 'legitimate attempt by the supplier to protect its own business interests'. The special circumstances were as follows: special legal rules for trade in sugar between Croatia and the EU under the SAA (prior to accession), whose aim was to prevent fraud with sugar imports to the EU.

---

282. Decision of the Croatian Competition Agency of 11 July 2013, *Competition Agency v. Zajednica prijevoznika na području Međimurske županije et al./Presečki grupa*, UP/I-034-03/2013-01/026, confirmed: Judgment of the High Administrative Court of the Republic of Croatia of 20 February 2014, *Presečki grupa d.o.o. v. Competition Agency*, UsII-72/2013-7.

283. Decision of the Croatian Competition Agency of 13 January 2011, *Competition Agency v. AZ d.o.o. et al.*, UP/I-030-02/2010-01/037.

284. Decision of the Croatian Competition Agency of 28 June 2012, *Competition Agency v. Udruga hrvatskih putničkih agencija*, UP/I-034-03/2012-01/010.

285. Decision of the Croatian Competition Agency of 12 June 2014, *Competition Agency v. Viro tvornica šećera d.d. i Konzum d.d.*, UP/I-034-03/13-01/019; Decision of the Croatian Competition Agency of 12 June 2014, *Competition Agency v. Viro tvornica šećera d.d. i Stridon-promet d.o.o.*, UP/I-034-03/13-01/021.

191. No-poaching agreement was not found in breach of Article 8 of the CA, as the Competition Agency, in its decision dismissing the initiative to start an infringement case, held that the agreement between companies whereby each company agrees not to attempt to recruit employees from each other was not to be considered a restriction of competition but rather as an ancillary restraint which is directly related, proportionate and objectively necessary to the implementation of the agreement.[286]

§6. Monopolization and Abuse of Dominance

192. Abuse of a dominant position by one or more undertakings in the relevant market is prohibited, and the relevant provision is almost identical to Article 102 TFEU.[287], [288] In particular, the following conduct is prohibited:

(1) directly or indirectly imposing unfair purchase or selling prices or other unfair trading conditions;
(2) limiting production, markets, or technical development to the prejudice of consumers;
(3) applying dissimilar conditions to equivalent transactions with other undertakings, thereby placing them at a competitive disadvantage; and
(4) making the conclusion of contracts subject to acceptance by the other parties of supplementary obligations which, by their nature or according to commercial usage, have no connection with the subject of such contracts.[289]

193. Article [13] of the CA, which prohibits abuse of a dominant position, has 'identical content as Article 102 TFEU'.[290]

194. There has to be a significant restriction of competition in order to find abuse of a dominant position.[291]

286. Decision of the Croatian Competition Agency of 14 November 2018, UP/I 034-03/18-01/009.
287. *See* Ch. 3 §2 Dominant Undertaking, Ch. 3 §5 Tests of Illegality, Ch. 4 §3 Market Power/Dominant Position, *supra*.
288. Article 13 CA.
289. *Ibid.*
290. Decision of the Croatian Competition Agency of 16 June 2011, *Competition Agency v. Adris grupa d.d. and TDR d.o.o.*, UP/I-030-02/2006-01/082, Official Gazette no. 103/2011; confirmed: Judgment of the High Administrative Court of the Republic of Croatia of 22 April 2015, *TDR d.o.o. i Adris grupa d.d. v. Competition Agency*, UsII-9222/2011-4.
291. Decision of the Croatian Competition Agency of 24 February 2011, *Kino Zadar Film d.d. v. Blitz d.o.o. and Duplicato Media d.o.o.*, UP/I-030-02/2008-01/080. For a similar point *see* the decision of the Croatian Competition Agency of 19 April 2019, Competition Agency v. Hrvatski taekwondo savez, UP/I-034-03/17-01/005.

§7. Concentrations

195. The definition of 'concentration' is an essential element of merger control. The purpose of this definition is to identify those transactions that are 'suitable' for merger review[292] and that will be subject to control by competition authorities.[293] There are essentially two types of criteria that are used in different jurisdictions to define what constitutes 'concentration': 'objective', numerical, and more 'economic' criteria that seek to align the definition of a merger transaction more closely with the changes in the relationship between parties that could lead to competition concerns.[294]

196. Croatian legislation relies on the second criteria. Article 15 of the CA provides for the notion of 'concentration' and is practically the same as Article 3 of Regulation 139/04.

197. Article 15(1) of the CA provides that:

> A concentration between undertakings shall be deemed to arise where a change of control on a lasting basis results from:
>
> 1. a merger of two or more independent undertakings or parts thereof;
> 2. acquiring control or a decisive influence of one or more undertakings over one or more other undertakings, or of one or more undertakings or a part of an undertaking, or parts of other undertakings, in particular by:
>   - the acquisition of the majority of shares or share capital; or
>   - obtaining the majority of voting rights; or
>   - in any other way in compliance with the provisions of the Companies Act.

198. As can be seen from the above provision, the notion of 'concentration' covers only those operations that result in a permanent[295] change of control between or over previously independent undertakings. The acquisition of control means in essence the ability to exert 'permanent decisive influence' over one or more undertakings.[296]

199. Thus, a change of control occurs in the case of:

---

292. Definition of Transaction for the Purpose of Merger Control Review, OECD, DAF/COMP(2013)25, 5, http://www.oecd.org/daf/competition/Merger-control-review-2013.pdf (accessed 13 Apr. 2018).
293. ICN, Merger Guidelines Workbook, 2006, available at http://www.internationalcompetitionnetwork.org/uploads/library/doc321.pdf (accessed 13 Apr. 2018).
294. Definition of Transaction for the Purpose of Merger Control Review, OECD, DAF/COMP(2013)25, 14, available at http://www.oecd.org/daf/competition/Merger-control-review-2013.pdf (accessed 13 Apr. 2018).
295. The wording used in the Competition Act is 'on a lasting basis'.
296. Article 15(2) CA.

- a merger of two or more independent undertakings or parts of those undertakings;
- by the acquisition of direct or indirect control or a decisive influence of one or more undertakings over one or more other undertakings, or of a part or of parts of other undertakings;
- by acquiring the majority of shares or stakes; or
- by acquiring the majority of voting rights or in any other way in accordance with the Companies Act.[297]

The definition is broad enough to cover different factual situations of a change in control over previously independent undertakings, including a change in control emanating from agreements or by the purchase of assets.[298]

200. This was, for example, addressed in the case of the concentration between Tommy d.o.o. and Kerum d.o.o in which the Competition Agency fined Tommy d.o.o. because it failed to notify the Competition Agency about an already implemented merger. Tommy d.o.o. argued that the conducted transaction does not constitute a concentration as referred to in Article 15(1) of the CA since the parties only entered into a pre-contract on the sale of business premises and a lease agreement. Moreover, Tommy d.o.o claimed that there was no obligation to notify concentration since the parties had not reached the threshold for mandatory notification. After examining all the relevant facts, the Competition Agency concluded that the implemented transactions would result in a lasting change of control over a previously independent undertaking (Kerum d.o.o.) and as such are considered a concentration within the meaning of Article 15 of the CA.[299]

201. Furthermore, the notion of concentration from the CA specifically refers to situations of 'sole control'[300] and 'joint control'[301] (Article 15(3) of the CA). While the concept of 'sole control' refers to situations where a single undertaking has the possibility of exercising decisive influence over the whole or part of another undertaking, 'joint control' exists in the case where, following the merger, two or more undertakings jointly control the previously independent undertaking.

202. The Competition Agency examined whether as a result of a concentration the parties of the concentration would gain joint control in the concentration

---

297. Article 15(1) CA.
298. The acquisition of assets will be considered a 'merger transaction' only if it results in structural changes with a certain durability. The definition of Transaction for the Purpose of Merger Control Review, OECD, DAF/COMP(2013)25, 8, available at: http://www.oecd.org/daf/competition/Merger-control-review-2013.pdf (accessed 13 Apr. 2018). For an interpretation of when the purchase of assets is considered to be a concentration, *see also* Case M.7940 *Netto/Grocery Store at Armitage Avenue Little Hulton*, C(2016) 1340 final.
299. Decision of the Croatian Competition Agency of 27 June 2013, *Tommy d.o.o. and Kerum d.d.*, UP/I-034-03/13-02/001.
300. Slaughter and May, *The EU Merger Regulation: An Overview of the European Merger Control Rules* 3 (January 2018), available at https://www.slaughterandmay.com/media/64572/the-eu-merger-regulation.pdf (accessed 13 Apr. 2018).
301. *Ibid.*

between the undertakings Ivan Granić, Europapress Holding, Veltrade, Adris Grupa, and Distri-press.[302] In this case, prior to the implementation of the concentration, the acquired company Distri-press had two members, Europapress Holding and Ivan Granić. Although each of them had 50% of the share capital, Europapress Holding exercised the decisive influence, and thus, it was considered that it had sole control. In the proposed concentration, two new members were entering the group, Veltrade and Adris Grupa. Following the concentration, each member of the group would hold 25% of the share capital. Therefore, the Competition Agency concluded that the concentration would result in structural change in control and that sole control over Distri-press following the concentration would change into joint control.

203. In Competition Agency's practice there has been only a few concentrations where several undertakings gained joint control over other undertaking. One or the most recent case concerns several Slovenian undertakings who gained indirect joint control over Croatian undertaking Šubic-Diabetologija Interna Medicina d.o.o.[303] Concentration was cleared following the phase I procedure.

204. The Competition Agency explicitly lists transactions that should not be regarded as a concentration within the meaning of Article 15(5) of the CA: when credit institutions or other financial institutions or insurance companies hold, on a temporary basis, securities with a view to reselling them, when the acquisition of shares is related to the internal consolidation of undertakings belonging to the same group, and when control is acquired by an office-holder according to liquidation, winding-up, and insolvency proceedings.[304]

§8. Joint Ventures

205. When it comes to joint ventures, the Croatian CA is also aligned with the EU Merger Regulation. It differentiates between a full function and partial function joint venture (non-full function joint venture).[305] A joint venture is considered to be full function if cumulatively the following conditions are met: (1) two or more undertakings exercise decisive influence over the joint venture; (2) the joint venture

302. Decision of the Croatian Competition Agency of 12 January 20 05, *Distri Pres d.o.o. and Ivan Granić, Zagreb, Europapress Holding, Zagreb, Adris grupa d.d., Rovinj*, UP/I-030-02/2004-01/17, available at http://www.aztn.hr/uploads/documents/odluke/TN/UPI-030-022004-01017.pdf (accessed 15 Apr. 2018).
303. Decision of the Croatian Competition Agency of 15 September 2021, *DC VILA BOGATIN d.o.o., Bled, R. Slovenija i ALFI PE d.o.o., SIS k.d., Ljubljana, R. Slovenija over MDT&T d.o.o., Maribor, R. Slovenija and i ŠUBIC d.o.o., Maribor, R. Slovenija*, UP/I 034-03/21-02/008.
304. Article 15(5) CA.
305. For a detailed discussion, *see* J. Pecotić, *Zajednički pothvat (joint venture) u pravu tržišnog natjecanja* (Sinergija, 2005).

functions on a lasting basis as an autonomous economic entity.[306] Being an autonomous economic entity essentially means that a joint venture must operate in a market, performing the functions normally carried out by undertakings operating in the same market.[307] In order to do so, the joint venture must have a management dedicated to its day-to-day operations and access to sufficient resources, including staff, finance, and assets.[308] When these conditions are met, the joint venture constitutes a concentration. On the contrary, the joint venture is considered to be partial function or non-full function when the joint venture, despite the fact that it is an autonomous economic entity, has as its object or effect the coordination of the competitive behaviour of the undertakings.[309] So, compared to a full function joint venture, in the case of a partial function joint venture there is the risk of the coordination of competitive behaviour outside the joint venture of the parties who have established the joint venture.[310]

206. The relevant CA provision governing partial function joint ventures is contained in Article 15(6) of the CA which states that 'the creation of a joint venture by two or more independent undertakings performing on a lasting basis all the functions of an autonomous economic entity shall also constitute a concentration, but the coordination itself will be appraised within the meaning of the criteria referred to under Article 8 paragraphs (1) and (3) of the Act' (general prohibition of restrictive agreements and cumulative criteria for exemption).

207. In assessing both types of joint venture, the Competition Agency relies on EU court rulings[311] and relevant interpretative documents, notably the Jurisdictional Notice under Council Regulation (EC) No. 139/2004 on the control of concentrations between undertakings.[312]

---

306. The creation of a joint venture by two or more independent undertakings performing on a lasting basis all the functions of an autonomous economic entity is considered as a concentration of undertakings (Art. 15(3) CA).
307. Commission Consolidated Jurisdictional Notice under Council Regulation (EC) no. 139/2004 on the control of concentrations between undertakings, 2008/C 95/01, 16 April 2008, 94.
308. *Ibid.*
309. A. Nourry, D. Harrison & C. Clifford, *Transactions and Practices: EU Joint Ventures* (Practical Law UK, Thomson Reuters, 2018), available at https://uk.practicallaw.thomsonreuters.com/1-107-3702?transitionType=Default&contextData=(sc.Default)&firstPage=true&comp=pluk&bhcp=1 (accessed 16 Apr. 2018).
310. *Ibid.*
311. In relation to this, it will be interesting to see how the Competition Agency will interpret rules on non-full function joint ventures following the ECJ judgment of 7 September 2017 in Case C-248/16 *Austria Asphalt* ECLI:EU:C:2017:643.
312. Commission Consolidated Jurisdictional Notice under Council Regulation (EC) no. 139/2004 on the control of concentrations between undertakings, 2008/c, 95/01, 16 April 2008.

Chapter 5. Consequences of Violations and Enforcement Institutions

§1. Administrative Enforcement

208. In Croatia, the administrative body entrusted with the enforcement of the Croatian CA, Articles 101 and 102 TFEU, and the EU Merger Regulation is the Competition Agency. There are a number of sector-specific regulators operating *ex ante* under sector-specific laws; however, they are not empowered to carry out *ex post* proceedings covering anticompetitive behaviour either under national or EU competition rules.[313]

I. Antitrust Authorities

A. *Formation, Composition*

209. The Competition Agency is a stand-alone, independent legal person vested with public authority, which as a general, national regulatory authority autonomously performs activities falling within the scope of the CA, Regulation 1/2003 in relation to the application of Articles 101 and 102 TFEU, and the EU Merger Regulation.[314] As of December 2017, the Competition Agency is entrusted with the enforcement of the Act on the prohibition of unfair trading practices in the business-to-business food supply chain as well.[315] The Competition Agency's work is public[316] and its independence from the executive branch is assured though its accountability to the Croatian parliament[317] and the explicit legislative prohibition of any form of political[318] or other type of influence that may impede its independence and autonomy.[319] The seat of the Competition Agency is in Zagreb,[320] and it currently employs fifty-two people, mostly lawyers and economists.[321] It was funded by the state with the annual budget of HRK 13.6 million (EUR 1.8 million) in 2020. Competition Agency's annual budget has often been criticized for being too low to secure the efficient performance of all the Competition Agency's activities. However, following the transposition of the ECN+ Directive, the agency should be ensured enough resources to cover qualified staff, financial means, technical and

313. For more details, *see* Ch. 2, §2 Special Sectors, *supra*.
314. Article 26(1) CA.
315. Official Gazette 117/2017.
316. Article 26.a(2) CA.
317. Article 26(6) CA.
318. Article 26(11) CA.
319. Article 26(10) CA.
320. Article 26(12) CA.
321. Annual report of the Competition Agency for 2020, available at https://www.aztn.hr/ea/wp-content/uploads/2015/05/Summary-Annual-Report-of-the-Croatian-Competition-Agency-for-2020.pdf (accessed 7 Feb. 2022).

technological expertise and equipment, necessary for its effective performance, of course, within the capacity of the state budget.[322]

210. The internal structure of the Competition Agency, as shown in Figure 1, is laid down by the CA and detailed by its statute,[323] which is subject to the Parliament's approval.[324] The main managing and decision-making body of the Competition Agency is the Competition Council consisting of five members, including the president,[325] who is the highest-ranking official of the Competition Agency, currently performed by Mirta Kapural. The Competition Council collectively decides on all competition matters,[326] while the primary duty of the president is to represent and speak for the Competition Agency as well as to manage and supervise its activities. The president is responsible for the legality of decisions and the expert performance of the Competition Agency,[327] which is supervised by the Croatian Parliament on a yearly basis on the ground of the Competition Agency's annual reports.[328]

211. All members of the Council including its president are appointed and relieved of duty by the Croatian Parliament upon the proposal of the Croatian Government,[329] while the Vice President of the Council is elected on the proposal of the President of the Council by a majority of votes of the Council.[330] All members of the Council are appointed for a term of five years with the possibility of reappointment.[331] In order to ensure the independence of the Competition Agency and autonomy in its decision-making, the members of the Council may not be 'state officials, persons who perform duty in any administrative body of a political party, members of supervisory boards and executive bodies of undertakings, or members in any kind of interest associations, which could lead to conflict of interest'.[332]

212. Administrative and professional activities related to competition law are performed by the expert teams of the Competition Agency, organizationally divided into divisions and departments. There are five divisions, the Council's Office, the Office of the Chief Economist, the Competition Division, and the General Affairs Division and the Unfair Trading Practices Division. The Competition Division is further divided into departments respectively responsible for restrictive agreements,

---

322. Article 26.a(5) CA.
323. Official Gazette nos 22/2011, 74/2014, 60/2018.
324. Article 26(8) CA.
325. Article 27(1) and (2) CA.
326. All the activities of the Council are enumerated in Article 30 CA, and they range from decision-making powers in concrete cases before the Competition Agency, either based on the CA or articles 101 and 102 TFEU, to activities related to legislative initiative, advocacy, international cooperation, and more.
327. Article 27(3) CA.
328. Article 26(6)CA.
329. Article 27(4) CA.
330. Article 27(5) CA.
331. Article 28(3) CA.
332. Article 28(5) CA.

abuse of dominance, mergers, legislation and comparative practice, and international and EU cooperation. In addition, the Restrictive Agreements Department has a special forensic and IT unit mostly used in the investigations of cartels. The General Affairs Division consists of the General Affairs Department, the Finance Department, and the Public Relations Office. All acts and decisions of the Competition Agency are prepared by responsible divisions but are finally rendered by the Competition Council by a majority of votes in sessions of at least three members, one of whom must be the president or the vice president of the Competition Council.[333]

Figure 1 Internal Structure of the Competition Agency[334]

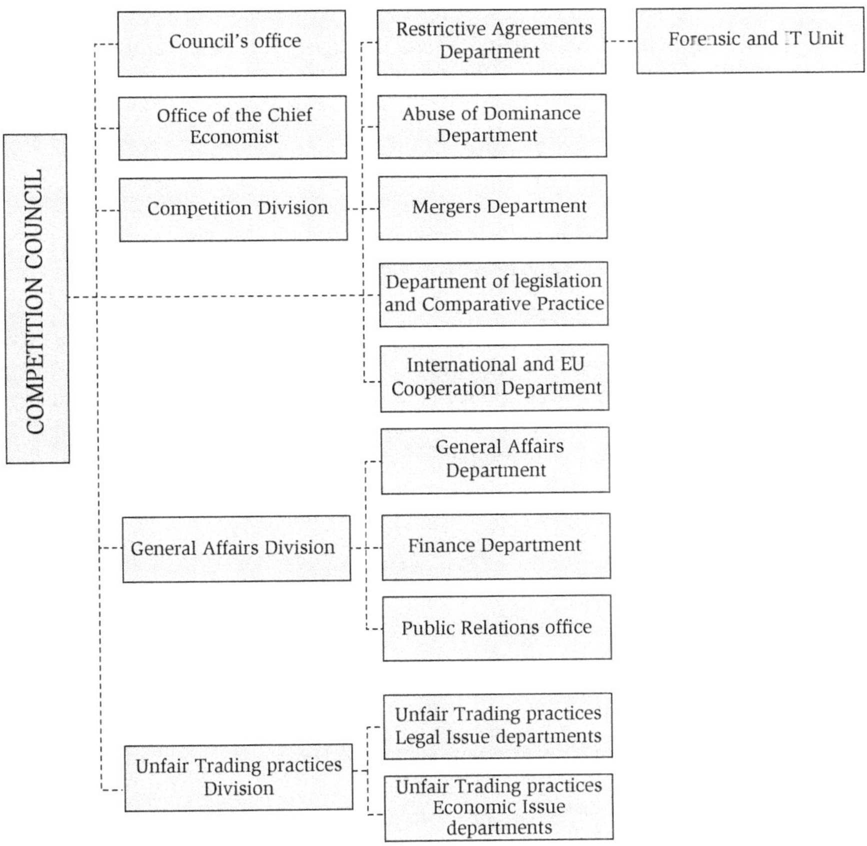

333. Article 19 Statute of the Competition Agency.
334. Sourced from the Competition Agency, http://www.aztn.hr/ea/wp-content/uploads/2015/05/Capture-1.png (accessed 2 Feb. 2022).

B. Investigating Powers

213. The competition law procedure is regulated by the CA as a *lex specialis* which is complemented by the General Administrative Procedure Act as a *lex generalis,* the latter thus being applicable where the CA does not regulate a particular matter. The main investigative powers prescribed by the CA are the collection of data, dawn raids, and the temporary seizure of objects. These investigative powers of the Competition Agency are very wide, and they resemble the powers of public prosecutors in criminal cases.[335]

C. Adjudicating Powers (Ascertaining and Sanctioning)

214. The Competition Agency has broad powers in both ascertaining and sanctioning antitrust violations. In particular, it has the power to:

- find and bring to an end an infringement of Articles 8[336] and 13[337] of the CA and/or Articles 101[338] and 102 TFEU;[339]
- accept commitments;[340]
- accept settlement proposals;[341]
- order interim measures;[342] and
- impose fines[343] and daily penalties.[344]

215. Besides these basic decisions, the Competition Agency is empowered to: withdraw the benefit of the block exemption either under national or EU law,[345] assess agreements of minor importance,[346] assess the compatibility of concentrations,[347] accept remedies,[348] and impose measures aimed at the restoration of effective competition in cases of incompatible concentrations and impose adequate fines.[349]

335. For a detailed overview of the Competition Agency's investigative powers, *see* Part III, Ch. 1, §2 Powers.
336. Articles 9(1) and 30(2) CA.
337. Articles 14(1) and 30(2) CA.
338. Articles 9(1) and 30(2) CA.
339. Articles 14(1) and 30(2) CA.
340. Articles 30(2) and 49 CA.
341. Articles 30(5) and 52.a CA.
342. Article 51(1) CA.
343. Articles 9(3), 14(1) and (4), 30(2) CA.
344. Article 63.a CA.
345. Articles 10.a(2) and (3) CA.
346. Article 11(4) CA.
347. Article 21 CA.
348. Article 22(6) CA.
349. Article 24 CA.

1. Finding and Bringing to an End an Infringement of Competition Rules

216. The main power of the Competition Agency is to find and bring to an end any infringement of national and EU rules on prohibited agreements and abuse of a dominant position. The finding of an infringement is carried out within an administrative procedure.

217. When it comes to prohibited agreements, in order to render an infringement decision, the Competition Agency must prove the existence of such an agreement, specify the parties involved, define the category of the agreement, as well as the goods and/or services concerned, the relevant geographic market, the duration of the agreement, and its object and implementation.[350] Agreements in violation of competition law are *ex lege* null and void and thus a decision to that effect is of a declaratory nature.[351] Once the violations have been ascertained, the Competition Agency can impose suitable remedies to restore efficient competition on the market and impose a fine.

218. A decision on the abuse of a dominant position includes the determination of whether an undertaking is dominant in the relevant market and whether its abusive conduct is capable of distorting competition, including the duration of such conduct. Where the Competition Agency finds the existence of abuse of dominance, it immediately orders a cessation of such conduct and imposes a fine on the undertaking concerned.[352]

219. In Croatia, as in other EU Member States, when a particular behaviour threatens to affect trade between Member States, the national authority is obliged to apply Articles 101 and 102 TFEU together with national antitrust provisions. This duty arises from Regulation 1/2003 and, for the Competition Agency, from Articles 2.a, 9 and 14 of the CA. This implies that the Competition Agency will carry out a single procedure, using the same analytical tools and render a single decision in which it will decide on the grounds of both national and EU competition law in cases where a particular behaviour affects trade between Member States. The relationship between the application of national and EU competition law is detailed by Regulation 1/2003 so as to avoid differences of outcome.[353] In order to safeguard the efficiency and uniformity of application of Articles 101 and 102 TFEU, the Competition Agency must comply with the general principles of EU law and the EU Charter of Fundamental Rights.[354]

220. Prior to the latest amendments to the CA, a serious enforcement problem was arising when proceedings against an undertaking did not lead to an infringement decision. Namely, according to the former Article 58 (1) 13 of the 2009 CA,

350. Article 9(1) CA.
351. Article 8(4) CA.
352. Article 14(1) CA.
353. For more details, *see* Part I, Ch. 1, §4 Relation and Hierarchy of Sources.
354. Article 2.b (2) CA.

the Competition Agency, had the authority to find that competition in the relevant market is not restricted in terms of the CA and/or Articles 101 and 102 TFEU. In other words, the Competition Agency was empowered to decide on the merits, even in cases of the non-violation of both national and EU competition laws. Obviously, such wording of the CA was in conflict with Article 5 of Regulation 1/2003 and its interpretation given by the European Court of Justice (ECJ) in the famous *Tele2 Polska* case.[355] According to the ECJ, when a national authority cannot prove the existence of an infringement of Article 102 TFEU (and by analogy Article 101 as well), it is not allowed to adopt a decision to that effect, even in situations where national law gives it the authority to do so, as is the case in Croatia. Adopting such a decision is under the exclusive jurisdiction of the Commission. National competition authorities should instead suspend the proceedings without deciding on the substance. The ECJ argued that the:

> [e]mpowerment of national competition authorities to take decisions stating that there has been no breach of Article 102 TFEU would call into question the system of cooperation established by the Regulation and would undermine the power of the Commission.
>
> Such a 'negative' decision on the merits would risk undermining the uniform application of Arts 101 TFEU and 102 TFEU, which is one of the objectives of the Regulation highlighted by recital 1 in its preamble, since such a decision might prevent the Commission from finding subsequently that the practice in question amounts to a breach of those provisions of European Union law.[356]

221. The problem transpired in *Hrvatski Telekom* [357] where the High Administrative Court took the position that, in accordance with Article 5(2) of Regulation 1/2003, after initiating proceedings the Competition Agency may only terminate the proceedings by the adoption of a decision on the merits as envisaged in former Article 58 of the CA. The reasoning of the High Administrative Court rested mostly on the erroneous translation of Article 5(2) of Regulation 1/2003 into Croatian and the non-observance of the duty of judges to consult other official languages and the EU in the case of doubt about the meaning of a particular provision.[358] Namely, instead of the original wording in Article 5(2) '[...] there are no grounds for action on their part' the official translation into Croatian read '[...] there are no grounds for *initiating proceedings* (emphasis added)'. The High Administrative Court thus

355. Judgment of 3 May 2011, Case C-375/09 *Tele2 Polska* ECLI:EU:C:2011:270.

356. *Ibid.*, paras 27–28.

357. Judgment of the High Administrative Court of the Republic of Croatia of 16 October 2014 UsII-65/2014-9

358. 'Each language version is authentic and is used as a source text for judicial interpretation, and application. Where a doubt about meaning arises all language versions should be looked at, but even if no doubt arises from one text, it cannot be taken alone, as all should be taken into account.' C. Robertson, *How the European Union Functions in 23 Languages* 20 (Council of the EU - Legal Service, Directorate for the Quality of Legislation, SYNAPS 28, 2013), available at https://brage.bibsys.no/xmlui/bitstream/handle/11250/2393842/Robertson_28.pdf?sequence=1 (accessed 2 May 2018).

reasoned that this provision is not applicable to situations where proceedings have already been initiated by the Competition Agency. The Competition Agency tried to argue its position by referring to *Tele2 Polska*. However, the High Administrative Court failed to take this into account as well, without explaining why it found the ECJ ruling inapplicable to the case. The subsequent decision of the Competition Agency was annulled again with the High Administrative Court ordering retrial.[359]

222. Considering that the misinterpretation of Article 5(2) of Regulation 1/2003 by the High Administrative Court was the result of the incorrect translation of that provision into Croatian, in 2016 the Competition Agency successfully sought an official change of translation to correspond to other official languages of the EU.[360] Following the official change of translation of Article 5(2), in 2017 the High Administrative Court upheld the decision of the Competition Agency to the same effect in another case (*Hrvatska pošta d.d)*.[361] This led the High Administrative Court to uphold the retrial decision in the *Hrvatski Telecom* case suspending proceedings on the ground of Article 102 TFEU.[362]

In order to prevent such misinterpretation of EU law in the future, Article 58(1)13 has been changed by the newest revisions of the CA from 2021, specifying that where there are no grounds for any further steps in the proceeding within either national or EU antitrust rules, Competition Agency renders a decision on the suspension of the proceeding. Accordingly, just like other national competition authorities, the Competition Agency is now able to terminate proceedings without rendering a decision on the merits of the case, whenever, on the basis of the information in its possession, it cannot find an infringement of Articles 101 and 102 TFEU or 8 and 13 CA. [363]

2. Commitment Decisions

223. In order to restore effective competition in the market in the most suitable and fastest manner, the CA envisages the possibility for parties to the proceedings to propose to the Competition Agency measures and conditions they consider suitable for neutralizing the competition law concerns, and to set time limits for the implementation of the measures and conditions proposed. The parties to the proceedings may take up on that procedural possibility after the proceeding has been

359. Decision of the Croatian Competition Agency of 17 December 2014, *Competition Agency v. Hrvatski Telekom d.d.*, UP/I-034-03/2013-01/007; Judgment of the High Administrative Court of the Republic of Croatia of 29 October 2015, *H1 Telekom d.d. v. Competition Agency*, UsII-8/15-10.
360. The Corrigendum was published in the Official Journal of 30 June 2016. *See* the annual report of the Competition Agency for 2016, 65, available at http://www.aztn.hr/ea/wp-content/uploads/2015/05/AZTN-GI-2016-.pdf (accessed 25 Sep. 2018).
361. Judgment of the High Administrative Court of the Republic of Croatia of 22 September 2017, UsII-15/16-19.
362. Judgment of the High Administrative Court of the Republic of Croatia UP/I 034-03/2013-01/007 of 14 November 2018.
363. See also Article 30 (4) CA.

initiated and prior to the issuing of a statement of objections.[364] Following their proposal, if satisfied, the Competition Agency may adopt a decision to that effect by which the voluntarily proposed commitments become binding on the parties.[365] A commitment decision specifies the conditions and measures to be implemented, the time limits for carrying them out, and obliges the parties to furnish proof to that effect.[366] The choice of commitments are fully in the hands of the parties as the CA does not specify the types of commitments suitable for the restoration of competition. However, from the practice of the Competition Agency, it can be concluded that both structural and behavioural commitments are acceptable as long as they are to meet the demands of the specific case at hand. The biggest motivation for the parties to propose commitments arises from the fact that the commitment decision does not contain a finding of an infringement; instead, it is a type of conditional clearance decision which determines that upon the completion of the commitments within the specified time frames, there are no further grounds for action on the part of the Competition Agency. For the same reason, however, such a decision is not available in all situations, particularly in cases of cartels or other hardcore violations of long duration. Article 49(4) of the CA stipulates that such a decision is available where the infringement is of short duration and where the undertakings concerned cooperate and propose commitments during the first six months of the proceedings, and where the infringement involves a large number of parties or where the Competition Agency finds this is appropriate for reasons of efficiency and for restoring effective competition without involving unnecessary lengthy procedures.[367]

224. When deciding on the proposed commitments, the Competition Agency has to take into account the interests of third parties as well. In order to ensure such rights will not be hampered by a commitment decision, the Competition Agency has the obligation to publish its intention to adopt the commitment decision, including its content, on its official website. Such an announcement is intended for all interested parties that are given twenty days to submit objections, which are then taken into consideration by the Competition Agency when deciding whether to accept the proposed commitments by the parties.[368]

225. The Competition Agency may reopen proceedings if the undertakings do not comply with the undertaken commitments or if the decision has been adopted on the grounds of incomplete, incorrect or misleading information given by the parties, or the circumstances have changed considerably.[369] In any case, the Competition Agency monitors the proper implementation of its decisions and imposes the appropriate sanctions in the case of non-compliance. In fact, the CA expressly provides that where the undertaking concerned does not comply with the commitments and the set time limits, such conduct is considered a violation of the CA and/or of

364. Article 49(1) CA.
365. Article 49(2) CA.
366. Article 49(3) CA.
367. Article 49(4) CA.
368. Article 49(5) CA.
369. Article 49(6) CA.

Articles 101 and 102 TFEU, triggering the right of the Competition Agency to immediately adopt a prohibition decision and impose a fine.[370]

3. Fining

226. Besides being empowered to accept or impose commitments for the restoration of efficient competition in the relevant market, where the infringement of either national or EU competition law has been established, the Competition Agency may impose fines upon the infringing parties, termed 'administrative-penal measures' as they combine the administrative and penal functions of a fine. By the wording of Article 60 of the CA, the objective of the fine is to ensure effective competition, to sanction the infringements, to eliminate the consequences of anti-competitive behaviour, and to deter other undertakings from engaging in such practices. For this reason, the CA specifies the manner of calculating the fines, taking into account the goals to be achieved. Special treatment is given to undertakings under the Leniency Programme. In addition, with the 2021 CA amendments, the Competition Agency is allowed to impose daily penalties[371] for a number of reasons related to non-cooperation of undertakings in the proceedings. This novelty is the result of the transposition of the ECN+ Directive and it is meant to empower the Competition Agency with an additional procedural tool for the efficient conduct of proceedings before it. [372]

D. Other Institutional Tasks (Consultancy to Parliament/Government)

227. One of the very important powers and duties of the Competition Agency relates to issuing expert opinions regarding the compliance of draft legislation and other legal acts with competition rules. Such expert opinions may be issued by the Competition Agency upon the request of the Croatian Parliament, the Government of the Republic of Croatia, central administration authorities, as well as local and regional self-government units.[373] Where a specific piece of draft legislation threatens to distort competition, the Competition Agency may also issue the expert opinion on its own initiative. In the latter situation, the Competition Agency is allowed to request from public authorities the delivery of draft legal acts for an evaluation of their compliance with competition law.[374] The evaluation of compatibility with competition law is not restricted to future legal acts. The Competition Agency may give an expert opinion on the legislation already in force as well. In addition, the Competition Agency may issue opinions promoting competition culture, and advocating and raising awareness of competition law and policy.[375]

370. Article 49(7) CA.
371. Article 63.a CA.
372. For more details, *see* Part I, Ch. 5, §1, IV Administrative Fines, *infra*.
373. Article 25(1) CA.
374. Article 25(2) CA.
375. Article 25(3) CA.

228. After evaluating the compatibility of existing or planned rules with competition law, the Competition Agency adopts recommendations suggesting how to bring them into compliance with competition rules. Although the expert opinions are not binding, they still have a significant influence on the shape of legislation and other legal acts. One example of successful advocacy in this regard relates to changes made to legislation regulating driving school services and the provision of taxi drivers' services.[376]In 2020 alone, the Competition Agency adopted seventy-five expert opinions and observations,[377]

II. Government Direct Enforcement Activities

229. There are no direct enforcement activities by the government, as competition law is envisaged to be enforced and applied independently of the executive branch.

III. Other Administrative Agencies Applying Antitrust Rules

230. The Competition Agency is the only institution entrusted with the application of national and EU competition rules. Other agencies are empowered to observe the protection of competition through sector-specific rules and legislation and thus are by their very nature regulatory agencies for a specific sector acting *ex ante* on the respective markets.[378]

IV. Administrative Fines

A. *Introduction*

231. Prior to the enactment of the CA 2009, competition law infringements were considered to be misdemeanours and thus, by the application of the Misdemeanour Act, were subject to a fining procedure before a misdemeanour court. This system proved to be extremely inefficient as misdemeanour courts were '[…] lavishly applying the general rule of criminal law on immunity from fines and the reduction of fines, and thereby perversely distorting the efficient prosecution of undertakings that breach competition rules'.[379] Between 2004 and 2008, the Competition Agency found over a hundred infringements of competition law, most of them hardcore infringements for which the Competition Agency envisages fines of up to 10% of

376. Competition Agency, Annual Report 2016, 4.
377. Competition Agency, Annual Report 2020, 12.
378. For more, *see* Part I, Ch. 2, §2 Special Sectors.
379. D. Mlikotin Tomić & J. Pecotić Kaufman, *Evolution of Cartel Practice in Croatia*, in *Economic Integration, Competition and Cooperation/Integrations Économiques, Concurrence et Cooperation, Research Monograph* (V. Kandžija & A. Kumar eds., University of Rijeka, Faculty of Economics, 2010), available at http://bib.irb.hr/datoteka/390283.evolution_of_cartel_practice_in_Croatia.pdf (accessed 25 Sep. 2018).

the overall yearly turnover, and yet in the same period misdemeanour courts imposed overall fines of only HRK 1 million (approx. EUR 130,000).[380] It is only with the enactment of the CA in 2009 that the Competition Agency was granted the power to fine undertakings for violating competition rules, rendering the system of fines and its purpose effective.[381] The powers of the Competition Agency were reinforced with the introduction of daily penalties introduced by the 2021 CA amendments.

B. Amount of Fines

232. The CA differentiates between three groups of fines according to their amount, each of them reflecting the severity of the infringement. The first and highest group of fines is set in Article 61 of the CA, to a maximum of 10% of the total worldwide annual turnover of the undertaking concerned and is intended for severe infringements of competition rules relating to a negligent or intentional:

- the conclusion of prohibited agreements;[382]
- abuse of a dominant position;[383]
- participation in the implementation of a prohibited concentration;[384] and
- failure to comply with the decisions of the Competition Agency aimed at restoring efficient competition on the market (including commitment decisions and orders for interim measures).[385]

233. Lower fines, up to 1% of the annual turnover of the undertaking concerned, are prescribed in Article 62 of the CA, for less severe infringements of competition rules, namely for:

- failure to notify a concentration, where the notification was obligatory under the CA;[386]

380. J. Pecotić Kaufman & V. Butorac Malnar, *The Interaction Between EU Regulatory Implants and the Existing Croatian Legal Order in Competition Law*, in *Economic Evidence in EU Competition Law, European Studies in Law and Economics* 340 (M. Kovač & A. Vendenberghe, eds., Cambridge-Antwerp-Portland, Intersentia, 2016).
381. The first fine ever to be imposed by the Competition Agency related to a cartel agreement of a limited geographic scope (only one Croatian region). A symbolic fine of HRK 50,000 was imposed on the Association of Craftsmen Osijek facilitating the conclusion of the agreement; bakeries who actually raised prices were fined HRK 1,500, while those who participated in the agreement but did not raise their prices after the meeting were fined HRK 500 each. *See* Decision of the Croatian Competition Agency of 26 July 2012, *Competition Agency v. Obrtnička komora Osječko-baranjske županije, Udruženja obrtnika, Osijek, Sekcije pekara i sedamnaest poduzetnika koji su prisustvovali sastanku*, UP/I-030-02/11-01/039.
382. In violation of Art. 8 CA and/or Art. 101 TFEU cartel agreements.
383. In violation of Art. 13 CA and/or Art. 102 TFEU.
384. In violation of Art. 16 CA.
385. In violation of Art. 58(1) points 1-11 CA.
386. In violation of Art. 19(1).

- giving incorrect or misleading information while notifying a concentration;[387]
- failure to comply with the request of the Competition Agency for the collection of data;[388]
- obstructing the enforcement of the High Administrative Court order for a dawn raid;[389] and
- implementing a concentration prior to the issuing of a clearance decision.[390]

234. The third group of fines, defined by Article 63 of the CA, set between HRK 10,000 and HRK 100,000 (approx. EUR 1,350 and EUR 13,500) is prescribed for other infringements of competition rules against undertakings that are not parties to the proceedings before the Competition Agency and who fail to comply with the request for information during the market inquiry.[391]

C. Calculating Fines

235. Methods for calculating a fine are set by Article 64 of the CA and are detailed by the Regulation on the Method of Setting Fines.[392] The methodology consists of a two-step procedure of defining a fine. In the first step, the Competition Agency determines a basic amount for each undertaking and, in the second step, this basic amount is increased or reduced depending on the established mitigating and/or aggravating circumstances in the proceedings, such as the degree of gravity of the infringement, the duration of the infringement, and the damage caused for competing undertakings and consumers.[393]

236. The basic amount of the fine is determined and set at a level of up to 30% of the undertaking's turnover generated exclusively from its activity carried out in the market where the infringement took place.[394] Fines for cartel members will usually be set at the higher end of the scale, because a cartel is the most damaging and serious infringement of competition rules. As for other infringements, their place on the scale of 30% of turnover depends on different factors taken into account by the Competition Agency, such as the nature and the geographic scope of the infringement, the combined market share of all the undertakings involved, and the actual implementation of anticompetitive measures.[395]

237. The amount determined on the basis of turnover is then multiplied by the number of years of participation in the infringement. In the case of price-fixing, market sharing, and agreements limiting production, instead of taking into account

387. In violation of Art. 20 CA.
388. In violation of Art. 41(1) and (3) and 41.a CA.
389. In violation of Arts 42–46 CA.
390. In violation of Article 19(5) CA.
391. In accordance with Articles 32(1)(a) and (b) and 41.a CA.
392. Official Gazette nos 129/2010, 23/2015.
393. Article 64 (10) CA.
394. Article 64 (11) CA.
395. Article 6(2) of the Regulation on the Method of Setting Fines.

the duration of the infringement, the Competition Agency includes in the basic amount of the fine an additional amount of up to 25% of the turnover of the undertakings concerned.[396] This approach to the most damaging violations of antitrust rules serves the purpose of the fine as a deterrent. The basic amount reached in the first step of determining the fine is subsequently, in the second step, increased or decreased depending on the aggravating or mitigating circumstances established by the Competition Agency.

238. Mitigating circumstances referred to by Article 64(12) of the CA are in particular:

- evidence of the prompt termination of anticompetitive behaviour on the opening of infringement proceedings;
- evidence that anticompetitive behaviour was the result of negligence;
- evidence that the participation of the undertaking concerned in a prohibited agreement was not substantial as it avoided applying anticompetitive conduct during its involvement in the prohibited agreement; and
- effective cooperation with the Competition Agency during the proceedings.

239. Aggravating circumstances referred to in Article 64(13) are in particular:

- a continued or repeated anticompetitive offence following the delivery of the infringement decision, in which case the basic amount may be increased by up to 100% for each such infringement established;
- refusal to cooperate with or obstruction of the Competition Agency in carrying out its investigations; and
- leading, instigating, or coercing another to participate in an antitrust infringement.

240. The amount reached following the two-step method described above may be additionally adjusted by the Competition Agency. The fine may be further increased in order to reflect the gains made from the antitrust violation,[397] or may be reduced if it would irreparably jeopardize the economic viability of the undertaking and cause its assets to lose all their value.[398] In any event, the fine must not exceed the maximum of 10% of the undertaking's turnover in the previous financial year.[399]

241. As a result of the transposition of the ECN+ Directive, the 2021 CA contains detailed rules on fining associations of undertakings where they have been found liable for infringing competition rules with their decisions. The amended Article 64 CA prescribes that where the fine is imposed on an association of undertakings, it must not exceed 10% of the sum of the total worldwide turnover of each

396. Article 7(1) of the Regulation on the Method of Setting Fines.
397. Article 64 (14) CA.
398. Article 64(15) CA.
399. Article 64(1) CA.

of its members operating in the market on which the antitrust injury took place.[400] In case the association of undertakings cannot pay the fine due to insolvency, it must turn to its members for additional funds necessary to cover the fine.[401] If the association of undertakings is unable to collect the funds, the Competition Agency may directly impose the fine on the members of the association whose representatives were members of the decision-making bodies of the association at the time of the infringement,[402] and if not successful, of each undertakings operating on the market where the infringement took place.[403] Rightly so, this power does not extend over undertakings which demonstrate they did not implement the infringing decision because they were either unaware of its existence or have distanced themselves from it before the investigation started.[404] The financial liability for any member should not be higher than 10% of its total annual turnover in the preceding financial year.[405]

242. Finally, the Competition Agency may decide to impose only a symbolic fine in a situation where it establishes that the antitrust violation did not substantially distort competition or where it did not have negative effects on competition.[406] The Competition Agency makes regular use of this statutory possibility both in cases of antitrust violation and violations in the ambit of control of concentrations.[407]

D. Enforcement of Fines

243. The decision to impose a fine forms an integral part of the decision on the merits, against which no appeal is allowed. However, the injured party may bring an action against the Competition Agency before the High Administrative Court of the Republic of Croatia,[408] on the ground of, *inter alia*, an allegedly inappropriate fine.[409] Bypassing regular legal remedies within the general administrative procedure is a particularity of competition law enforcement, envisaged to speed up the

400. Article 64 (2) CA.
401. Article 64 (4)
402. Article 64 (6)
403. Article 64 (7) CA.
404. Article 64 (8) CA.
405. Article 64 (5) CA.
406. Article 64(16) CA.
407. Recent examples of symbolic fines: failure to notify a concentration *Competition Agency v. Totalni radio*, UP/I-034-03/2014-03/004 of 11 June 2015 – 0.09% of combined annual turnover amounting to HRK 10,000 (approx. EUR 1,342) and *Competition Agency v. UMA radio* UP/I-034-03/2016-02/004 of 20 December 2016 – 0.60% of the UMA radio turnover amounting to HRK 1,000 (approx. EUR 134.20); for a prohibited vertical agreement (RPM), *see Competition Agency v. Carlsberg Croatia d.o.o. and KTC d.d.*, UP/I-034-03/2013-01/018 of 23 October 2014 – fine of HRK 500,000 (approx. EUR 67,116) for Carlsberg, and HRK 100,000 (approx. EUR 13,420) for KTC; *Competition Agency v. Kujevo d.d. and KTC d.d.* UP/I-034-03/2013-01/017 of 30 July 2014, a fine of HRK 130,000 (approx. EUR 17,450) for Kutjevo d.d. and HRK 100,000 (approx. EUR 13,420) for KTC.
408. Article 67(1) CA.
409. Article 67(1)(4) CA.

process and enable the swift reaction of the Competition Agency aimed at restoring normal competitive conditions in the market. This ability is reinforced by the fact that a claim against a decision of the Competition Agency before the High Administrative Court does not postpone its enforcement, save in the part related to the fine.[410] Thus, where an action is brought against a decision on a fine, the parties' right to a suspensive legal remedy is secured because such a fine may not be executed until the judgment confirming the fine imposed by the Competition Agency becomes final.[411] On the contrary, such a claim will not have a suspensive effect on other parts of the decisions, which might contain specific measures for the restoration of competition. This legislative solution effectively balances the demands for legal protection of the parties and the public interest for healthy competition.

244. The final amount to be paid by the undertaking concerned includes interest, which starts running from the day of delivery of the Competition Agency decision until the day of payment. The Competition Agency may grant payment of the fine by instalments. If the undertaking fails to pay the imposed fine including interest within the prescribed deadline, the Competition Agency may seek the assistance of local tax authorities, which then enforce the payment in accordance with the rules related to the enforcement of taxes. This solution is very effective and logical, as the payments made by the parties on the account of fines and interest contribute directly to the state budget.[412]

245. Finally, when it comes to the enforcement of fines, it is worth mentioning the limitation periods set in the CA. According to Article 72(1), the enforcement of fines is subject to a five-year limitation period from the date of delivery of a final enforceable decision of the Competition Agency or the final and enforceable judgment of the High Administrative Court. This limitation period is interrupted by any enforcement action, which means that after the interruption, the limitation period starts running from the beginning. In order to provide legal certainty, the CA provides a limitation cap of ten years overall.[413]

246. Mirroring the solutions of the Directive ECN+, the 2021 CA includes detailed rules on the enforcement of final decisions imposing fines or periodic penalty payments rendered by a competition authority of another Member State. The enforcement may be requested in situations where the undertaking does not have sufficient assets for the payment of the fine or periodic penalty payment in the country of the decision's origin,[414] irrespectively of its place of establishment. [415] In order to be afforded enforcement, the applicant authority must have made tried to

410. Article 67(4) CA.
411. Because the High Administrative Court is the second instance court, the finality of its judgments take place upon their adoption as there is no regular legal remedy against such judgments.
412. Article 70 CA.
413. Article 72 CA.
414. Article 70.a (1) CA.
415. Article 70.a (2) CA.

ascertain the lack of undertaking's assets to cover the fine.[416] The enforcement itself is carried out according to the Croatian law,[417] immediately upon receipt of a uniform instrument (containing a list of legally prescribed information) [418] and a copy of the decision to be enforced,[419] without subjecting it to any act of recognition.[420]Although these rules are introduced to make the enforcement system more efficient, the Competition Agency is allowed to refuse enforcement on public policy grounds.[421] Finally, it should be noted that the Competition Agency may be compensated for the costs connected with the enforcement either by the undertaking itself, or where the execution of the fine has not been successful, by the applicant competition authority.[422]

E. Fines Within the Leniency Programme

247. With the enactment of the CA in 2009, for the first time in Croatian competition law a Leniency Programme was introduced through Article 65 and the accompanying Regulation on Immunity from Fines and Reduction of Fines (hereinafter Leniency Regulation). [423] Following the 2021 transposition of the ECN+ Directive into the CA, the rules on leniency are much more detailed and will certainly require amendments to the Leniency Regulation as well. Pending such changes, this section relies on the Leniency Regulation currently in force.

248. Because the purpose of the Leniency Programme is to encourage cartel members to come forward and provide information on the existence of a cartel, the Competition Agency is empowered to grant either full immunity from fines or their reduction. According to Article 65(1) of the CA, full immunity may be granted to the first cartel member which:

(a) comes forward and informs the Competition Agency of the existence of a cartel and supplies evidence enabling the Competition Agency to initiate proceedings or conduct a targeted unannounced inspection (dawn raid); or
(b) submits information and evidence enabling the Competition Agency to find the existence of a cartel in proceedings already initiated by the Competition Agency.

416. Article 70.a (1) CA.
417. Whereas disputes on the legality of the decision imposing the fine or the uniform instrument permitting enforcement in the Republic of Croatia are governed by the law of the Member State of the applicant competition authority. See Article 70.c (1) and (2) CA. The same applies to limitation periods for the enforcement of fines or daily penalties according to Article 70.a (4) CA.
418. Articles 70.b (3) and (4) CA.
419. Article 70.a (2) CA.
420. Article 70.a (7) CA.
421. Article 70.a (9) CA.
422. Articles 70.a (11) and (12) CA.
423. Regulation on Immunity from Fines and Reduction of Fines, Official Gazette nos 129/10, 96/2017.

The latter is possible only where the Competition Agency is not in possession of sufficient evidence and information to initiate proceedings or conduct a dawn raid, or where the proceedings have already been initiated, to prove the existence of a cartel on its own. The immunity may be granted both where the proceedings are conducted under Article 8 of the CA or together with Article 101 TFEU; in both cases, the instigators of the cartel[424] are not eligible for immunity.[425]

249. Undertakings which disclose their participation in a cartel but do not meet the conditions for immunity from the fine are eligible for a reduction of the fine in accordance with Article 65(4) of the CA. Such a benefit is available where the undertakings concerned provide evidence with significant added value to the existing evidence and substantially contribute to finding an infringement.[426] Evidence with significant added value is evidence that enables the Competition Agency to find an infringement or to find it much earlier than in the absence of such evidence. The reduction of a fine is relative to the fine that would otherwise have been imposed on the undertaking concerned under the CA. Provided the applicants fulfil all the statutory criteria:

- a reduction of 30–50% is granted to the first applicant;
- a reduction of 20–30% is granted to the second applicant; and
- a reduction of up to 20% is granted to any subsequent applicant.[427]

While leaders and instigators of a cartel may not be granted immunity, they may benefit from a reduction of the fine.[428]

250. Finally, regardless of whether an application is made for immunity or for a reduction of a fine, in both cases, in order to qualify, the applicant:

- must cooperate genuinely, fully, and continuously with the Competition Agency;
- must end its involvement in the cartel immediately, unless the Competition Agency considers the involvement to be reasonably necessary in order not to jeopardize the unannounced inspection; and
- must neither have destroyed, falsified, or concealed evidence of the cartel nor have disclosed its intended application or its content.[429]

251. A very misleading normative situation occurred as a result of the implementation of the ECN+ Directive in 2021 CA, most precisely its Article 23 (1) providing for the MS' obligation to extend, under certain conditions, the leniency

424. According to Art. 2(d) of the Regulation on Immunity from Fines and Reduction of Fines, 'instigator or coercer' means an undertaking which has taken active steps to coerce other undertakings – its competitors – in illegal activity or compelled other undertakings to subsequently take part in the cartel, in particular by using direct or indirect methods of coercion or threat.
425. Article 65 (2) CA.
426. Article 17(2) of the Leniency Regulation.
427. Article 19(3) –(5) of the Regulation on Immunity from Fines.
428. Article 17(5) Regulation on Immunity from Fines.
429. Article 3(4) Regulation on Immunity from Fines.

protection over sanctions imposed in administrative and non-criminal judicial proceedings to current and former directors, managers, and other members of staff of applicants for immunity. Obviously, this article of the ECN+ Directive creates an obligation for those MS which provide under national law sanctions of this type. Croatian law does not envisage sanctions for natural persons in any capacity in neither administrative nor non-criminal judicial proceedings. Yet, the 2021 CA includes a new Article 65.a (1) replicating fully the Article 23 (1) of the ECN+ Directive. Its meaning could be easily misconstrued by an interpretation *a contrario*, wrongfully leading to a conclusion that natural persons will be fined for their participation in a cartel where they do not meet the prescribed condition. Such an outcome is however not possible as no sanctions for natural persons are envisaged under the CA. Being associated with non-existent sanctions, Article 65.a (1) is superfluous and should be taken out of the CA.[430]

252. The 2021 CA contains new provisions on the relationship between Leniency Programme and criminal prosecution of natural persons as well. This time the provisions are welcomed as there is one criminal offence related to Art 8 CA infringements – the bid-rigging – defined by Article 254 (1) of the Criminal Code.[431] According to the new Article 65.a (3) of the CA, the decision about the criminal prosecution rests with the State Attorney, who may decide not to press criminal charges or if it does, it may propose to the court to mitigate of the criminal sanction where the contribution in the detection and investigation of the cartel outweighs the interest of sanctioning the responsible person.[432]

253. Finally, it is worth mentioning that these rules do not affect in any way the right of injured persons to pursue damages for the loss suffered as a result of antitrust violations.[433]

F. Daily Penalties

254. With the 2021 CA amendment, the Competition Agency has been granted the power to impose daily penalties on undertakings in the situation where they:

- fail to respond to the Competition Agency's written request to submit data;
- fail to appear at the interview they were summoned to by the Competition Agency;
- obstruct the execution of a dawn raid;
- fail to comply with imposed remedies, commitments, and interim measures.[434]

430. Pecotić Kaufman, J. 'Sankcioniranje fizičkih osoba za povrede tržišnog natjecanja, pokajnički program i novi čl. 65.a ZZTN-a', *Zbornik Pravnog fakulteta u Zagrebu*, 2022, pp. 00-00, 12.
431. For more on criminal sanctions for antitrust violations see *infra* para 317 et seq.
432. Article 65.a (4).
433. Article 65.a (5) CA.
434. Article 63.a (1) CA

255. The daily penalty is calculated by dividing the undertaking's total worldwide annual turnover in the preceding financial year with the number of days in the financial year. Thereby obtained daily amount is multiplied by the number of infringement days.[435] The amount of daily penalty may not exceed 5% of the undertaking's average daily total worldwide turnover in the preceding business year. [436] When deciding on the imposition of a daily penalty the Competition Agency must take into account the gravity and to the duration of the infringement and the ramifications of the infringement. In principle, daily penalties are effective and dissuasive against short-term infringements, in which case they may replace the fine for the same infringement.[437]

G. Settlement in Cartel Proceedings

256. The novelty in fighting cartels under Croatian law is the introduction of a settlement between cartelists and the Competition Agency. It is a well-known procedural instrument positively tested by its wide use in the practice of the EU Commission. Pursuant to the new Article 52.a CA, undertakings against which the Competition Agency is conducting antitrust proceedings for their participation in a cartel in violation of Articles 8 CA and /or 101 TFEU may, in a written settlement submission, voluntarily admit their participation in the cartel and waive their right to dispute the decision on the infringement.[438] Should the Competition Agency decide to accept the settlement submission, it will reduce the fine by 10% to 20% of what it would have otherwise imposed on the settling party.[439] On the contrary, should it decide not to accept the settlement submission, the Competition Agency is not allowed to rely on it as a sole evidence of the infringement.[440] In addition, settlement may be combined with leniency,[441] and just like leniency applications, settlement submissions are shielded from disclosure to third parties,[442] which is of utmost importance in cases of private actions for damages initiated against the cartelists. All these benefits combined form a great additional incentive for cartelists to come forward and admit their participation in the cartel, without taking too many risks.

V. Administrative Injunctions and Other Restrictive Orders

257. Where the Competition Agency establishes an infringement of the CA or Articles 101 and 102 TFEU, it may require the parties to bring the infringement to

435. Article 63.a (2) CA.
436. Article 63.a (3) CA.
437. Articles 63.a (5) and (6) CA.
438. Such a possibility is available only until thirty days after the receipt of the Statement of Objections. Articles 52.a (1) and (2) CA.
439. Article 52.a (3) CA.
440. Article 52.a (7) CA.
441. Article 52.a (6) CA.
442. Article 47.a CA.

an end and may decide to impose measures and conditions and deadlines for restoring effective competition on the market.[443] The prohibition decision thus combines the determination of an infringement with a cease-and-desist order and the imposition of remedies called measures and conditions under Croatian statutory language. The provisions related to prohibited agreements specifies that behavioural and, where this is not efficient structural measures and conditions could be imposed on the parties[444]

258. When it comes to the abuse of a dominant position, the situation is no different, so the competition authority here as well uses its statutory power to impose restrictive orders to neutralize the negative effects of anticompetitive behaviour. To begin with, the Competition Agency will order a cessation of any abusive practices by the dominant undertaking.[445] Unlike some other national competition laws of the Member States, the CA does not specifically authorize the Competition Agency to order the undertaking concerned to refrain from future infringements.[446] In addition, the infringement decision may be combined with the imposition of remedies that are proportionate to the infringement and necessary to bring it to an end.[447] In fact, the CA provides that the Competition Agency may impose both structural and/or behavioural measures, the latter having precedence over the former.[448] Article 14(4) emphasizes that a structural measure may be imposed only if no behavioural measure would be as efficient or if the behavioural measure would be more burdensome on the dominant undertaking. Having in mind the above, it comes as no surprise that the practice of the Competition Agency shows that remedies have mostly been used in the context of abuse of a dominant position,[449] while, in the context of prohibited agreements, in most cases the Competition Agency limits itself to declaring their nullity and imposing a fine.

259. When it comes to merger control, the CA is much more detailed regarding applicable injunctions and other restrictive orders.[450] Both behavioural and/or structural remedies are available in the following cases: the revocation of a conditional clearance decision,[451] the implementation of a prohibited concentration, and the implementation of a concentration prior to, or without, a mandatory notification.[452] The CA specifies that in such cases the Competition Agency may in particular order

443. Articles 9, 14, 22, 24, 58(1), 58(4), 58(5), 58(8) CA.
444. Articles 9(2) and (3) CA.
445. Article 14(1)(2) CA.
446. Unlike BE, CZ, CY, DE, DK, EE, EL, ES, FR, HU, IT, LT, LU, SK. *See* ECN Working Group Cooperation Issues and Due Process Decision-Making Powers Report 13 (31 October 2012), available at http://ec.europa.eu/competition/ecn/decision_making_powers_report_en.pdf (accessed 20 Jul. 2018).
447. Article 14 (4) CA.
448. Article 24 CA.
449. *See* Decision of the Croatian Competition Agency of 20 October 2005, *Ponikve*, UP/-030-02/2004-01/66; Decision of the Croatian Competition Agency of 12 July 2007, *T-mobile*, UP/I-030-02/2005-01/50.
450. *See* more on remedies in merger cases, Part III, Ch. 2, §3, *infra*.
451. Article 23(2) CA.
452. Article 24 CA.

a transfer or divestiture of acquired shares or interest, prohibit or restrict the exercise of voting rights of shares related to the concentration, and order a termination of control of a joint venture which led to a prohibited concentration.[453] In any case, a restrictive order includes a decision on the appropriate fine.[454]

VI. Interim Measures

260. During the course of antitrust proceedings, the Competition Agency may adopt a decision ordering interim measures on the basis of sufficient circumstantial evidence of an infringement, in cases of urgency due to the risk of serious and irreparable damage to competition.[455] Usually, with such a decision, the Competition Agency orders the suspension of a particular behaviour and requires the fulfilment of certain measures and conditions necessary for the elimination of negative effects on competition.[456]

261. In principle, the interim measure may not exceed the duration of twelve months. However, its duration may be prolonged where the Competition Agency finds it indispensable.[457] The prolongation of the duration of interim measures is not a regular procedure, and because the Act envisages this opportunity only in indispensable cases, such decisions are rather rare. However, on at least one occasion, the interim measure was prolonged twice by the Competition Agency, and its duration was ultimately extended until the end of the infringement procedure.[458] This was the interim measure imposed in the *Peugeot* case.[459] The investigation dealt with the possible abuse of a dominant position by Peugeot Croatia on the market for the repair and maintenance services of Peugeot cars and the selling of its spare parts, which allegedly applied non-transparent and discriminatory selective criteria for joining the network of authorized Peugeot repairers. Peugeot allegedly discriminated against Auto Maksimir by excluding it from the network. The Competition Agency ordered an interim measure against Peugeot Croatia, requiring it to include Auto Maksimir in the Peugeot dealer's authorized service network and to enable it to exercise all associated rights and obligations, including access to equipment, and to enable it to acquire the elements of the brand's new brand image, NIM. The Competition Agency argued that further prolongation of the duration of this interim measure was indispensable because the exclusion from the market of Auto Maksimir, a long-time servicer of motor vehicles, risked the occurrence of significant and irreparable damage to competition to the detriment of consumers.

453. Article 24(2) CA.
454. Article 24(3) CA.
455. Article 51(1) CA.
456. Article 51(2) CA.
457. Article 51(4) CA.
458. It is important to note that this case was decided on the former CA where the length of interim measures was set to six months.
459. Decision of the Croatian Competition Agency of 9 July 2015, *Competition Agency v. Peugeot*. UP/I-034-03/2014-01/005.

262. If the parties fail to comply with the interim measure, the Competition Agency may impose a fine. Such non-compliance is considered to be the most severe type of infringement, for which the CA envisages the highest fine of up to 10% of the annual turnover of the undertaking concerned.[460] Finally, it should be stressed that decisions imposing interim measures may not be appealed; instead, just as in cases of a decision on the merits, the injured party may bring an action against such a decision before the High Administrative Court.

263. A good example of a recent interim measure decision is the case of a funeral service provider Flora VTC.[461] This provider was ordered to temporarily repeal part of its price list by way of which a special 10% discount was offered for funeral services to those clients who had bought funeral equipment from that same undertaking. The temporary measure included the restriction of marketing the named discount. This implied a temporary restriction of placing advertisements, sharing or leaving them in visible spots, removing them from visible places (including existing posters, leaflets, reminders, etc.) if they contained information about the named promotion. The interim measure was ordered for a then maximum duration of six months.

§2. Civil Enforcement

I. Competent Civil Courts

264. In Croatia, courts competent to hear antitrust damages disputes, and other claims of private relief, are commercial courts. This legislative solution in relation to actions for damages had already been introduced in the 2013 CA,[462] restating the general subject-matter jurisdiction of commercial courts as regulated by Article 34(b)9 of the CPA,[463] and has recently been reaffirmed by the new Act on Actions for Damages Arising out of Antitrust Infringements.[464] These are specialized courts within the Croatian judicial structure and are thus the most suitable to hear antitrust damages cases. Opting for commercial over general courts was meant to accommodate for the need to provide courts capable of hearing complex issues related to competition law infringements.

460. Article 61(4) CA.
461. Decision of the Croatian Competition Agency of 4 April 2016, *Competition Agency v. Flora VTC*, UP/I-034-03/2015-01/045.
462. Article 69.a (1) CA.
463. Commercial courts in civil disputes in the first instance adjudicate, *inter alia*, on disputes arising out of acts of unfair market competition, monopolistic agreements, and disruption of equality on the single market of the Republic of Croatia.
464. Act on Actions for Damages Arising out of Antitrust Infringements, Official Gazette no. 69/17.

II. Sanctions

A. Nullity

265. Competition rules are mandatory rules, and thus any contract concluded in contravention of those rules is *ex lege* null and void. This general principle is stipulated in Article 322(1) of the OA according to which nullity is the legal consequence of any agreement that is contrary to the Constitution of the Republic of Croatia, mandatory rules, or moral principles. Article 8(4) of the CA, which follows the wording of Article 101(2) TFEU, expressly provides for nullity of agreements, decisions, and concerted practices that are prohibited by the CA, while the same cannot be found in relation to agreements that are the expression of the abuse of a dominant position. In those cases, the general rule of Article 322 of the OA applies, producing the same effects as Article 8(4) of the CA.

266. Because nullity takes place *ex lege*, any legal act to that effect is only declaratory by nature. The court must control ex officio the nullity of contracts,[465] thus any condemnatory request for the fulfilment of a contractual duty arising from a contract that is prohibited by the CA should not be granted, irrespective of whether the other contractual party has invoked nullity as a defence. The issue of the nullity of a contract may also arise as a result of litigation aimed at obtaining such a declaratory judgment. Article 327 of the OA stipulates that any interested party may invoke the nullity of a contract. This corresponds to the general rules on standing regulated by Article 187 of the CPA according to which the power to seek declaratory protection is recognized for every person having legal interest. As a rule, the plaintiff is only required to make probable the existence of his/her concrete legal interest.[466]

267. The legal consequences of nullity of contracts in general, including those in contravention of the CA, are defined by the OA. In the case of the nullity of a contract, each of the contracting parties must return to the others all that it has received under such a contract. Where this is not possible, an appropriate remuneration must be given, based on the prices existing at the time of the court decision.[467] Finally, where possible, the partial nullity of the contract applies. This is the case whenever the contract may survive the nullity of one or more of its clauses.[468] This might, for example, be the case with vertical agreements having an anticompetitive clause, while it is not likely to be the case with hardcore cartel agreements.

465. Article 327 OA.
466. For more on declaratory judgments under Croatian civil procedure, *see* S. Triva & M. Dika, *Građansko parnično procesno pravo* 398 (7th ed., Narodne novine, 2004).
467. Article 323(1) OA.
468. Article 324(1) OA.

B. Damages[469]

268. As already mentioned, in Croatia actions for damages resulting from competition law infringements are regulated by the Act on Antitrust Damages,[470] which is the result of the implementation of the Antitrust Damages Directive[471] in the Croatian legal order. The Act on Antitrust Damages is a *lex specialis* in relation to the general provisions of the CPA[472] and the OA.[473] Therefore, any issue not regulated by the Act on Antitrust Damages remains to be regulated by the general rules of civil procedure and civil law.[474]

269. Although the Act on Antitrust Damages for the first time elaborates in detail the legal framework for antitrust damages actions, it is worth mentioning that these procedures had already been explicitly recognized in the 2013 CA. In fact, Article 69.a of the CA provides that undertakings that have infringed national or EU competition rules (Articles 101 and 102 TFEU) are liable for compensation of damages thereby induced.[475] Most procedural and substantive aspects of these procedures were left out of the CA (to be regulated by general tort and civil procedure rules contained respectively in the OA and CPA), although some important aspects of antitrust damages cases were addressed. The CA touched upon the role of infringement decisions in follow-on cases, in the suspension of proceedings and the interruption of limitation periods, and in the obligations of the commercial courts to inform the CCA of any initiated antitrust damages cases. Since some of the solutions envisaged by the CA neither conformed to the Directive, and consequently nor to the Act on Antitrust Damages, in 2021 the CA was amended in that regard, and is now fully aligned with all relevant legislation.

270. Generally, the Act on Antitrust Damages follows the normative structure of the Directive and, for the most part, it faithfully takes over its solutions (and pitfalls). It consists of twenty articles and, just like the Directive on antitrust damages, it establishes the right to full compensation of damages resulting from antitrust infringements, and it regulates the disclosure of evidence in general, the disclosure of evidence contained in the file of the competition authority, the limits to such disclosure, the penalties for non-compliance, the effects of national decisions, the limitation periods, the suspension of procedure, the joint and several liability, the

469. A more extended version of this chapter was previously published by V. Butorac Malnar, *Croatia*, in *Implementation of the EU Damages Directive in Central and Eastern European Countries* (A. Piszcz, ed., University of Warsaw, Faculty of Management Press, 2017).
Act on Actions for Damages Arising out of Antitrust Infringements, Official Gazette no. 69/17.

470. Act on Actions for Damages Arising out of Antitrust Infringements, Official Gazette no. 69/17.

471. Directive 2014/104/EU of the European Parliament and of the Council of 26 November 2014 on certain rules governing actions for damages under national law for infringements of the competition law provisions of the Member States and of the European Union Text with EEA relevance, OJ L 349/1, 5.12.2014.

472. Civil Procedure Act, Official Gazette nos 53/91, 91/92, 58/93, 112/99, 88/01, 117/03, 88/05, 02/07, 84/08, 123/08, 57/11, 148/11, 25/13, 89/14, 70/19, 80/22.

473. Obligations Act, Official Gazette nos 35/05, 41/08, 125/11, 78/15, 29/18, 126/21.

474. Article 4 of the Act on Antitrust Damages.

475. Article 69.a(2) CA.

passing-on of overcharges, the passing-on of defence, actions for damages by claimants from a different level of the supply chain, and, finally, the quantification of damages and consensual dispute resolution.

1. Scope of Application

271. The Act on Antitrust Damages as defined in Article 1 covers claims for damages incurred as a result of an infringement of competition law, defined as the infringement of rules establishing prohibited agreements, the abuse of dominance, and Articles 101 and 102 TFEU. Consequently, the Act on Antitrust Damages is narrow in scope. It leaves out actions for damages resulting from anticompetitive concentrations of undertakings and other infringements such as the violation of state aid rules, or unfair commercial practices.

272. As for the personal scope of application, the Act follows the linguistic definitions of the Directive. The 'injured' party is any person that has suffered harm by an antitrust infringement. This wording is in line with the general tort rules recognizing the right of any individual or legal person to be compensated for a legally recognizable harm suffered. On the contrary, the 'infringer' is defined as an undertaking or association of undertakings which has committed an infringement of competition law.[476] The notions of undertaking and association of undertakings are derived from the CA.[477] Therefore, the same criteria apply – the autonomous functional interpretation developed in the context of Articles 101 and 102 TFEU, taken over by the CA and so far applied consistently by the Competition Agency. With this in mind, any person engaged in production and/or trade in goods and/or the provision of services, thereby participating in economic activity, might be a tortfeasor in civil proceedings. The application of the notion of an undertaking as defined by the CA also implies the application of the concept of a single economic unit as developed by the Court of the EU in public enforcement.[478] It was unclear whether the autonomous interpretation provided by the Court of the EU would apply, just as it does to the notion of an undertaking in more general terms, or whether the general rules of company law[479] would be applicable. This issue has recently been resolved by the Court of the EU in Skanska[480] whereby it has been confirmed that the concept of undertaking is an autonomous term of the EU and therefore national

476. Article 3(2) of the Act on Antitrust Damages.
477. Article 3(3) of the Act on Antitrust Damages.
478. Article 3 (4) CA provides:
"For the purpose of application of this Act and the imposition of fines or periodic penalty payments for the infringements of this Act and/or Articles 101 and 102 TFEU on the parent company and its legal and economic successors the Agency shall take into account the concept of undertaking as defined by case law of the Court of Justice of the European Union (CJEU)."
479. Companies Act, Official Gazette nos 111/93, 34/99, 121/99, 52/00, 118/03, 107/07, 146/08, 137/09, 125/11, 152/11, 111/12, 68/13, 110/15, 40/19, 34/22.
480. Judgment of the Court, of 14 March 2019, C-724/17 - Skanska Industrial Solutions and Others, ECLI:EU:C:2019:204.

courts should not rely on the general rules of company law but should instead follow the interpretation provided by the Court of the EU. This implies that in civil enforcement the parent company may be held liable for antitrust damages caused by an infringement of competition rules committed by its subsidiaries and, as recently confirmed by the Court of the EU in Sumal,[481] under certain circumstances, the other way around as well.

2. Substantive Law Issues

273. The Act on Antitrust Damages establishes the right to full compensation encompassing both material and non-material damages, which under the general rules of the OA may be granted to legal persons as well.

274. The Directive on Antitrust Damages did not establish the type of liability to be applicable in cases of antitrust damages. In fact, the Directive expressly states, 'where Member States provide other conditions for compensation under national law, such as imputability, adequacy or culpability, they should be able to maintain such conditions in so far as they comply with the case law of the Court of Justice, the principles of effectiveness and equivalence'. The Act on Antitrust Damages opted for strict liability, notwithstanding the general tort rule of liability based on presumed fault.

a. Limitation Periods

275. The Act on Antitrust Damages brought novel solutions with regard to limitation periods for bringing actions for damages. Namely, under the general rules of the OA, Article 230, a time limit for bringing actions for damages is set at three years from the time the injured party becomes aware of the damage and of the person causing the damage, while the objective limitation period is set at five years from the moment the damage was caused. These general limitation periods, coupled with the general rules on their suspension and interruption, are unsuitable for antitrust damages actions, particularly for cases involving continuous or repeated antitrust infringements, as their application would hamper the bringing of antitrust damages action.[482]

276. Following the legislative solution of the Directive, the Act on Antitrust Damages now provides tailor-made limitation periods for antitrust damages claims. According to Article 12 of the Act on Antitrust Damages, a claim for damages may be brought within five years of the date the infringement of competition law ceased or the date when the injured party knew or should have known about the infringement of competition law, the harm suffered, and the identity of the infringer. The

481. Judgment of the Court of 6 October 2021, C-882/19 – Sumal, ECLI:EU:C:2021:800.
482. V. Butorac Malnar, M. Mataija & S. Petrović, *National Report: Croatia*, in *Private Enforcement and Collective Redress in European Competition Law* (G. Bándi Gyula et al., eds., Wolters Kluwer, Budapest, 2016).

limitation periods are interrupted where the competent competition authority initiates proceedings with respect to the infringement to which the action for damages relates. In this case, the limitation period restarts running[483] from the date when the infringement decision of the competition authority becomes final and binding[484] (decisions of national competition authorities confirmed by a review court or those which were not subject to review and a final decision of the EU Commission), or the proceeding is otherwise finalized. This wording is somewhat imprecise, as the rules triggering the initiation of infringement proceedings might differ substantially across Member States. For the sake of legal certainty, the term 'initiation of proceedings' should be interpreted to refer only to the formal opening of proceedings and should not include actions for the purpose of an investigation. The suspension of limitation periods is envisaged in situations of consensual dispute resolution in relation to the parties involved and lasts for the duration of such a process, after which it continues to run.

277. No specific rules on limitation periods are envisaged for victims who are neither direct nor indirect customers of the immunity recipient, such as direct or indirect customers of other co-infringers, umbrella claimants, or competitors. Such victims, according to the rules on joint and several liability, may lodge a claim against the immunity recipient only if they were unsuccessful in claiming compensation from other co-infringers.[485] In this regard, the Directive expressly states that Member States must ensure that any limitation periods in such cases are reasonable and sufficient to allow injured parties to bring such actions.[486] In other words, it would have been appropriate to introduce a rule whereby limitation periods for these victims are suspended for bringing an action against the immunity recipient for the duration of proceedings against other co-infringers.

278. Croatia took up the possibility granted by the Directive and provided an absolute limitation period of fifteen years from the date the infringement ceased. This period, however, serves the purpose of legal certainty for the infringers, and cannot efficiently solve the potential problem for the injured persons who are neither direct nor indirect purchasers of the immunity recipient.

b. Joint and Several Liability

279. Rules on joint and several liability are very complex and follow rather truthfully the wording of the Directive on antitrust damages. According to Article 14(1) of the Act on Antitrust Damages, tortfeasors that have infringed competition law by joint behaviour are jointly and severally liable for the harm caused. In

483. On the differentiation between interruption and suspension of limitation periods under Croatian law, *see* J. Čuveljak, *Zastoj i prekid zastare*, 3 Hrvatska pravna revija 16 (2003).

484. On the effects of decisions in Croatian administrative procedure, *see* M. Sikić, *Pravomoćnost, konačnost i izvršnost u upravnom postupku*, 33 Zbornik Pravnog fakulteta Sveučilišta u Rijeci 205 (2012).

485. Article 11(4)(b) Directive 2014/104 and Art. 14(2)(2) of the Act on Antitrust Damages.

486. Article 11(4) of Directive 2014/104.

essence, this means that in circumstances in which a number of persons/ undertakings are liable for the same harm caused by the joint behaviour, the injured party may claim compensation for the entire harm suffered from any of the infringers, irrespective of its relative share in the overall harm caused.[487] Following the *verbatim* of the Directive, as an exception to this rule, the Act on Antitrust Damages limits joint and several liability of the immunity recipient, i.e., the undertaking that has been granted full immunity under the Leniency Programme, only to its direct and indirect purchasers or providers. To other injured parties, the immunity recipient is jointly and severally liable only where full compensation cannot be obtained from other tortfeasors/infringers.[488] This rule accommodates the requirement of the Directive, whose purpose was to protect an immunity recipient 'from undue exposure to damages claims' as a preferential target of litigation, given the fact that an infringement decision against it becomes final sooner than decisions related to other co-infringers.[489] Here, however, it is very unclear what the determining moment is when the claim against other co-infringers will be deemed unsuccessful, consequentially triggering the right of such victims to request compensation from the immunity recipient. Although this solution of the Directive has already been criticized for imprecision and ambiguity,[490] the Act on Antitrust Damages does not attempt to provide more clarity here.[491]

280. When one of the joint tortfeasors compensates the entire amount of damages, the obligation of the other tortfeasors towards the injured party ceases to exist. In such a situation, the tortfeasor/co-infringer that has paid more than its share of the harm by the application of the rules on joint and several liability is entitled to recover a contribution from the other tortfeasors/co-infringers.[492] The Act on Antitrust Damages explicitly sets out exemplary objective criteria for determining the relative co-infringers' share in the overall harm. Such a determination is based on all the circumstances of the case, such as market share, turnover, role in a cartel or some other infringement and the like, and this is irrespective of whose purchasers or providers are affected by the infringement.[493] In essence, this provision codifies Recital 37 accompanying Article 11 of the Directive and will provide very useful guidance for national courts in attributing relative shares in the harm to co-infringers. In addition, the Act on Antitrust Damages establishes that where the

---

487. V. Gorenc et al., *Komentar Zakona o obveznim odnosima* 1852 (Narodne novine, 2014).
488. Article 14(2) of the Act on Antitrust Damages.
489. Recital 38 of Directive 2014/104.
490. A. Howard, *Too Little, Too Late? The European Commission's Legislative Proposals on Anti-trust Damages Actions*, 4 Journal of European Competition Law & Practice 458 (2013); S.O. Pais & A. Piszcz, *Package on Actions for Damages Based on Breaches of EU Competition Rules: Can One Size Fit All?* 7 Yearbook of Antitrust and Regulatory Studies 200 (2014).
491. Most likely, it will be considered to be the moment when a final judgment against the co-infringers will prove to be unenforceable because of liquidity problems and lack of assets. However, because rules on debt enforcement envisage several possible rounds of debt enforcement, it is unclear at which point of the enforcement procedure it will be considered that the compensation was unsuccessful. This ambiguity might jeopardize the right to obtain full compensation from the immunity recipient, particularly when coupled with the limitation periods discussed above.
492. Article 14(3) of the Act on Antitrust Damages.
493. *Ibid.*

relative shares of the co-infringers in the overall harm cannot be established (by the application of the objective criteria), all the co-infringers will be attributed an equal share in the overall harm unless this is unjust in a particular case. [494] This wording is taken over from the general legislative solution of Article 1109(3) of the OA regulating the relationship between jointly and severally liable tortfeasors. The possibility of allocating evenly the shares in the overall harm between co-infringers might prove to be a very practical tool in situations where the objective criteria do not produce decisive results. However, it remains very unclear when such an even distribution would be considered unjust – especially given the strict form of liability both for the infringement of competition law and the harm caused. The possibility for deciding on the grounds of fairness under the OA is limited to exceptional circumstances, such as those involving minors, persons with diminished mental capacity, and persons with poor economic status or the like.[495] It seems implausible that any of the situations in antitrust damages cases would qualify for decision-making based on fairness. This wide discretion is superfluous and, even if only theoretically, makes room for arbitrary decisions leading to legal uncertainty.

281. As an exemption to these rules on establishing the co-infringers' relative share in the overall harm, Article 14(5) of the Act on Antitrust Damages establishes that the relative share of an immunity recipient infringer may not exceed the amount of harm caused to its direct or indirect purchasers or providers. A different rule applies when the harm was caused and when compensation was made to persons other than the direct or indirect purchasers or suppliers of any of the co-infringers, such as umbrella customers or competitors. In such situations, Article 14(5) establishes that the relative share of an immunity recipient cannot be higher than the amount of its part in the harm.

282. Similar to immunity recipients, under certain circumstances Small and Medium Enterprises (SMEs) have limited joint and several liability. Following the wording of the Directive, the Act on Antitrust Damages provides that an SME is jointly and severally liable only to its direct and indirect purchasers or providers when its market share was below 5% of the relevant market during the infringement and if the general rules on joint and several liability would irreversibly jeopardize its economic viability and cause the complete loss of its assets.[496] These are cumulative criteria, and thus if any of them are not met, the general rules on joint and several liability apply. This rule, however, would not apply if the SME in question was an initiator or instigator of the competition law infringement that caused the harm (particularly using coercion) or if that SME had already been found to have infringed competition law.[497]

494. Article 14(4) of the Act on Antitrust Damages.
495. V. Gorenc et al., *Komentar Zakona o obveznim odnosima* 1859 (Narodne novine, 2014).
496. Article 14(6) of the Act on Antitrust Damages.
497. Article 14(7) of the Act on Antitrust Damages.

c. Quantification of Harm

283. Croatia opted for the introduction of a very general and simple rule, procedural in nature, which allows national courts to accommodate the particular circumstances of the case, guaranteeing that the difficulties in calculating the amount of damages will not result in non-compensation, when the liability of the infringers has been established. Accordingly, Article 17 of the Act on Antitrust Damages provides that where the right to compensation has been determined, and the amount of damages cannot be established based on the available evidence, or when such a determination would be possible only with disproportional difficulties, the court shall, by free evaluation, estimate the amount of damages to be compensated. This rule is *ad verbatim* taken from the CPA (Article 223), which constitutes an exemption to the general rule whereby each party is obliged to provide facts and present evidence on which his or her claim is based, or to refute the statements and evidence of his or her opponent. [498] With this in mind, the legislative solution of the Act on Antitrust Damages is not new, and fits well the general civil procedure framework. The Act on Antitrust Damages is intentionally silent on the applicable methods for calculating the amount of damages in order not to limit the courts in this regard, as different methods may be suitable depending on the circumstances of a particular case. It is expected that judges will avail themselves of the Practical Guide on the Quantification of Harm published by the Commission.

284. The novelty of the Act on Antitrust Damages is the possibility for national courts to require help in quantifying harm from the National Competition Authority (NCA). Although the Act on Antitrust Damages does not provide explicitly which competition authority it refers to, if one is to look at its definitions the term NCA covers the Competition Agency, the NCAs of other Member States, and the Commission.[499] This is a very novel solution, unprecedented in Croatian civil procedure. It is ambiguous whether it may be interpreted in such a way, or whether this right should be confined to the assistance of the Competition Agency only. The other side of the coin is the right or the obligation of the Competition Agency to provide assistance to national courts of other Member States in their antitrust damages cases. In this regard, no national legal basis exists. In addition, on the grounds of general civil procedure rules, the court may also use expert opinions for the quantification of damages.[500]

498. Article 219 CPA.
499. Article 3(12) of the Act on Antitrust Damages. A very interesting case appeared before the Competition Agency even prior to the enactment of the Antitrust Damages Act – *Media-ideja d.o.o. v. Tisak d.d. and Distri-Press d.o.o.,* UP/I-030-02/2005-01/43 of 15 October 2007, confirmed by the Administrative Court USRH 12765/2007-5 of 30 June 2010. The Competition Agency rejected the request by Media-ideja d.o.o. to determine the financial loss that it suffered due to the abusive conduct of the jointly dominant firms, since it found that in absolute terms Media-ideja d.o.o. paid a lower distribution price per copy in comparison to its competing publishers. Indeed, the Competition Agency held that because of its lower retail price the publisher would always suffer from a higher financial burden in terms of distribution, and there was no liability of distributors in this part since the publisher was free to set its retail price and bear any commercial risks arising therefrom.
500. Article 250 CPA.

d. Passing-on of Overcharges

285. Rules on the passing-on of overcharges are certainly the most innovative rules in Croatian tort law and they pretty much follow the wording of the Directive. The Act on Antitrust Damages regulates in a single article the passing-on defence and indirect purchasers. As for the passing-on defence, the Act on Antitrust Damages provides that the infringer/tortfeasor may invoke as a defence against a claim for damages the fact that the victim passed on the whole or part of the overcharge down the supply chain, thereby reducing the amount of its actual loss. This reduction of harm is, however, without prejudice to the right to full compensation of indirect purchasers, including the loss of profit caused by the passing-on of overcharges.[501] The burden of proof rests with the respondent, and, for that purpose, it may require disclosure of evidence from the claimant of a third party.[502]

286. When it comes to indirect purchasers, the Act *ad verbatim* takes on the wording of Article 14 of the Directive. To begin with, it defines an indirect purchaser as a natural or legal person that purchased goods or services which were the object of an infringement (or products or services containing them or derived therefrom) from the infringers' direct purchaser, or a subsequent purchaser. An indirect purchaser is deemed to have proven that a passing-on to him occurred where he or she shows that: (a) the respondent committed an infringement of competition law; (b) the infringement resulted in an overcharge for the direct purchaser; and (c) the indirect purchaser purchased goods or services that were the object of the infringement, or goods or services derived from or containing them.[503] Following the basic principles of civil procedure and the Directive, the Act on Antitrust Damages states that the infringer may refute the statements of the claimant by proving that the overcharge was not passed on to him or her, or that is was passed on in a smaller amount.[504]

287. According to the general rules on civil procedure, the decision on whether the standard of proof has been met is left to the 'discretion of the judge after conscientious and careful assessment of all the evidence presented individually and as a whole and taking into consideration the results of the entire proceedings'.[505] Additional guidance is given by Article 15 of the Act on Antitrust Damages according to which for that purpose the judge may take into account pending cases related to the same infringement, initiated by claimants from other levels of the supply chain, judgments rendered in such proceedings, and publicly available information arising from the public enforcement of competition law.[506] This rule is meant to safeguard the principle of full compensation while avoiding overcompensation, expressly provided for by Article 16 of the Act on Antitrust Damages. In addition, the Directive expressly provides that in order to avoid overcompensation, Member States must lay dawn appropriate rules 'ensuring that the compensation of actual loss at any

501. Article 15(1) of the Act on Antitrust Damages.
502. Article 15(2) of the Act on Antitrust Damages.
503. Article 15(3) of the Act on Antitrust Damages.
504. Article 15(4) of the Act on Antitrust Damages.
505. Article 8 CPA. Relevant are also Arts 8, 219 and 220(2) CPA
506. Article 15(5) of the Act on Antitrust Damages.

level of the supply chain does not exceed the overcharge harm suffered at that level'.[507] Yet the Croatian Act on Antitrust Damages only restates this principle[508] without attempting to lay down additional rules to avoid overcompensation, save those referred to above which may prove to be insufficient.

288. Avoidance of overcompensation will necessitate intensive coordination and cooperation between courts hearing these disputes and prompt the availability of information in this regard. Likewise, some of the cases might be pending before the courts of other Member States, additionally complicating the issue, and there is no specific mechanism envisaged to tackle these situations. Coupled with the problem of the quantification of the passing-on of overcharges, these difficulties will render claims by indirect purchasers very burdensome for the parties and courts alike, while the principles of full compensation and avoidance of overcompensation might be jeopardized. Overall, the Act on Antitrust Damages fails to overcome the pitfalls and vagueness of the Directive itself.[509] In addition, neither the Directive nor the Act on Antitrust Damages addresses the issue of causation, which is particularly important in cases involving indirect purchasers. Finally, most of the indirect purchasers suffer small and scattered harm, particularly consumers, and thus their incentive to initiate proceedings and their ability to obtain compensation will depend upon the availability of procedural rules regulating collective redress. As there is no such mechanism under the Croatian civil procedure for competition law related claims, but only collective declaratory and injunctive relief,[510] it is likely that these types of proceedings will not play a major role in private enforcement in Croatia.

3. Procedural Issues

a. Standing

289. According to the general rule of the OA, every person is obliged to refrain from taking any action that may cause damage to others.[511] This rule essentially establishes one of the basic principles of the law on obligations[512] and provides a

507. Article 12(2) of Directive 2014/104.
508. Article 16(2) of the Act on Antitrust Damages.
509. For a more detailed analysis of the passing-on of overcharges, *see* E. Büyüksagis, *Directive on Antitrust Damages Actions*, 1 Schweizerische Zeitschrift für Wirtschaftsrecht (SZW) 18 (2015); M. Reppo, *EU Private Competition Law Enforcement: Rethinking the Impact of the Passing-on Defence and Indirect Purchaser Standing*, JAEM01 Master Thesis (Faculty of Law, Lund University, 2015).
510. For a summary on collective relief in Croatia, *see* V. Butorac Malnar, J. Pecotić Kaufman & S. Petrović, *Pravo tržišnog natjecanja, Manualia Universitas Studiorum Zagrabiensis* (Pravni fakultet Sveučilišta u Zagrebu, 2013); for a more detailed discussion, *see* Z. Jelinić, *Instrumenti zaštite kolektivnih interesa i prava u hrvatskom pravu – između stvarne potrebe za jačanjem vladavine prava i efikasnog pravosuđa te mogućih nesnalaženja*, 5 Godišnjak Akademije pravnih znanosti Hrvatske 116 (March 2014); M. Pavlović, *Značaj tužbe za zaštitu kolektivnih interesa i prava*, 52 Zbornik radova Pravnog fakulteta u Splitu 799 (2015).
511. Article 8 OA.
512. V. Gorenc et al., *Komentar Zakona o obveznim odnosima* 19 (Narodne novine, 2014).

base ground for rules regulating the right to compensation and the obligation to compensate the harm caused.[513] Standing to sue is given to any person having a legal interest to pursue his or her claim before the courts. The legal interest is derived from the existence of a legally recognizable harm. According to the general rules of the OA, legally recognizable harm is the loss of a person's assets (actual loss), the halting of an increase in assets (loss of profit), and a violation of an individual's and a legal person's privacy rights (non-material damage).[514] The Act on Antitrust Damages decided to recognize all these types of harm, which, in addition to interest, represent full compensation.[515] In condemnatory claims, such as claims for damages, the legal interest of a claimant is presumed.[516] Accordingly, under Croatian law, any person who claims to have suffered damages resulting from an antitrust infringement will have standing to sue without having to demonstrate the existence of his or her legal interest. The Act defines the injured party as any person who has suffered damages due to a competition law infringement. Consequently, in Croatia, standing to sue is given to any person who has suffered damages, irrespective of how far removed from a competition law infringer he or she is, including indirect purchasers, umbrella claimants,[517] and competitors.

b. Disclosure of Evidence

290. The disclosure of evidence was the most challenging part of the implementation, as the Directive provides very detailed rules, of which some are difficult to implement given the general legal framework on disclosure that is narrower in scope. General rules of the CPA provide that each party is obliged to provide facts and present evidence supporting their claims.[518] Court-assisted disclosure is available in cases when the document is in the possession of a state authority, the opponent or a third person.[519] When it comes to documents in the possession of a state authority, court-assisted disclosure will be available only upon showing that a party requesting disclosure was unable to obtain those documents by himself or herself (e.g., thorough the general rules on access to documents).[520]

513. Any person who causes damage to another is obliged to make compensation. Arts 1045 et seq. OA.
514. Article 1046 OA.
515. Article 5 Act on Antitrust Damages.
516. *See* Triva et al., *Građansko parnično procesno pravo* 248 (Narodne novine, 1986).
517. Specifically, on umbrella claimants, *see* V. Butorac Malnar, *The Kone Case . A Missed Opportunity to Put the Standard of Causation Under the Umbrella of the EU*, in *EU Competition and State Aid Rules: Public and Private Enforcement* (V. Tomljenovic et al., eds., Series Europeanisation and Globalisation (3) Springer-Verlag, 2017).
518. Article 219 CPA. Which of the proposed evidence is to be presented to establish the decisive facts is left to the assessment of the court.
519. Articles 232–233 CPA. When one party refers to a document and claims that it is in the possession of the other party, the court shall order the latter to furnish the document, giving him or her a time limit to do so. The court, in view of all the circumstances and according to its conviction, shall assess the significance of the fact that the party who has possession of the document refuses to act according to the court ruling ordering him or her to furnish the document or, contrary to the conviction of the court, denies that the document is in his or her possession.
520. Article 8(2) of the Act on Antitrust Damages.

291. A different situation arises in the context of the court-ordered disclosure of documents held by the opposing party. According to the general rules of the CPA, the opposing party may resist court-ordered disclosure for a number of justifications such as attorney-client privilege, religious confession, professional secrecy, or if there is a risk of exposing himself or herself or a close family member to criminal prosecution or significant material damage. These are justifications pertinent to witness privileges that apply *mutandi mutandis*.[521] The Act on Antitrust Damages maintained these rules on opposing party disclosure, explicitly giving full effect of the legal professional privilege,[522] while specifying that the interest of a respondent to avoid actions for damages or to avoid compensation is not a justifiable reason for withholding evidence.[523] While the court cannot enforce the disclosure order against the opposing party, it may draw inferences from the fact that evidence was withheld by the party that was ordered to disclose it.[524]

292. The Act on Antitrust Damages sanctions non-compliance with a court order for disclosure in the following manner: (a) facts that should have been determined by the evidence will be considered established;[525] and (b) the party opposing discovery or that has destroyed or tried to destroy evidence may be heavily fined – undertakings from HRK 10,000 (approx. EUR 1,342) up to a maximum of 1% of total turnover in the last year for which financial statements were completed, and responsible persons or individuals from HRK 500–HRK 50,000 (approx. EUR 67–EUR 6,700).[526]

293. A major obstacle in implementation relates to court assistance in the disclosure of 'relevant categories of evidence'. Attempting to make sure that parties are not unduly barred from making such a motion, while trying not to interfere in the general rules on civil procedure which do not recognize the disclosure of 'categories of documents', the Act makes it possible for the parties to obtain court-assisted disclosure of specified or specifiable evidence[527] (circumscribed as narrowly as possible considering the circumstances of the case[528]). This wording is

521. Articles 237–238 CPA.
522. Article 6(4) of the Act on Antitrust Damages.
523. Article 6(6) of the Act on Antitrust Damages.
524. Article 233 CPA.
525. Article 6(8) of the Act on Antitrust Damages.
526. Article 10(2) of the Act on Antitrust Damages.
527. Article 6(1) of the Act on Antitrust Damages. Given the interpretation of relevant categories of evidence in Recital 16 of the Directive, the term 'specifiable evidence' could be adequate to accommodate the interpretation of 'relevant categories of evidence'. According to Recital 16, a category should be identified by reference to the common features of its constitutive elements, such as nature, object, or content of the documents or other criteria, so long as they are relevant and defined as precisely and narrowly as possible. These elements render evidence sufficiently specifiable to be identified and ordered for disclosure. It will be very important for the judges to follow the interpretation of the Directive in this regard, otherwise a major obstacle will arise in antitrust damages cases.
528. Article 6(5)(2) of the Act on Antitrust Damages.

meant to cover the term 'relevant categories of evidence' but it remains to be seen how the application of this rule will evolve in court practice.[529]

294. Disclosure may be obtained when the party requesting it makes it plausible that the opponent or a third party holds such evidence. If the party requesting disclosure is the claimant, he or she has to demonstrate the plausibility of his or her claim for damages as well. The standard of showing plausibility is not explicitly defined in the Act on Antitrust Damages. However, it is a common term in civil procedure corresponding to the explanation given in the Directive, whereby the standard of plausibility is met by presenting 'reasonably available facts in a reasoned justification'.

295. The Act on Antitrust Damages provides that while deciding on disclosure requests, the court must apply the principle of proportionality, i.e., it has to balance 'opposing interests in a given situation – the interests which would be favoured by the disclosure of the documents in question versus those which would be jeopardized by such disclosure'.[530] Pursuant to Article 6(5) of the Act on Antitrust Damages, the court should balance the interest of all parties involved and in particular their interest: (a) to avoid disclosure where relevant facts contained therein may be established though other available evidence; (b) to specify evidence as precisely as possible considering the circumstance of the case and to order the disclosure only of evidence relevant for the case; (c) to make sure that the scope and cost of discovery is not disproportionate to the value of the facts being established; and (d) to safeguard the protection of business secrets.

c. Protection of Business Secrets

296. A very difficult issue for implementation relates to the protection of business secrets because the Directive demands effective measures in this regard. However, given that the Croatian civil procedure is adversarial in nature, and thus all of the evidence presented by one party has to be available to the other for the latter to be able to respond to it in court proceedings, the introduction of a data room or the like was not an option. Consequently, there is no measure to prevent a competitor that is a party to the action for damages from using information obtained during a damages procedure to gain a competitive advantage without necessarily infringing the duty of secrecy.

529. 'The closest general procedural rule is the possibility for a plaintiff that is unable to obtain the information needed to formulate his claim to 'rely on the rules on multistep complaints' ('*stupnjevite tužbe*') in Art. 186.b CPA. He or she could request the court to order the respondent to present accounts or submit an overview of assets and liabilities or say what he/she knows about concealed or hidden assets, if it is proven that there is an underlying legal obligation for the respondent to do so. Also, if the plaintiff is unable to specify the extent of damages sought without obtaining information held by the respondent (which he or she is either obliged to give according to the contents of their civil law relationship or which may be deemed to be common to both parties), the complaint may state that the amount will be defined only after obtaining the relevant information.' Butorac Malnar, Mataija & Petrović, *supra* n. 486.

530. A. Galič, *Disclosure of Documents in Private Antitrust Enforcement Litigation*, 8 Yearbook of Antitrust and Regulatory Studies 105 (2015).

297. Overall, there are only few measures that may be granted upon the motion of a party. The first is the exclusion of the public from the entire or parts of the proceedings. However, based on the general rules of civil procedure, this may be done only when this 'would be unconditionally necessary in special circumstances in which the public could be harmful to the interests of justice'.[531] It remains unclear whether this condition of the CPA would be applicable. The second measure relates to the avoidance of the use of the e-notice board, which is followed by a prohibition of copying documents containing confidential information.[532] In addition, the court may order confidential information to be sealed in an envelope that may be opened only in court, in which case the envelope would be sealed again, when it has been specified who inspected the documents contained therein, and when they were inspected.[533] Before allowing the inspection of documents containing confidential information, the court will instruct those present that they are 'obliged to treat as a secret anything they come to know' who will then have to sign a statement that they are aware of their legal obligations of secrecy.[534] According to the general rules, violating this rule can result in criminal liability.[535]

298. The most effective measures are found, most probably, in heavy fines for the breach of the duty of secrecy. Legal persons may be fined from HRK 10,000 (approx. EUR 1,342) to up to a maximum of 1% of the total turnover in the last year for which financial statements were completed, and responsible persons or individuals may be fined from HRK 500 to HRK 50,000 (approx. EUR 67–EUR 6,700).[536]

d. Disclosure of Evidence Contained in the File of a Competition Authority

299. When it comes to the disclosure of evidence contained in the file of the Competition Agency, the Act on Antitrust Damages follows faithfully the Directive. It specifies that the national court may order disclosure of the following evidence only after the proceedings before the competition authority have been finalized: (a) information prepared specifically for the proceedings; (b) information drawn by the competition authority for the parties; (c) withdrawn settlement submissions.[537]

300. The Act specifies that a motion for disclosure must be specific, i.e., it must contain the description of the nature, subject, or content of the files or documents whose disclosure is requested; it must relate to the damages case; the party must prove that it failed to obtain the documents by itself prior to requesting disclosure, and must ensure the protection of the efficient public enforcement of competition

531. Article 307(1) CPA.
532. Article 7(4) and (2) of the Act on Antitrust Damages.
533. Article 7(3) of the Act on Antitrust Damages.
534. Article 7(2) point 4 of the Act on Antitrust Damages.
535. Articles 262 and 307 of the Criminal Code, Official Gazette nos 125/2011, 144/2012, 56/2015, 61/2015.
536. Article 10(3) of the Act on Antitrust Damages.
537. Article 8(1)(2) of the Act on Antitrust Damages.

law.[538] This rule provides a clear guidance for the parties requesting disclosure while leaving untouched the right of the courts to observe that proportionality of disclosure is being observed.

301. Given that the Directive regulates exemptions from disclosure via a maximum harmonization rule, those have been implemented fully and precisely. Accordingly, documents that may never be disclosed are settlement submissions and leniency statements. Here it is important to note that as of 2021 CA amendments Croatian competition law envisages a settlement procedure in public enforcement. Therefore, this provision no longer safeguards only settlement procedures before the Commission or any other NCA.[539]

302. When it comes to penalties for infringing the rules on disclosure, according to the Article 10 (3) of the Act on Antitrust damages, the court may impose significant fines, for legal persons from HRK 10,000 (approx. EUR 1,342) to up to maximum of 1% of total turnover in the last year for which financial statements have been completed, and for responsible persons or individuals from HRK 500 to HRK 50,000 (approx. EUR 67–EUR 6,700).

e. Effect of National Infringement Decisions

303. The Act on Antitrust Damages provides that domestic infringement findings (both those based only on domestic competition law, or combined with Articles 101 and 102 TFEU) have a binding effect in antitrust damages cases. This is a very practical rule, as prior to the implementation of the Directive, the CA only provided that in such situations the competent commercial court must take into account such decisions.[540] There was no binding effect and the finding of an infringement could have been relitigated in civil proceedings.

304. A completely different situation arises in the context of the effects of the infringement decision rendered by the competition authorities of other Member States. Here, the Directive provides a minimum harmonization rule whereby final decisions that are based on Articles 101 and 102 TFEU should have at least the effect of prima facie evidence that an infringement of competition law has occurred, and may be assessed along with other evidence. Thus, minimum harmonization requires giving only an evidentiary effect to the infringement findings of the NCAs of other Member States in situations where they are based on EU competition law. The Directive completely leaves out the issue of legal effects of the infringement findings of the NCAs of other Member States based purely on national competition law as this issue falls outside the EU's legislative competence. Having in mind the functioning of minimum harmonization, in regulating this situation the Member States had several alternative options at their disposal.

538. Article 8(1) of the Act on Antitrust Damages.
539. Article 3(26) of the Act on Antitrust Damages.
540. Article 69a(3) CA.

305. The Croatian Act on Antitrust Damages adopted a solution whereby infringement findings of other Member States' NCAs based on EU law are deemed to be proven. This is a rebuttable presumption and thus may be rebutted. On the contrary, findings based on national competition law are given no legal effect. The minimum harmonization rule, and the resulting differences in treatment across EU countries, will be a strong incentive for forum shopping,[541] as it will be much more attractive for claimants to initiate proceedings in countries giving binding effect to the infringement findings of foreign NCAs. Given the chosen standards of the legal effects of other Member States' NCAs in the Act on Antitrust Damages, Croatia will not be a likely forum of choice for antitrust damages cases.

4. Consensual Dispute Resolution

306. According to the Act on Antitrust Damages, consensual dispute resolution is defined as any form of out-of-court dispute resolution between the parties.[542] In Croatia, these may include out-of-court settlement, mediation, conciliation, and arbitration. However, given the nature of arbitration, it may be concluded that the rules regarding consensual dispute resolution in the Act on Antitrust Damages would not refer to it. This is so because parties to an arbitration agreement must arbitrate rather than litigate their dispute. The arbitral award is final and binding, and has a *res judicata* effect, unless of course 'the award is invalid and is set aside by a court of a competent jurisdiction'.[543] Therefore, the rules of the Directive pertinent to limitation periods in the case of consensual dispute resolution and the suspension of court proceedings for the duration of consensual dispute resolution would not be applicable to arbitration. The Directive, and as a result the Act on Antitrust Damages, 'deal in essence, with situations when the parties attempt to resolve the case primarily through mediation or conciliation without referring to arbitration/ litigation'.[544] 'In case the parties do not resolve their dispute through mediation, arbitration/litigation follows.'[545]

307. The Act on Antitrust Damages provides that where the parties reach a settlement, the overall amount of damages should be reduced by the settling co-infringer's share of the harm.[546] The remaining part of the claim may be claimed

---

541. M. Merola & L. Armati, *The Binding Effect of NCA Decisions under the Damages Directive: Rationale and Practical Implications*, 1 Rivista Italiana di Antitrust 87, 100 (2016).

542. Article 3(22) of the Act on Antitrust Damages.

543. A. Redfern, M. Hunter, *The Law and Practice of International Commercial Arbitration*, 396 (3d ed., Sweet & Maxwell, 1999).

544. M. Driessen-Reilly, *Private Damages in EU Competition Law and Arbitration: A Changing Landscape*, 31 Arbitration International 567 (2015), available at http://dx.doi.org/10.1093/arbint/aiv007 (accessed 6 May 2015).

545. R. Moisejevas, *The Damages Directive and Consensual Approach to Antitrust Enforcement*, 8 Yearbook of Antitrust and Regulatory Studies 181, 187–188 (2015).

546. The relative share is determined by the application of the rules of Art. 14 of the Act regulating contributions between co-infringers.

only against non-settling co-infringers. In addition, non-settling co-infringers cannot recover a contribution for the remaining claim from the settling co-infringer.[547] As an exemption, the injured party may claim from the settling co-infringer the remaining claim when non-settling co-infringers 'cannot pay' the damages.[548]

308. In addition, the Act on Antitrust Damages specifies that in determining the amount of the contribution that an infringer may recover from other infringers, in accordance with their relative share in the overall harm, the court shall take into account the damages paid pursuant to consensual settlements.[549] The limitation periods are suspended for the duration of consensual dispute resolution with regard to the parties involved in such a process. When the parties have already entered into litigation, they may request the court to suspend its proceedings for the purposes of the consensual settlement of their dispute and the suspension may last for up to two years.[550] The court proceedings will restart following the motion of the parties, or ex officio when the period of two years has lapsed.[551]

C. *Interim Measures*

309. Interim measures are a very important and useful procedural tool at the disposal of the parties that suffered harm as a result of anticompetitive behaviour. Because there are no specific rules on interim measures related to private claims arising out of competition law infringements, the general rules of the Enforcement Act (EA) apply.[552]

310. According to Article 341(1) of the EA, an interim measure may be proposed before the opening of judicial or administrative proceedings, during the course of such proceedings, and after its termination up until the enforcement of the claim. In a motion to order an interim measure, the applicant must: (i) make a request specifying the claim to be secured; (ii) determine the type and duration of the requested interim measure; (iii) when necessary, define the object of security and the means of its enforcement; (iv) present facts on which the request is based; and (v) propose and present evidence in support of the applicant's statements.[553] An interim measure may be issued to secure non-matured and conditional claims as well;[554] however, it is not permitted to order interim measures where the same effect may be achieved by way of preliminary measures.[555]

547. Article 18 of the Act on Antitrust Damages.
548. Article 18(3) of the Act on Antitrust Damages.
549. Article 18(5) of the Act on Antitrust Damages.
550. Article 13(1) and (2) of the Act on Antitrust Damages.
551. Article 13(4) of the Act on Antitrust Damages.
552. Enforcement Act, Official Gazette nos 112/2012, 25/2013, 93/2014, 55/2016, 73/2017, 131/20. (hereinafter: EA).
553. Article 341(2) EA.
554. Article 343(1) EA.
555. Article 343(2) EA.

311. The EA distinguishes between interim measures securing pecuniary[556] and non-pecuniary claims.[557] Which type of interim measure is best suited in the individual case depends on the type of competition law infringement and the related private claim.

312. An interim measure securing pecuniary claims may be ordered by the court upon the request of the applicant, where the applicant demonstrates that the existence of the main claim is plausible and that without the proposed interim measure there is a plausible risk that the debtor will prevent or impede the enforcement of the claim by either transferring, concealing, or otherwise disposing of his or her assets.[558] However, this would not be necessary where it is likely that the proposed interim measure would result in an insignificant loss of the debtor.[559] In addition, when the claim is to be enforced abroad, the existence of this risk is presumed.[560]

313. The EA enumerates a number of different types of interim measures securing pecuniary claims that the court may order. The list is non-exhaustive, and the court may choose the one that is best suited to protect the concrete claim, and in particular:

- prohibiting the debtor from disposing of his or her movable property and seizing of such property;
- seizing and depositing of cash, securities and the like with the court or a notary public;
- prohibiting the debtor from transferring or encumbering his or her immovable property or rights in rem and noting this prohibition in the land register;
- prohibiting the debtor's debtor from voluntarily fulfilling his or her obligation and prohibiting the debtor from recovering debts and disposing of them; and
- instructing a bank to refuse payment from the debtor's account in the amount secured by the interim measure.[561]

314. When it comes to interim measures securing non-pecuniary claims, the EA makes their availability conditional on the applicants' demonstration of the plausibility of the existence of the claim; the plausibility that, without the proposed interim measure, the debtor would prevent or impede the enforcement of the claim by altering the current situation; and the plausibility that the measure is necessary to prevent violence or the occurrence of irreparable damage.[562] Just as with motions for ordering interim measures securing pecuniary claims, the applicant does not have to prove the plausibility of the described risks if the interim measure would

556. Article 344 EA.
557. Article 346 EA.
558. Article 344(1) EA.
559. Article 344(2) EA.
560. Article 344(3) EA.
561. Article 345(1) EA.
562. Article 346(1) EA.

cause only insignificant loss to the debtor, and such risks are considered to be demonstrated if the claim is to be enforced abroad.[563]

315. In order to secure a non-pecuniary claim, the court may order any appropriate interim measure achieving that goal. Besides the types of measures equally suitable for securing pecuniary claims, the EA exemplifies other types of measures specific for securing non-pecuniary claims, such as prohibiting the debtor's debtor from handing over an object, transferring a right, or undertaking any other non-pecuniary obligation to which the claim refers, prohibiting the debtor from undertaking anything that might cause damage to the applicant, and prohibiting any alterations to the objects to which the claim refers, and similar measures.[564] In addition, where this is necessary in order to prevent violence, the occurrence of irreparable damage, or to safeguard the legal order, the court may order a measure by which it temporarily regulates the disputed relationship between the parties.[565]

316. Depending on the particular circumstance of the case, the court may order several interim measures.[566] Where more than one measure would achieve the same result, the court will order the measure that is the least onerous for the debtor.[567]

§3. Criminal Enforcement

I. Criminal Sanctions for Antitrust Violations

317. As a rule, antitrust offences are not treated as criminal offences under Croatian law, save for bid-rigging in public procurement markets, which will be discussed in more detail below. As an introduction, it is first necessary to describe the context and the development of the existing legislative solution.

318. Up until 2009, the CA classified antitrust infringements as misdemeanours[568] and, accordingly, such offences were subject to a fine that could have been imposed on both the undertaking concerned and the responsible person. The competent body to impose the fine was misdemeanour courts. Essentially, this institutional structure of competition law enforcement combined two types of proceedings: the administrative, infringement proceeding conducted by the Competition Agency and the misdemeanour, fines proceeding, conducted by misdemeanour courts, the latter being initiated following the finality of the Competition Agency's infringement decisions. Soon it became evident that this division of powers between

563. Article 346(2) EA.
564. Article 347(1) EA.
565. Article 347(2) EA.
566. Article 350(1) EA.
567. Article 350(2) EA.
568. 2003 CA.

the Competition Agency and misdemeanour courts was very unsatisfactory for a variety of reasons,[569] all of them resulting in the overall inefficiency of antitrust enforcement.

319. This problem was solved by the 2009 CA, which gave the Competition Agency the necessary powers to impose fines for antitrust infringements, bringing together the infringement and fine proceedings under the authority of a single body. The procedure remained administrative in nature, save the oral hearing, which is conducted under the rules of the Misdemeanour Act so as to safeguard the rights of the parties.[570] In order to achieve this goal and bypass the involvement of the misdemeanour courts, antitrust violations ceased to be categorized as misdemeanours, and became offences sui generis, subject to fines and other restrictive orders jointly termed administrative-penal sanctions by the CA, pointing to their combined sanctioning and deterrent function. The drawback of this, otherwise good and necessary, institutional change was the perceived need to omit from the new CA the possibility of fining the responsible persons of the infringing undertakings. Initially, this was not a problem, because at that time the Criminal Code contained two provisions criminalizing conduct that could have been traced back to what constitutes restrictive agreements and abuse of dominance[571] and thus could have been used against the responsible persons of infringing undertakings. However, in 2011 a new Criminal Code was enacted, bringing many novelties, including the deletion of the two criminal offences in relation to anticompetitive market behaviour. Ironically, this deletion took place on account of the enactment of the 2009 CA, the latter being considered more suitable and sufficient means for sanctioning this kind of behaviour. Instead, a legal gap was created. Under the combined new rules, save in the

569. For a detailed analysis of the Croatian historical background of antitrust law in the EU context, *see* J. Pecotić Kaufman & V. Butorac Malnar, *The Interaction between EU Regulatory Implants and the Existing Croatian Legal Order in Competition Law*, in *Economic Evidence in EU Competition Law* (M. Kovač & A. Vandenberghe, eds., Cambridge-Anwerp-Portland, Intersentia, 2016).

570. Article 135(2) CA.

571. Article 280 of the former Criminal Code defined as a criminal offence the violation of equality in the execution of economic activities in the following manner:

(1) Whoever, by abusing his official position or authority, limits the free movement of capital and labour within a certain area, withholds or limits the right of a legal or natural person to be engaged within a certain area in trading with goods and services, places a company in a disadvantageous position in relation to other legal and natural persons regarding the conditions of work or trading with goods and services, or limits the free exchange of goods and services shall be punished by imprisonment for six months to five years.

(2) The same punishment as referred to in paragraph 1 of this Article shall be inflicted on whoever exploits his social position or influence so that the offence referred to in paragraph 1 is committed.

Article 288 of the former Criminal Code defined as a criminal offence the creating of a monopolistic position on the market in the following manner:

Whoever, in a legal person, concludes an agreement by which another legal or natural person is restricted in the free movement of goods or services within a certain area or with certain legal or natural persons, or concludes an agreement that otherwise creates the monopolistic position of legal or natural persons on the market, shall be punished by imprisonment for between six months and five years.

case of bid-rigging cartels, the responsible persons of undertakings infringing competition rules are free of any kind of liability for their anticompetitive conduct. Consequently, it is safe to conclude that while the overall efficiency of antitrust enforcement has been improved remarkably with the sanctioning powers granted to the Competition Agency, the sanctions themselves became less efficient. The CA explicitly provides in its Article 65(5) that imposing a fine or other measures under the CA has no effect on the criminal responsibility of the person who was subject to the fine in the administrative procedure. The only problem is that there is no criminal responsibility except in cases of bid-rigging in public procurement. Treating antitrust violations as criminal offences might be a suitable method of achieving a high level of competition law compliance.[572]

320. Let us now turn to the only criminal offence regarding antitrust violations under Croatian law – the public procurement bid-rigging cartel. Article 254(1) of the Criminal Code specifies that whoever, in the public procurement procedure, makes a bid based on a prohibited agreement between economic operators with the aim of ensuring that a particular operator is chosen, shall be punished by imprisonment for between six months and five years. Where the offender acquires considerable property gains or causes material damage, punishment by imprisonment is stricter as it ranges between one and ten years.[573] However, where the offender voluntarily prevents a contracting authority from accepting the offer resulting from a prohibited agreement, the offender may be released from punishment.[574] This is a very important solution as it is meant to work together with the Leniency Programme, which was enacted the same year as the Criminal Code, and thus they complement each other. This means that in cases of public procurement bid-rigging cartels, whistleblowers cooperating with the Competition Agency might not only gain immunity from a fine but may also be released from criminal punishment. The big difference between the two is that immunity from fines is possible regardless of whether the bid-rigging cartel was successfully implemented, while release from criminal sanctions can be granted only where the bid-rigging cartel was prevented from being successfully implemented by the defendant himself.

II. Other Applications of Criminal Law to Relevant Conduct

321. There is no other application of criminal law besides what has been described above.

---

572. *See* P. Novoselec & S. Vidlička Roksandić, *Gospodarska kaznena djela u novom Kaznenom Zakonu*, 17 Hrvatski ljetopis za kazneno pravo i praksu, 699 (2010); I. Tot, *Kazna zatvora za kaznena djela protiv slobode tržišnog natjecanja u hrvatskom pravu de lege ferenda,* in *Pravo tržišnog natjecanja- novine u hrvatskom i europskom zakonodavstvu i praksi* (J. Pecotić Kaufman, ed., Ekonomski fakultet Zagreb, 2012).

573. Article 254(2) of the Criminal Code, Official Gazette nos 125/11, 144/12, 56/15, 61/15, 101/17, 118/18, 126/19, 84/21.

574. Article 254(3) of the Criminal Code.

III. Role of Prosecutors

322. In addition to regular prosecuting powers, when it comes to public bid-rigging cartels, public prosecutors may also conduct special investigative measures envisaged for the most serious criminal offences as they provisionally restrict certain constitutional rights of citizens.[575] These include:

- surveillance and technical recording of telephone conversations and other remote communications;
- intercepting, collecting, and recording computer data;
- entry into premises for conducting surveillance and technical recording of premises; secret surveillance and technical recording of persons and objects;
- the use of undercover investigators;
- the simulated sale and purchase of items, offering, and accepting bribes;
- providing simulated legal services or concluding simulated legal transactions; and
- supervised transportation and delivery of items, objects of criminal offences.[576]

323. Such measures are available only where the investigation could not have been carried out in any other way or, if it could, it could be done only with disproportionate difficulties. These types of measures may be conducted only on the grounds of a court order issued by the investigative judge, upon a written and reasoned request by the State Attorney.

IV. Competent Criminal Courts

324. The competent criminal courts to hear bid-rigging cartel cases are municipal courts as first instance courts and county courts as appellate courts.[577]

575. Article 332(1) of the Criminal Procedure Act, Official Gazette nos 152/2008, 76/2009, 80/2011, 91/2012, 143/2012, 56/2013, 145/2013, 152/2014, 70/2017 126/19, 126/19, 80/22.
576. Article 332(1) of the Criminal Procedure Act, Official Gazette nos 152/2008, 76/2009, 80/2011, 91/2012, 143/2012, 56/2013, 145/2013, 152/2014, 70/2017,126/19, 126/19, 80/22.
577. Articles 19a and 19c of the Criminal Procedure Act.

Part II. Application of Prohibitions

Chapter 1. Restrictive Agreements

§1. Horizontal Agreements

I. Cartels

325. Cartels are prohibited under the Croatian CA and are considered as the gravest competition law infringement. Looking at the period of more than twenty-five years of Competition Agency practice, we observe that almost all cartels prosecuted by the Competition Agency took place within a trade association, with the association serving as a cartel facilitator or simply as a meeting point allowing for anticompetitive contact. Whereas the frequency of cartel proceedings was relatively rare in the first ten to fifteen years of the Competition Agency's existence, in more recent times, especially after the new fining regime was put into place by the CA 2009, more cartel cases are being brought forward and prosecuted.[578] However, in the post-accession period we observe stagnation in cartel enforcement.[579] Most cartel cases decided by the Competition Agency have concerned explicit collusion, with direct evidence of anticompetitive contact between competitors. In late 2010s, in a devastating blow to the Competition Agency's enforcement efforts, a number of cartel decisions of the Competition Agency were annulled by the courts, including two cases where the Constitutional Court of the Republic of Croatia controversially annulled its decisions.[580] The rationale of the courts, both the Constitutional Court and the High Administrative Court, used in the above-mentioned judgments, cast an unpleasant light on the capacity of the courts to take in EU law, especially post-accession.

578. J. Pecotić Kaufman, *Fighting Against Cartels in Croatia: More Than a Decade of Enforcement Practice* (GCP: The Online Magazine for Global Competition Policy, June 2009), available at http://bib.irb.hr/datoteka/418374.Kaufman-JUNE-09_1_.pdf (accessed 27 Sep. 2018).

579. J. Pecotić Kaufman, *On the development of (not so) new competition systems—findings from an empirical study on Croatia*, *Journal of Antitrust Enforcement*, 2021; jnab018, https://doi.org/10.1093/jaenfo/jnab018

580. Decision of the Croatian Competition Agency of 17 March 2015, *Competition Agency v. Sokol Marić d.o.o. et al.*, UP/I-034-03/2014-01/002, confirmed: Judgment of the High Administrative Court of the Republic of Croatia of 22 April 2016; *Sokol Marić d.o.o. v. Competition Agency*, UsII-40/15-10 (and other cases), annulled: Judgment of the Constitutional Court of the Republic of Croatia of 1 February 2018, *Sokol Marić d.o.o.*, U-III-2791/2016 (and other cases). For the Presečki saga *see* fn 635.

326. Cartels are, as a rule, secret horizontal agreements between two or more independent undertakings or decisions of an association of undertakings or concerted practices of all undertakings operating at the same level of production or distribution, with the aim of distorting competition between competitors through the mutual determination of purchase or selling prices, markets and customers, limiting production and/or sales and technological development, making agreements on participation in public procurement procedures, and the like, and the consequence of cartel agreements is detrimental to consumers in terms of price increases and reduced choice of goods and/or services.[581]

327. In its practice, the Competition Agency regularly defines cartels as:

> secret horizontal agreements between two or more independent undertakings or decisions of associations of undertakings or concerted practice of undertakings dealing at the same level of market, which have as their object the distortion of competition between competitors by fixing prices, allocating markets, limiting production and or sales and technologic development, public bid-rigging and similar, and its consequences are detrimental effects as regards consumers due to elevated prices and lesser choice of goods and or services.[582]

328. Under the CA 2003, the notion of cartel covered tacit agreements. For example, in the *Bus cartel* case, a cartel was defined as an explicit or tacit agreement between two or more undertakings – direct competitors – whose aim is to fully exclude competition between cartel participants, for the purpose of inflating the prices and achieving extra profit for cartel members; a cartel may also result in erecting barriers to market entry, or in eliminating from the market competitors that are not part of the cartel.[583] A cartel results in the elimination or diminishing of consumer welfare.[584]

329. In cartel cases, the Competition Agency typically holds that the agreement in question is prohibited by its object, with no need to prove its effect. In addition, no exemption is available for hardcore restraints, and *de minimis* rules are not applicable in cartel cases.

330. Explaining the underlying reasons to prohibit an agreement restrictive by object, in a typical cartel decision, the Competition Agency would state that:

581. Article 2g of the Regulation on the Method of Setting Fines, Official Gazette no. 129/10.
582. For example, Decision of the Croatian Competition Agency of 22 December 2015, *Competition Agency v. Bolus d.o.o. et al.*, UP/I-034-03/2015-01/010, annulled: judgment of the High Administrative Court of the Republic of Croatia of 8 July 2016, *Super Sport d.o.o. et al. v. Competition Agency*, UsII-22/16-11.
583. Decision of the Croatian Competition Agency of 24 September 2007, *Competition Agency v. Autobusni promet d.d. Varaždin et al.*, UP/I-030-02/2006-1/39.
584. *Ibid.*

price fixing, market allocation and other similar activities between competitors were contrary to the very nature and purpose of a market economy; they prevented an optimal allocation of resources, eliminated competition between competitors and they acted as one 'collective' monopolist; as a result, end consumers had to pay what can be called a 'private tax' to these undertakings in the form of higher prices, since the goal was to secure survival also to the least efficient undertakings, and an extra profit for those with a more efficient business model; in those circumstances, there is no incentive to compete regarding the quality of service or introducing innovations; thus, those undertakings remain on the market which would not survive if there was efficient competition on the market.[585]

331. The Competition Agency also typically argues that:

> in an open market each undertaking is accountable for its business decisions and each undertaking autonomously decides on its conduct in the market. Its autonomy and freedom go as far as until its conduct infringes upon mandatory rules which prohibit coordination and agreements between competitors regarding their dealings on the market. Therefore, there is no justification for an arrangement whereby competitors agree to stop competing on price and to divide buyers since such arrangements between direct competitors result in a restricted choice of prices for the same service, and there is no incentive for undertakings to do their business cost effectively and to provide higher quality service. This precludes or restricts the optimal forming of prices in the relevant market and takes away the possibility for end customers to choose, and to be provided with the best possible service with the most convenient price. In the end, customers pay higher prices for lower quality of goods or service.[586]

332. A number of documents with cartel intent were treated as a single whole.[587] An agreement on the purchase of shares on the stock exchange between, *inter alia*, pension funds was not found to be a cartel within the meaning of competition rules.[588]

A. Price-fixing

333. Both direct and indirect price-fixing is explicitly prohibited by the CA.[589] Price-fixing is considered as a hardcore restraint which precludes the benefit of

585. For example, Decision of the Croatian Competition Agency of 21 July 2011, *Competition Agency v. BIRODOM d.o.o. et al.*, UP/I-030-02/2010-01/018.
586. *Ibid.*
587. Decision of the Croatian Competition Agency of 4 October 2005, *Competition Agency v. Mustela d.o.o. et al. (Demining companies cartel)*, UP/I-030-02/2004-01/095.
588. Decision of the Croatian Competition Agency of 13 January 2011, *Competition Agency v. AZ d.o.o. et al.*, UP/I-030-02/2010-01/037.
589. Article 8(1)(1) CA.

block exemption.[590] In its decisions the Competition Agency regularly finds that price-fixing agreements are a restriction by object, being null and void.

334. The majority of cartel decisions adopted by the Competition Agency were instances of explicit price-fixing arrangements, with direct evidence of collusion usually available, which occurred within the framework of an association of undertakings.[591]

335. In one such case, newspaper publishers simultaneously increased the price of daily general-information newspapers by the same amount.[592] As in other cases, the Competition Agency here used the opportunity to explain why such arrangements were prohibited. The Competition Agency held that:

> each undertaking should independently decide on its price policy in a market economy where the allocation of resources is made in the market and through economic laws, not through government intervention. The Competition Agency has no power to control prices or decide on this basic entrepreneurial freedom, provided the undertakings act in compliance with the laws and regulations. The free formation of prices vouches for the establishment of competition between competitors and for the optimal allocation of resources in the market, so undertakings which are the most cost effective, the most innovative and which enable consumers to have the biggest benefits (lower prices, better quality, more choice) have the biggest chances of long-term success and survival in the market. On the other hand, explicit price agreements, market division agreements and other forms of restricting competition are the biggest danger for the development of a market economy and are contrary to consumer interests. This is why they are explicitly prohibited pursuant to the Competition Act.

336. Direct contact between competitors was found in this case. It was found that they met regularly in their trade association, and discussed problems in the market, with the chairman of the association giving a public statement on the price-fixing meeting and the agreement they reached on the price increase. The fact that the minutes of this meeting were not submitted to the Competition Agency, despite its requests to have them submitted, additionally proved, according to the Competition Agency, that the meeting in question was crucial for reaching the agreement. Another element that helped to prove that the competitors concluded a prohibited

590. For example, *see* the Regulation on Block Exemptions and Horizontal Agreements – Hard Core Restraints, Arts 11 and 13.

591. For a detailed discussion see Pecotić Kaufman, J. & Šimić Banović, R. 'The Role of (In)formal Governance and Culture in a National Competition System: A Case of a Post- Socialist Economy', (2021), 44, *World Competition,* Issue 1, pp. 81-108.

592. Decision of the Croatian Competition Agency of 25 March 2010, *Competition Agency v. Datapress d.o.o. u stečaju et al.*, UP/I-030-02/2008-01/72, confirmed: Judgment of the Administrative Court of the Republic of Croatia of 21 December 2011, *Glas Slavonije d.d. et al. v. Competition Agency*, Us-4995/2010-6, Official Gazette no. 25/12.

agreement, in the view of the Competition Agency, was the fact that they increased the price after the move was announced in the media by the chairman of the association.

337. To state that the form of the agreement was irrelevant and that any contact regarding their business activities and market conduct (e.g., price-fixing, market allocation) between competitors was a risk for competition, the Competition Agency invoked EU case law,[593] stating that, although undertakings have the right to adjust to existing or anticipated competitors' conduct, there must be no direct or indirect contact between competitors which can influence their behaviour in the market or through which an undertaking reveals to its competitor its future course of conduct in the market.

338. Since all nine publishers increased prices simultaneously, the Competition Agency did not allow for the argument of parallel behaviour as defence.

339. In a typical move, despite its findings of direct collusion, the Competition Agency performed an economic analysis, finding that the structure of costs differed substantially between undertakings, and thereby concluded that it was not rational behaviour for each and every undertaking to increase prices by the same amount and at the same time.

340. In the *Bakers cartel* case, competitors discussed bread prices and the need to increase them at a meeting, agreeing finally on an 'orientation price' of HRK 8 for white bread.[594] The Competition Agency held that the meeting 'eliminated to a significant measure any uncertainty regarding their future behaviour on the relevant market'. It was held that:

> an exchange of strategic information, such as information on prices, quantities, production costs, buyers lists and similar, brings about coordination of behaviour between competitors since it diminishes the autonomy of undertakings on the market and their incentive to compete. An exchange of strategic information regarding future prices of products/services is a hard-core restriction of competition which is per se prohibited due to its goal of distorting competition.

341. As regards the actual outcome of the meeting in terms of a price increase, the Competition Agency held that it was not relevant for proving the existence of the prohibited agreement to prove that all undertakings present at the meeting actually increased their prices: 'Undertakings participating in the meeting have tacitly approved the prohibited agreement by their mere participation in talks on future prices, and they showed no explicit and clear reservation regarding the conclusions of the meeting, thus no exculpation from liability was available for not executing

593. Case C-7/95 *John Deere v. Commission* ECLI:EU:C:1998:256.
594. Decision of the Croatian Competition Agency of 26 July 2012, *Competition Agency v. Pekarstvo Kadulja d.o.o., Darda (Bakers cartel) et al.*, UP/I-030-02/11-01/039.

the increase of prices'.[595] The Competition Agency held that this can only be taken as a mitigating circumstance as regards the fine. In addition, it was not relevant that no sanctions for non-compliance were agreed between competitors.

342. The rationale for prohibiting such a cartel, according to the Competition Agency, was that:

> each individual undertaking must autonomously adopt its own business decisions, and must behave on the market in a manner that avoids any coordination and agreements between competitors which decrease uncertainty of future conduct, since thereby the risk of adopting business decisions within a competitive environment is decreased.

343. In another typical price-fixing case with direct evidence of a prohibited arrangement, but interesting for the communication channel between the competitors, the Competition Agency found that the CEOs of two major newspaper publishers exchanged messages on their mobile phones, thereby fixing prices.[596] The Competition Agency found out about this cartel through a criminal trial for the murder of one of the CEOs who was involved in this communication, and who was killed by a hit man. Once transcripts of the messages between the CEOs were revealed, the Competition Agency opened a cartel case. The Competition Agency held that:

> securing equal participation for all participants in the market is the basis of the protection of competition. Prices are determined by supply and demand. The parties may not abuse their freedom to compete by restricting competition between themselves. An explicit agreement on prices is a hard-core restriction of competition and is explicitly forbidden by the Competition Act. In modern economies, the prohibition of restrictive agreements is very important both for undertakings since it secures a competitive market and economic growth, and for consumers since it eliminates undertakings unable to compete and ensures lower prices.

The Competition Agency held that there was a causal link between the agreement and the price increase, with all the features of a cartel agreement: an increase in prices, within the same week, by the same amount, agreed by the CEOs of two newspaper firms. The object of the agreement, the Competition Agency found, was to distort competition in the relevant market of national weekly (general-information) newspapers in Croatia. The Competition Agency explained the rationale of its prohibition in the following way:

---

595. 542. *Ibid.*

596. Decision of the Croatian Competition Agency of 16 December 2010, *Competition Agency v. Europa Press Holding d.o.o. i NCL Media Grupa,* UP/I-030-02/2010-01/027; confirmed: Judgment of the High Administrative Court of the Republic of Croatia of 16 May 2012, *NCL Media Grupa d.o.o. i Europa Press d.o.o. v. Competition Agency*, Us-1189/2011-4.

> By implementing the agreement, risks inherent in competition were avoided, and, instead of mutual competition, it will be their mutual agreement that will govern the market. In this manner, market mechanisms that force undertakings to be cost effective and to produce higher quality newspapers were eliminated. There is no more incentive for the parties to compete on quality and innovations.[597]

To state that no exemption is available for cartel agreements, the Competition Agency held that:

> price agreement cannot be exempted since each publisher must determine its prices autonomously. Each undertaking is responsible for its own business decisions in market circumstances and it acts independently in the market, and this freedom to act autonomously is subject to 'mandatory' rules which prohibit coordination and agreement between competitors regarding their decisions on the market.[598]

344. In the *Residential Management* cartel case, the Competition Agency found a price-fixing agreement between firms providing residential buildings management services.[599] Typically, this was an explicit agreement/concerted practice, with a meeting of competitors taking place at one of the undertakings' premises where they discussed prices and agreed on a price increase, which followed after the meeting. Since this was an explicit price-fixing agreement/concerted practice between direct competitors which had a joint market share of more than 90%, the Competition Agency held that their goal was to eliminate any competition between themselves, thus making it a hardcore restriction of competition, not eligible for individual or block exemption. In line with the notion of an agreement as defined in the CA 2003, the Competition Agency defined the notion of a cartel in this decision as an 'explicit or tacit agreement'[600] between competitors whose object was to fully eliminate competition between its members, with the aim of increasing prices and making extra profit for its members.

345. The Competition Agency provided an economic analysis to further substantiate concrete negative anticompetitive effects. In particular, the negative effect

---

597. *Ibid.*
598. *Ibid.*
599. Decision of the Croatian Competition Agency of 24 November 2009, *Competition Agency v. Tehnoplast d.o.o. et al.*, UP/I-030-02/2008-01/03; confirmed: Judgment of the High Administrative Court of the Republic of Croatia of 13 December 2012, *Stano-uprava d.o.o. et al. v. Competition Agency*, Us-1700/2010-6, Official Gazette no. 20/13; *see* also, in the same industry but on a different local market, Decision of the Croatian Competition Agency of 23 December 2009, *Competition Agency v. EKI Inžinjering d.o.o. et al.*, UP/I-030-02/2008-01/78; confirmed: Judgment of the High Administrative Court of the Republic of Croatia of 13 March 2012, *Stambeni inžinjering d.o.o. et al. v. Competition Agency*, Us-2248/2010-6.
600. Article 9 CA 2003.

of the agreement for consumers was taken into account in this case. The Competition Agency held that since the managers of residential buildings had different suppliers and various numbers of clients and different cost structures, the prices for their services should also be different.

346. The Competition Agency reasoned that:

> coordination as to price leads to no choice in terms of prices for the same service, and undertakings feel no pressure to do their business more cost effectively and with higher quality. This restricts or prevents optimal prices being determined in the relevant market. As a consequence, consumers pay higher prices for lower quality … The implementation of the said agreement eliminated market mechanisms which forced undertakings to do their business more cost effectively and to provide services of a higher quality. There is no incentive to compete in terms of quality and innovations. Thus, those undertakings which would be unable to survive in the market if there was effective competition will now be able to do so.[601]

347. The Competition Agency invoked the criteria for concerted practice from the ECJ's case law[602] to show that there was a causal link between concerted practice and the conduct of undertakings in the market, even if the concerted practice ensued after only one meeting.

348. In the *Driving Schools cartel* case, an elaborate cartel between driving schools, including a punishing scheme for deviators, the Competition Agency found that an explicit written agreement between competitors to fix a minimum price had all the elements of a cartel agreement, the object of which was to eliminate competition in the relevant market.[603] Despite the fact that the relevant product market was partially regulated, the Competition Agency held that the price-fixing agreement had no justification in the relevant sector rules: the rules adopted by the Ministry of the Interior provided for a fixed minimum level of individual elements for the education of drivers, but this did not amount, according to the Competition Agency, to fixing the end price, and since different driving schools had different cost levels, this should be reflected in the end price. In this case, as in a number of other cartel cases, despite evidence of explicit collusion, the Competition Agency undertook an elaborate analysis of costs for each undertaking, finding (unsurprisingly)

601. Decision of the Croatian Competition Agency of 24 November 2009, *Competition Agency v. Tehnoplast d.o.o. et al.*, UP/I-030-02/2008-01/03; confirmed: Judgment of the High Administrative Court of the Republic of Croatia of 13 December 2012, *Stano-uprava d.o.o. et al. v. Competition Agency*, Us-1700/2010-6, Official Gazette no. 20/13.

602. Case C-8/08 *T-Mobile Netherlands* ECLI:EU:C:2009:343.

603. Decision of the Croatian Competition Agency of 30 July 2009, *Competition Agency v. Vlamal d.o.o. et al. (Driving schools cartel)*, UP/I-030-02/2008-01/68, confirmed: Judgment of the High Administrative Court of the Republic of Croatia of 24 October 2012, *Europa zajednički obrt autoškola et al. v. Competition Agency*, Us-10674/2009-4.

they all had a different cost structure. As in some other cases, the Competition Agency explained the notion of a cartel in such a way as to include the notion of a tacit agreement.[604]

349. No cartel was found in the context of a highly concentrated oligopolistic market where three mobile network providers increased their prices one by one despite the fact that all of them were members of an association that announced that 'measures' would be taken as a reaction to the introduction of a 6% tax on all telecoms in Croatia.[605] The firms changed the calculation units for voice calls in mobile telephony, effectively increasing the price of over half of all voice calls. The associations' reaction was explained as a lobbying activity directed towards the Croatian Government and the European Commission with the aim of having the newly introduced fee abolished. The Competition Agency accepted this explanation, and saw the 6% tax as an external trigger for all three undertakings to increase prices within a short time, thus the price increase was an autonomous decision ('a logical and independent choice for each of the parties, which could have been reached without any previous contact with competitors and without any exchange of sensitive information'). However, the Competition Agency used the opportunity to emphasize that no external circumstances (change of legislation, economic crisis, etc.) could ever be used as a justification for concluding prohibited agreements.[606] The Competition Agency noted that each competitor offered a wide variety of options in terms of different tariff schemes, which meant that consumers had a wide choice of options in terms of prices and products on the market.

350. In a number of cases, the Competition Agency stopped infringement proceedings against several professional associations (architects, construction engineers, mechanical engineers, electrical engineers) due to the fact that the law authorizing associations to adopt minimum and maximum price lists, which provides this authorization only until a new price list is adopted, failed to set a deadline for adopting new price lists, hence allowing the associations to keep their price lists indefinitely.[607] In such a situation, where the CA was not applicable, the Competition Agency decided to send its opinion to the ministry which was authorized to initiate a change of legislation. The agency invoked the position of the Commission and the ECJ that the fixing of (minimum) prices by professional associations was an infringement of competition rules, and that abolishing the price-fixing of services by associations resulted in lower prices for consumers. The Competition

604. This was not surprising since the CA 2003 defined the notion of restrictive agreement to include tacit agreements. *See supra* para. 181, 328.
605. Decision of the Croatian Competition Agency of 26 July 2012, *Competition Agency v. VIPnet d.o.o. et al.*, UP/I-030-02/2010-01/001.
606. *Ibid.*
607. Decision of the Croatian Competition Agency of 1 December 2011, *Competition Agency v. Hrvatska komora arhitekata*, UP/I-030-02/2011-01/035; Decision of the Croatian Competition Agency of 1 December 2011, *Competition Agency v. Hrvatska komora inženjera građevinarstva*, UP/I-030-02/2011-01/027; Decision of the Croatian Competition Agency of 1 December 2011, *Competition Agency v. Hrvatska komora inženjera elektrotehnike*, UP/I-030-02/2011-01/037; Decision of the Croatian Competition Agency of 1 December 2011, *Competition Agency v. Hrvatska komora inženjera strojarstva*, UP/I-030-02/2011-01/036.

Agency held that, instead of minimum prices, other conditions could be regulated in order to ensure both the quality of services and compliance with *ius cogens*.[608]

351. In another case related to price lists adopted by associations, the Competition Agency's decision finding a hardcore restriction was annulled by the High Administrative Court in a controversial judgment.[609] The case related to the Croatian Orthodontic Society, which drafted a minimum price list for orthodontic services, while not being authorized to do so by law. Instead, it was the higher-level association (the Chamber of Dental Medicine) which was authorized by law to adopt such price lists. The Competition Agency held that the Orthodontic Society acted in violation of Article 8(1) of the CA, rejecting as invalid the argument that the Orthodontic Society was merely putting up a proposal. The Competition Agency noted that the price list had been publicly displayed for three years on the society's website, which indicated that there was no doubt that its creation was the result of an agreement on prices between competitors. However, the court disagreed and, in a surprising judgment annulled the decision of the Competition Agency. Subsequently, the Supreme Court decided in favour of the agency, reversing the High Administrative Court judgment and, in a rare move, substituting it with its own decision.[610] Rightfully, the Supreme Court held that the right of the Chamber of Dental Medicine, as a higher-level organization, to regulate prices was immaterial in this case and that trade associations were exempted from competition law sanctions only if the right to regulate prices was stipulated by law in a manner that it directly related to that specific association of undertakings.

352. In the *Private Security Companies cartel* case, another trade association case, the Competition Agency's decision was confirmed by the High Administrative Court, but was annulled by the Constitutional Court of the Republic of Croatia.[611] Here, private security companies met to exchange views on prices and costs, agreeing finally on a minimum cost of a security guard per hour of HRK 32.50 as the lower limit of the viability of their businesses. The Competition Agency held that a hardcore agreement was concluded, which was detrimental to consumers since it eliminated incentives to compete on merits and eliminated uncertainty between competitors. The Competition Agency did not accept the argument of the parties that they were merely discussing the minimum cost level that had already been calculated within the CCC in 1999. The reply of the Competition Agency to this argument focused on the fact that, since the operating costs of firms were different, the

608. *Ibid.*

609. Decision of the Croatian Competition Agency of 12 June 2014, *Competition Agency v. Hrvatsko društvo ortodonata*, UP/I-034-03/2013-01/034, annulled: Judgment of the High Administrative Court of the Republic of Croatia of 5 March 2015, *Hrvatsko društvo ortodonata v. Competition Agency*, UsII-70/14-6.

610. Judgment of the Supreme Court of the Republic of Croatia of 2 March 2021, *Hrvatsko društvo ortodonata v. Competition Agency*, U-zpz 16/2015-4. For more details on this case see infra para 634.

611. Decision of the Croatian Competition Agency of 17 March 2015, *Competition Agency v. Sokol Marić d.o.o. et al.*, UP/I-034-03/2014-01/002, confirmed: Judgment of the High Administrative Court of the Republic of Croatia of 22 April 2016, *Sokol Marić d.o.o. v. Competition Agency*, UsII-40/15-10 (and other cases), annulled: Judgment of the Constitutional Court of the Republic of Croatia of 1 February 2018, *Sokol Marić d.o.o.*, U-III-2791/2016 (and other cases).

minimum cost per hour of a security guard cannot be equal in all firms. In what was later considered a highly controversial judgment by commentators,[612] the Constitutional Court held that the agreement on cost was not in breach of the CA, with the explanation that this was not an agreement on price. Furthermore, the Constitutional Court quashed the Competition Agency's decision since it had not looked into the actual implementation of the allegedly anticompetitive arrangement, while the Competition Agency in its decision stated that, since the object of the agreement was anticompetitive, there was no need to prove anticompetitive effects.

353. In another trade association and price-fixing cartel case, the *Sports Betting cartel* case, the decision of the Competition Agency was annulled by the High Administrative Court.[613] Here, a price-fixing agreement was concluded between sports betting firms, at their associations' meeting, where they agreed on the calculation of the 'manipulative cost' (a constituent part of the final price, and influencing the final price). It was relevant for the Competition Agency that manipulative cost was not regulated by law, holding thus that firms were free to compete. The Competition Agency did not accept the argument that there was no prohibited agreement since a change in the calculation of manipulative cost was reached individually by undertakings prior to the association meeting. The Competition Agency held that even if this was true, it would still be illegal as an exchange of information on future conduct on the market, which would eliminate uncertainty as to future dealings, thereby eliminating risks of competition. Individual undertakings must, the Competition Agency held, adopt business decisions on their own, and an agreement between competitors diminishes uncertainty of future conduct, diminishing the risk of adopting business decisions in a competitive environment.

354. In a typical price-fixing cartel case, involving fourteen driving schools of Split, the cartelists were engaged in frequent contacts with the aim of supporting and encouraging each other in the application of commonly agreed prices. The dawn raids allowed the Competition Agency to gather a large amount of evidence of their collusive behaviour, including their extensive communication via WhatsApp. In its decision the agency found that the driving schools concluded a prohibited agreement, restrictive by object and pronounced a total fine in the amount of HRK 465,000 (EUR 62,000).[614]

355. The other price-fixing cartel decision adopted by the Competition Agency in 2019 related to another regional collusive arrangement, this time between five

612. *See* S. Petrović, *Tržišno natjecanje u praksi Ustavnog suda Republike Hrvatske – osvrt na recentne odluke Ustavnog suda* (U-III-952/2017/'Presečki'/i U-III-2791/2016, U-III6196/2016, U-III-2826/2016, U-III-2820/2016/'zaštitari'/) (12 Jun. 2018), available at https://hdpptn.hr/wp-content/uploads/2018/06/usud-tr%C5%BE-natj.pdf (accessed 20 Jun. 2018).

613. Decision of the Croatian Competition Agency of 22 December 2015, *Competition Agency v. Bolus d.o.o. et al.*, UP/I-034-03/2015-01/010, annulled: Judgment of the High Administrative Court of the Republic of Croatia of 8 July 2016, *Super Sport d.o.o. et al. v. Competition Agency*, UsII-22/16-11.

614. Decision of the Croatian Competition Agency of 30 December 2019, *Competition Agency v. Fourteen Driving Schools of Split*, UP/I 034-03/18-01/002. Confirmed by the judgment of the High Administrative Court of 21 July 2021, *Bul d.o.o. et al. v. Competition Agency*, UsII-112/20-16.

competitors involved in septic tank and other sewage disposal in the Šibenik area, which adopted a price list and colluded in tendering procedures. The agency found an infringement by object and fined the firms with a total of HRK 131,00 (approx. EUR 17,500).

356. In a case related to the oligopolistic telecom market, the Competition Agency dismissed the initiative to start infringement proceedings against three largest telecom operators, which allegedly colluded on introducing a network access charge, as it found no direct anticompetitive contact between them.[615] The agency found that the firms' conduct was not illegal as the two smaller firms merely followed and adapted to the moves of the market leader, which was the first to announce the introduction of such a fee.

357. In a surprisingly lenient decision, the Competition Agency dismissed the initiative to start infringement proceedings for price-fixing arrangement between beekeeping associations in the area of Primorsko-goranska county.[616] Seemingly deviating from EU law standards, the agency held that the price alignment announcement posted in a Viber beekepeers' group was not relevant since there was no evidence that the members of that group explicitly agreed with the price increase. In addition, the agency alarmingly held that there was no indication that the Viber announcement resulted in prohibited concertation of the group members as regards the resale price of honey in the wake of the Viber announcement. Despite decrying the 'extreme inappropriateness' of the collusive Viber announcement, as well as of the subsequent instructions from the association to its members on how to respond to the individual requests for information from the Competition Agency, and of how both 'should not be regarded as a part of legitimate business communication', but how each economic agent must decide independently of its course of action on the market, the Agency nevertheless decided to dismiss the initiative to start infringement proceedings in this case. Instead, the Competition Agency announced it would later on adopt a separate statement with recommendations to all the beekeeping associations involved in how to increase the level of competition culture.

615. Decision of the Croatian Competition Agency of 3 July 2018, *Competition Agency v. Hrvatski Telekom d.d., VIPnet d.o.o. and Tele2 d.o.o.*, UP/I 034-03/18-01/001. In a similar older case the agency adopted a no-infringement decision, Decision of the Croatian Competition Agency of 26 July 2011, *Competition Agency v. VIPnet d.o.o., Hrvatski Telekom d.d. and Tele2 d.o.o.*, UP/I 030-02/2010-01/001.

616. Decision of the Croatian Competition Agency of 31 March 2021, *Competition Agency v. Pčelarska udruga „Učka" and Pčelarska udruga „Milutin Barač"/Udruženje pčelarskih udruga Primorsko-goranske županije*, UP/I 034-03/20-01/018.

B. Market/Client Allocation

358. 'Market division' and 'the division of sources of supply' are explicitly prohibited by the CA.[617] They are considered hardcore restraints in the Regulation on Block Exemption and Horizontal Agreements, denying the agreement the benefit of block exemption.[618]

359. In one of the older cartel cases, in which the CA 2003 was applied, the *Demining Companies cartel* case, the Competition Agency held that a written cartel agreement to divide markets, fix prices, and rig bids adopted between seventeen demining companies in Croatia under the auspices of their trade association amounted to an infringement of the CA.[619] This was an elaborate cartel, with an elaborate punishing mechanism for deviators. Upon finding about this agreement, international donors stopped funding demining activities in Croatia. The cartel included a cocktail of anticompetitive arrangements in one setting: the object was to divide the market, ensuring each cartelist had its own part of the market, and to fix prices for the provision of demining services; in addition, a bid-rigging mechanism was included in the agreement: each competitor was allotted its territory for the purpose of making offers on a public tender (collusive tendering). However, the Competition Agency decided not to ask the misdemeanour court to initiate proceedings for a fine with the argument that the agreement was concluded in 2002 and no similar agreements had been concluded since. Indeed, the Competition Agency held that this was an industry of special importance for Croatia, and that the state should in fact regulate this market.

360. In the *Presečki grupa* case, where different forms of hardcore cartel infringements were present – price-fixing, market division, limiting of production, and bid-rigging – the Competition Agency held that the parties (three bus operators: one holding 65% of the market, the other 25%, and the third 10%) divided the market between themselves, thus eliminating competition from the market.[620] Although the parties – providing bus transport for passengers in Međimurska County –

617. Article 8(1)(3) CA.
618. Articles 11 and 13 of the Regulation on Block Exemptions and Horizontal Agreements.
619. Decision of the Croatian Competition Agency of 4 October 2005, *Competition Agency v. Mustela d.o.o. et al. (Demining companies cartel)*, UP/I-030-02/2004-01/095.
620. Decision of the Croatian Competition Agency of 27 December 2012, *Competition Agency v. Presečki grupa d.o.o. et al.*, UP/I-030-02/2011-01/024, confirmed: Judgment of the High Administrative Court of 20 February 2014, *Presečki grupa d.o.o. v. Competition Agency,* UsII-65/2013-6. However, the Constitutional Court annulled the High Administrative Court judgment by its decision of 21 April 2016, U-III-1678/2014. The High Administrative Court adopted a new judgment of 19 January 2017, UsII-60/16-2, confirming the initial decision of the Competition Agency. Presečki grupa again went to the Constitutional Court which on 19 April 2018, U-III-952/2017 annulled the judgment of the High Administrative Court for the second time. Finally, the High Administrative Court annulled the Competition Agency decision with its judgment of 27 September 2018, UsII-171/18-2, requesting retrial. The Competition Agency adopted a new decision on 7 October 2021, UP/I-030-02/11-01/024, finding that Presečki grupa et al. concluded an illegal horizontal agreement and pronouncing a fine in the total amount of approximately HRK 1 million (EUR 133,000).

claimed there was no restriction of competition, since the right to transport passengers was obtained by the Presečki group, the biggest competitor, in a public tender launched by the County, the Competition Agency did not accept this as a defence. It was worrying for the Agency that Presečki divided the obtained licences among itself and two other competitors. The Competition Agency held that this amounted to a restriction of competition since, by explicitly putting this division of licences into an agreement, they made sure that they would not compete against each other. If a cartel agreement had not been concluded, Presečki could have been threatened by other competitors asking for a transport licence whereby they could compete with Presečki on the same line. The cartel agreement made sure that operators' market positions were solidified, and that any uncertainty that results from competition was eliminated. It was very important for the Competition Agency that Presečki was dividing the existing licences to transport lines obtained in a public tender, while this brought no advantage for customers, in terms of additional departures/arrivals within a certain line, and no price competition.

361. In another cartel case involving the division of a market, the *Office Supply Firms cartel* case, office supply companies cartelized within their trade association, agreeing on the method of price calculation and allocation of buyers. The Competition Agency found that the role of the association in facilitating and enforcing the cartel was of such importance that the association had to be regarded as a member of the cartel agreement.[621] Since the cartel agreement was concluded at the very beginning of setting up the association, the Competition Agency held that the aim of coming together within the association was to restrict competition, i.e., for its members to maintain existing the market share and to obtain profit in an anticompetitive environment. There was plenty of direct evidence of a cartel in this case: minutes from association meetings, a decision by the association to exclude two members who were 'cheating' on the agreement, and no member of the association or the association itself announcing any reservation or disagreement with regard to punishing the cheaters or the whole arrangement. As regards the role of the association in this case, the Competition Agency held that trade associations have a legitimate right to protect the interest of its members as long as there is no breach of *ius cogens*, including competition rules. However, in this case the Competition Agency noted that the role of the association was crucial: its liability lay in the fact that it was directly involved in shaping the rules of conduct which the members must obey, and which were a constituent part of the prohibited agreement, that it imposed an obligation on its members to abide by these rules or be punished for breaching them, and that it was itself involved in policing these rules.

362. The Competition Agency held that the ignorance or unawareness of the association and its members of the infringement of competition rules by such conduct could provide no justification and no release of liability. Furthermore, the fact that the undertakings involved had a low market share in the relevant market was

621. Decision of the Croatian Competition Agency of 21 July 2011, *Competition Agency v. BIRODOM d.o.o. et al.*, UP/I-030-02/2010-01/018; confirmed: Judgment of the High Administrative Court of the Republic of Croatia of 19 December 2012, Us-9383/2011-4, Official Gazette no. 13/13.

irrelevant from the point of view of competition rules, since no individual or joint exemption was available for horizontal agreements containing hardcore rules (price-fixing agreements and market/buyers allocation agreements), notwithstanding their market share.

C. Production/Innovation Limitation

363. 'Limiting production, markets, technological development and investment' is explicitly prohibited by the CA and labelled as a restrictive agreement.[622] It is also mentioned as a hardcore restraint in the Regulation on Block Exemption and Horizontal Agreements, denying the agreement the benefit of block exemption.[623]

364. In a case already discussed above, the *Presečki grupa* case, a variety of forms of cartel behaviour were involved: price-fixing, market division, the limiting of production and bid-rigging.[624] Pursuant to the cartel agreement, the parties were obliged to coordinate and register any new bus lines in Međimurska County, as well as to change the existing bus schedule collectively, not individually. They also agreed to continuously analyse demand for bus transport for passengers in that territory and collectively coordinate supply to meet demand. The Competition Agency held this was contrary to Article 8(1)(2) of the CA, which prohibits any restriction or control over production, markets, technological development, or investment.

D. Group Boycott

365. Group boycott is not mentioned explicitly in the CA, but the list of restrictions in Article 8 of the CA is not exhaustive ('in particular those ... '), so this form of horizontal collusion is also covered.

E. Collusion on Other Objects

366. The CA prohibits agreements which apply dissimilar conditions to equivalent transactions with other undertakings, thereby placing them at a competitive disadvantage, or which make the conclusion of contracts subject to acceptance by the other parties of supplementary obligations which, by their nature or according to commercial usage, have no connection with the subject of such contracts.[625]

367. No breach of competition rules was found in the *Green Card* case, where an association of insurance companies adopted a decision whereby the authorization to issue a green card (a document issued at the moment of vehicle registration

622. Article 8(1)(2) CA.
623. Articles 11 and 13 of the Regulation on Block Exemption and Horizontal Agreements.
624. *See* fn 635.
625. Article 8(1)(4) and (5) CA.

that allows the vehicle to travel abroad) was revoked from one of its members, which – immediately upon market liberalization – pursued an aggressive marketing campaign offering heavily discounted prices for mandatory car insurance.[626] Although in the early stages of the proceedings the Competition Agency investigated a possible cartel case scenario, where cartelists were punishing one of its members for 'cheating', the Competition Agency in the end held that no proof was found that a restrictive agreement by object was concluded. The Competition Agency held that the fact that the procedure for taking away the authorization to issue the green card of insurance was not entirely in accordance with the rules on insurance did not mean that it was in breach of competition rules on prohibited agreements. Rather, it was held that the decision by the association to take away the authorization from Generali osiguranje was motivated by its aggressive (and possibly illicit) marketing activities, which were prohibited by the insurance market regulator HANFA, and not with the aim of restricting competition. The Competition Agency held that, importantly, no detrimental effects on the relevant market were found, since the authorization to issue the green card of insurance had been in force for a very short time (only twenty-two days), and Generali osiguranje was able to conclude new insurance contracts during that time.

368. In another trade association case, the *Udruga Franak* case, the Competition Agency held that the fact that a trade association represented its members, the banks, in negotiations with the state and a consumer NGO that took place at the Ministry of Finance, where only some of the bank representatives were present along with the representative of the association, did not amount to a restriction of competition. The Competition Agency held that there were no grounds to open a case on possible coordinated behaviour by banks through their association in this case.[627]

369. The *Presečki grupa* case, already discussed above, also had a bid-rigging aspect worth mentioning here. The parties to the agreement agreed to participate in any future public tenders for servicing bus lines for pupils in elementary schools only as a consortium. The Competition Agency held that this amounted to a cartel agreement whereby they eliminated any form of competition between themselves and restricted competition in the relevant market.[628] Forming a consortium is allowed under public procurement rules, but here, the Competition Agency held, the consortium was not being formed for a concrete future bid, but it was agreed *pro futuro* to form such a consortium for every tender for bus line transport for school children, no matter who opened the tender and what the conditions were. The Competition Agency considered that this kind of discourse demonstrated the real nature of the contract, i.e., the elimination of any form of competition between the parties.

626. Decision of the Croatian Competition Agency of 17 July 2015, *Competition Agency v. Hrvatski ured za osiguranja et al.*, UP/I-034-03/13-01/046.

627. Decision of the Croatian Competition Agency of 23 October 2015, *Competition Agency v. Zagrebačka banka et al.*, UP/I-034-03/2015-01/026.

628. *See* fn 635.

370. In a case brought by the Central Government Public Procurement Office against consortiums bidding to supply cartridges, the Competition Agency held it was up to the tendering body to make sure that the conditions of the tender were drafted to detect any sign of possible collusion.[629] If the intention was to allow as many firms as possible to tender individually, it was up to the tendering body to create such conditions in the tender for this to be possible. The Competition Agency held that no antitrust proceedings could be opened, since consortiums were justified on account of the large volume of supplies and the fact that it was not possible to participate in the tender individually.

371. Joint bidding was not found restrictive of competition in *Messer Croatia Plin.*[630] The Competition Agency held that a consortium in public procurement was not per se contrary to competition rules, but that any agreement within the consortium framework with the aim or effect of distorting competition was prohibited. It was up to the public procurement bodies to draft conditions in the invitation to tender to leave as little space as possible for anticompetitive conduct. It is essential to know the market well to be able to draft a public tender in such a way that its enforcement was legal. Furthermore, the Competition Agency held that the conditions of the tender could be used to invigorate competition between bidders, for example, by separating different types of products in several tenders, to prolong or shorten (depending on the conditions of each tender) the duration of the contract, with the aim of increasing the number of bidders.[631]

II. Information Exchange Practices

372. Information exchange practices, although not explicitly mentioned in the CA, fall under Article 8 of this Act if they are restrictive of competition.

373. In *Marinas Cartel*, already discussed above, the one-time information exchange on future price trends between direct competitors, which occurred at a meeting of an association of firms running marinas, and which was recorded in the minutes of the meeting, was found to be a prohibited agreement.[632] The Competition Agency held that, since this was not an explicit agreement to increase prices by a fixed amount, but an exchange of information on future prices, it was not necessary for all the parties to increase prices by the same amount in order to show that

---

629. Decision of the Croatian Competition Agency of 31 May 2012, *Competition Agency v. Narodne novine d.d. et al.*, UP/I-030-02/2011-01/032.
630. Decision of the Croatian Competition Agency of 14 October 2016, *Competition Agency v. Messer Croatia Plin d.o.o. et al.*, UP/I-034-03/2015-01/014.
631. *Ibid.*
632. Decision of the Croatian Competition Agency of 17 March 2015, *Competition Agency v. Adriatic Croatia International Club d.d. et al.*, UP/I-034-03/13-01/047; annulled: Judgment of the High Administrative Court of the Republic of Croatia of 17 March 2016, *Ilirija d.d. et al. v. Competition Agency*, UsII-39/15-10; Decision of the Croatian Competition Agency of 13 December 2016, *Competition Agency v. Adriatic Croatia International Club d.d. et al.*, UP/I-034-03/13-01/047 (decision to suspend proceedings).

there was a prohibited agreement. The Competition Agency held that, although an exchange of information between competitors may have positive effects, such as more efficient operations of an individual undertaking, the exchange of strategic information, such as prices, quantities, production costs, buyer lists, and the like, can result in the concertation of conduct between competitors, since it decreases the autonomy of their actions on the market and the incentives to compete. Furthermore, the exchange of strategic information regarding future prices and quantities was deemed a hardcore restriction, prohibited per se, since its goal is to restrict competition, and amounts to a prohibited agreement. Therefore, no anticompetitive effects of the concerted practice on the market needed to be shown. The Competition Agency considered that each undertaking must act independently in adopting its business decisions and in acting on the market in such a way that there is no coordination and agreement between competitors, which decreases the uncertainty of any future conduct, since this diminishes the risk of making business decisions within a competitive context. In the concrete case, the parties, even in the absence of an agreement on prices, eliminated in advance any uncertainty regarding their future acts on the market and thereby eliminated any risks of competition.

374. The Competition Agency held that an association (the CCC), along with its members, was liable for a breach of competition rules. The Competition Agency held that the CCC had a special responsibility to ensure that its members were obeying by-laws and regulations, since it was an institution created by law, with mandatory membership for all legal persons performing economic activity in Croatia. In this case, a meeting was held under the auspices of the CCC, and representatives of the CCC participated in the meeting.

375. However, the High Administrative Court repealed the decision of the Competition Agency and remanded it for retrial, finding that the facts of the case had not been determined to a satisfactory extent, which prevented the court from going into substantial issues. Controversially, the court noted it was relevant that the prices discussed at their October 2012 meeting were already defined for the 2013 season.

376. In its first dawn raid case ever, the *Croatiastočar* case, the Competition Agency decided to eventually stop the proceedings, finding there was no proof that the conduct of the biggest milk processing firms in Croatia and their association amounted to a prohibited agreement.[633] An association of milk producers initiated the case, claiming that the milk processing companies functioned as a cartel via their trade association, collectively pushing down the price of milk which they were paying to primary producers. No evidence of a cartel was found during the dawn raid, however. An analysis of individual milk prices paid to primary producers by milk processors also showed no indication of an illicit agreement. The Competition

633. Decision of the Croatian Competition Agency of 19 September 2013, *Competition Agency v. Dukat mliječna industrija d.d. et al.*, UP/I-034-03/13-01/013; annulled: Judgment of the High Administrative Court of the Republic of Croatia of 5 June 2015, *Udruga stočara i proizvođača mlijeka 'Bilogora' v. Competition Agency*, UsII-98/13-13; decision of the Croatian Competition Agency of 7 October 2015, *Competition Agency v. Dukat mliječna industrija d.d. et al.*, UP/I-034-03/13-01/013.

Agency established that discussions on milk prices between milk producers and processing companies took place at meetings in the Ministry of Agriculture, with the ministry as a mediator. The Competition Agency held that the application of competition rules in this sector still allowed for the active role of the Ministry of Agriculture, even after the liberalization of the market, as a mediator between the two sides. In 2009, representatives of milk manufacturers and milk processors, at a meeting held at the Ministry of Agriculture, agreed on a new method of calculation of the price of milk; and in February 2012 a new agreement between those two sides on the calculation of the milk price was also reached in the Ministry of Agriculture, a method which was applied until September 2012. In October 2012, the Milk Council decided that this agreement would no longer be applied and that each milk processor would determine its price for milk purchased from primary producers.

377. The court annulled the decision of the Competition Agency on procedural grounds, holding that it did not explain which legal conditions for the continuation of proceedings ceased to exist, and that it should have adopted a substantive decision.[634] In a new decision, the Competition Agency decided that there was no infringement of competition by concluding a prohibited agreement within the meaning of Article 8 of the CA since there was no evidence that those undertakings and associations of undertakings had concluded an agreement on the purchase prices of milk in Croatia.[635]

III. Cooperation Agreements

378. Cooperation agreements are block exempted provided the conditions laid out in relevant regulations are met.[636] As already discussed above, several regulations have been adopted that cover cooperation agreements.[637] The Competition Agency may revoke the benefit of block exemption after individually assessing the effects of the agreements if it finds that the conditions under Article 8(3) of the CA have not been met.[638]

A. *Research and Development*

379. Research and development cooperation agreements are block exempted under Article 10 of the CA, provided the conditions found in the Regulation on Block Exemptions and Horizontal Agreements are met.[639]

634. Judgment of the High Administrative Court of the Republic of Croatia of 5 June 2015, *Udruga stočara i proizvođača mlijeka 'Bilogora' v. Competition Agency*, UsII-98/13-13.
635. Decision of the Croatian Competition Agency of 7 October 2015, *Competition Agency v. Dukat mliječna industrija d.d. et al.*, UP/I-034-03/13-01/013.
636. Article 10(1) CA.
637. Vertical agreements, horizontal agreements, technology transfer agreements, distribution and repair of motor vehicles, insurance agreements, transport – Art. 10(2)(2) CA.
638. Article 10(4) CA.
639. Regulation on Block Exemption and Horizontal Agreements.

B. Specialization

380. Specialization agreements are block exempted under Article 10 of the CA, provided the conditions found in the Regulation on Block Exemptions and Horizontal Agreements are met.[640]

C. Standardization

381. Standardization agreements are block exempted under Article 10 of the CA, provided the conditions found in the Regulation on Block Exemptions and Horizontal Agreements are met.[641]

D. Joint Production

382. Joint production agreements are block exempted under Article 10 of the CA, provided the conditions found in the Regulation on Block Exemptions and Horizontal Agreements are met.[642]

E. Joint Purchasing

383. Joint purchasing agreements are block exempted under Article 10 of the CA, provided the conditions found in the Regulation on Block Exemptions and Horizontal Agreements are met.[643]

F. Joint Selling

384. Joint selling agreements are block exempted under Article 10 of the CA, provided conditions found in the Regulation on Block Exemptions and Horizontal Agreements are met.[644]

385. Joint selling of football broadcasting rights was the crux of the matter in the case against the Croatian Football Federation. The agency took the position that joint selling arrangement might be exempted from the general prohibition found in Article 8(1) of the Competition Act provided it was based on an open, transparent, and non-discriminatory tendering procedure. After extensive assessment of legal

640. *Ibid.*
641. Regulation on Block Exemption and Horizontal Agreements.
642. *Ibid.*
643. *Ibid.*
644. *Ibid.*

and economic context of the arrangement and its effects on competition, the agency found that it did not restrict competition.[645]

§2. VERTICAL AGREEMENTS

386. The prohibition of restrictive agreements applies both to vertical and horizontal agreements (Article 8(1) and (2) of the CA). Block exemptions are applicable to vertical agreements (Article 10 of the CA as a legal basis for the adoption of BERs), as well as to horizontal agreements. The general BER is applicable to selective distribution, exclusive distribution, franchising, and single branding.[646] Some more specific vertical arrangements are covered by other BERs.[647] As with other areas of Croatian competition law, the rules governing vertical agreements also mirror EU rules.

387. Vertical agreements are defined as a contract, a single contract clause, an oral or written agreement, or concerted practice as a result of those agreements, the decisions of undertakings or of associations of undertakings, general terms of contract and other documents by undertakings, concluded between undertakings active at different levels of production and/or distribution, and which govern the conditions under which the contract parties purchase, sell, or resell goods and/or services.[648]

388. Vertical restraints are competition restraints contained in a vertical agreement which is encompassed by Article 8(1) of the CA.[649]

389. The BER is applicable to vertical agreements which contain vertical restraints, but they have to meet the conditions from the BER in order to be exempted.[650] If other BERs apply, the general BER on vertical agreements is not applicable.[651]

390. A large proportion of vertical restraint cases in the practice of the Competition Agency relate to vertical restraints in the motor vehicles sector.[652]

391. The issue of RPM, considered as one of the hardcore restrictions in vertical agreements, has been tackled in several cases by the Competition Agency. In the

645. Decision of the Croatian Competition Agency of 31 July 2020, *Competition Agency v. Croatian Football Federation*, UP/I-034-03/20-01/013.
646. Official Gazette no. 37/2011, Uredba o skupnom izuzeću vertikalnih sporazuma između poduzetnika.
647. Such as the BER on the Distribution of Motor Vehicles, Official Gazette no. 37/2011, Uredba o skupnom izuzeću sporazuma o distribuciji i servisiranju motornih vozila.
648. Article 2 point a of the Regulation on Block Exemptions and Vertical Agreements.
649. BER on Vertical Agreements, Art. 2 point b.
650. Articles 3 and 4 BER on Vertical Agreements.
651. Article 4 BER on Vertical Agreements.
652. BER on the Distribution of Motor Vehicles.

Kraš/NTL case, the Competition Agency looked at a sales contract between a retailer and a supplier whereby the retailer agreed not to sell the supplier's products for a price which was above the price determined by the suppliers' price lists, and where the retailer would suffer punishment in the case of non-compliance.[653] The Competition Agency held this was a prohibited agreement which, since it contained a hardcore vertical restriction, was not available for exemption or for the *de minimis* rule.

392. In a very similar case, the Competition Agency looked at vertical hardcore restraints in a sales contract between a retailer and a supplier whereby the retailer agreed not to sell the supplier's products below agreed minimum prices, which were attached to the contract, and where a unilateral termination of contract was allowed if the retailer breached this clause.[654] The Competition Agency held that the CA, the Regulation on Vertical Restraints, and other pieces of legislation in the area of competition law were 'mandatory' rules whose application could not be trumped in favour of contractual freedom. If the contract contains hardcore restrictions, it is presumed that it is unlikely that conditions for exemption, pursuant to Article 8(3) of the CA, would be met. Finally, the Competition Agency held that *de minimis* rules were also unavailable in this situation.

393. In another similar case, the Competition Agency looked at a vertical agreement between a retailer and a supplier, with hardcore restrictions: minimum prices, and territorial restriction of sales, no discounts if the retailer does not obey minimum prices, termination of the agreement if the products are resold outside Croatia.[655] The Competition Agency held that fixed or minimum resale prices, and territorial restrictions for reselling the goods, were 'always prohibited and a hardcore infringement of competition rules, whether they were applied in practice or not'. Competition rules, which are 'mandatory' rules, were not trumped by the freedom to arrange freely one's contractual relationship. As in other hardcore restraints cases, no exemption or application of *de minimis* rules was allowed.

394. In another typical hardcore vertical restraints case, where a retailer was obliged by a contract to obey the suggested minimum wholesale and retail prices as set by the supplier, or where otherwise the supplier reserved the right not to supply the retailer, the Competition Agency held that no exemption, and no *de minimis*

653. Decision of the Croatian Competition Agency of 3 December 2014, *Competition Agency v. Kraš d.d. and Narodni Trgovački Lanac d.o.o.*, UP/I-034-03/13-01/016, Official Gazette no. 7/2015; confirmed: Judgment of the High Administrative Court of the Republic of Croatia of 16 July 2015, *Narodni Trgovački Lanac d.o.o. i Kraš d.d. v. Competition Agency,* UsII-4/15-5.

654. Decision of the Croatian Competition Agency of 30 July 2014, *Competition Agency v. Kutjevo d.d. i KTC d.d.*, UP/I-034-03/2013-01/017; confirmed: Judgment of the High Administrative Court of the Republic of Croatia of 18 May 2016, *Kutjevo d.d. v. Competition Agency,* UsII-85/14-5.

655. Decision of the Croatian Competition Agency of 23 October 2014, *Competition Agency v. Carlsberg Croatia d.o.o. i KTC d.d.,* UP/I-034-03/2013-01/018.

treatment were available.[656] Here, two consecutive contracts with the same hardcore restrictions were regarded by the Competition Agency as 'one agreement with uninterrupted duration'. The Competition Agency noted that competition rules, as *jus cogens*, and their application cannot be excluded on the basis of the freedom to arrange freely one's contractual relationship. Thus, the Competition Agency held that rules governing contracts could not be invoked to justify restrictions of competition.

395. In a more complex RPM case, *M SAN v. Rivulus*, the supplier exerted pressure on the retailer not to depart from the 'recommended' prices by charging lower prices, and further supplies depended on complying with this demand.[657] Pursuant to the Regulation on Vertical Agreements, the maintenance of any direct or indirect resale price is considered as a hardcore restriction, unavailable for exemption or *de minimis* treatment, and is prohibited and null and void under Article 9 of the CA. The Competition Agency held that the retailer in this situation was restricted in its freedom to set resale prices within the meaning of Article 9(1)(a) of the Regulation on Vertical Agreements. The Competition Agency noted that recommended prices were in general not prohibited by competition rules, since they can be beneficial in terms of positive economic effects for the retailer (to organize a sales network, to maintain the reputation of products, etc.). However, price recommendations may not be obligatory and conditions may not be placed on them (i.e., no further supply if the recommended prices are not obeyed). The retailer's actions must not result from any pressure or incentive on the side of the supplier, but must entirely reflect the retailer's free will to achieve its own economic interests. Free determination of resale prices is one of the basic principles of free competition, since undertakings compete in the market primarily by setting the prices of products and services.

396. The Competition Agency held that in this case the potential horizontal effects should also be taken into account in the sense that limiting the freedom of the retailer to set resale prices has a potential detrimental effect on competition at the horizontal level, since it incentivized coordinated behaviour among other retailers and eliminated competition between them. In this case, enforcing hardcore vertical restraints served to maintain a broader business policy of maintaining retail prices (by other retailers) at a certain level. Awareness by the retailers of the supplier or another competitor making sure that a certain price level was maintained, and was being policed, creates pressure for other retailers to maintain the price level, even in the absence of an explicit mutual agreement thereon. The Competition Agency held, in this sense, that the fact competitors do nothing to challenge the existing price level amounts to coordinated practice, which does not result from an autonomous business decision, but from outward illicit pressure.[658]

---

656. Decision of the Croatian Competition Agency of 30 July 2014, *Competition Agency v. Dukat d.d. i Konzum d.d.*, UP/I-034-03/2013-01/015.

657. Decision of the Croatian Competition Agency of 7 October 2010, *Competition Agency v. M SAN grupa d.d. i Rivulus d.o.o.*, UP/I-030-02/2008-01/61; confirmed: judgment of the High Administrative Court of the Republic of Croatia of 7 March 2012, *M SAN grupa d.d. v. Competition Agency*, Us-12531/2010-7.

658. *Ibid.*

397. By disciplining the retailer for 'cheating', i.e., breaching a tacit agreement, the supplier – the biggest wholesaler of IT products in Croatia – demonstrated its market power by threatening to stop supply to this retailer. In this sense, it was intended as an example to others. It should be noted that it was the other retailers that demanded action from the wholesaler. The Competition Agency held that this kind of concerted practice by the supplier and its retailers was highly detrimental, since it eliminated competition between the retailers as regards prices, and end consumers bore the consequences of this behaviour by paying higher prices.[659]

398. Increasingly typical for its approach in the post-accession period, the Competition Agency adopted a commitments decision in an RPM case where the distributor imposed fixed resale prices on its dealers.[660]

399. In an older hardcore vertical restraints case, the Competition Agency held that since the duration of the infringement was very short, and since the parties on their own initiative, before the proceedings were commenced, concluded new and revised agreements which did not contain restrictive clauses, it was not opportune to demand the initiation of misdemeanour proceedings against the undertakings.[661]

400. An elaborate and comprehensive illegal vertical practice of monitoring and disciplining its distributors in order to maintain fixed or minimum prices was found to be in breach of the CA in the *Gorenje* case, where the affiliated company of the manufacturer of household appliances based in Slovenia was fined HRK 1,577,000 (approx. EUR 213,000).[662] In this high-profile case which started off by a dawn raid at Gorenje, the Competition Agency held that the proceedings could not be conducted against the distributors, since their participation in the illegal practice, as weaker parties upon which Gorenje Zagreb imposed pressure to make them obey fixed or minimum price levels, did not necessarily reflect their actual will. The Competition Agency found that Gorenje Zagreb refused to supply distributors which failed to obey the set price levels, but also by means of its rebate policy it stimulated buyers to maintain set resale prices, thereby punishing buyers which failed to act in accordance with its business strategy.[663]

659. *Ibid.*
660. Decision of the Croatian Competition Agency of 4 May 2018, *Competition Agency v. Motonavis*, UP/I 034-03/17-01/007. For a similar case, related to an RPM situation with minimum prices imposed on a restaurant by a beer manufacturer, which was also concluded by a commitments decision, *see* decision of the Croatian Competition Agency of 27 November 2020, *Competition Agency v. Pivovara Daruvar*, UP/I 034-03/20-01/003.
661. Decision of the Croatian Competition Agency of 15 September 2005, *Competition Agency v. Tradexco*, UP/I-030-02/2005-01/005.
662. Decision of the Croatian Competition Agency of 20 December 2016, *Competition Agency v. Gorenje*, UP/I-034-03/13-01/035, Official Gazette no. 26/2017.
663. *Ibid.*

401. In the *Croatia osiguranje* case, the Competition Agency looked at leasehold agreements concluded between Croatia osiguranje, the largest insurance company in Croatia, as lessee, and various lessors, including car inspection stations.[664] For example, clauses providing that the car inspection station must not give lease to other competitors were deemed problematic. The case was closed with a commitments decision, with Croatia osiguranje *inter alia* pledging to sign new agreements with its lessors, which would not include anticompetitive clauses.

I. Distribution

402. Distribution agreements which contain vertical restraints can be block exempted if conditions set out in BERs are met.[665]

A. *Exclusive Distributorship*

403. An exclusive distribution agreement is defined as a vertical agreement by which the supplier is obliged to sell goods that are the object of an agreement to only one distributor chosen in a specific territory or to a specially selected group of buyers which is exclusively allotted to this distributor.[666]

404. In an exclusive distributorship case, the Competition Agency held that a clause in the distribution agreement in the pharma sector between a supplier and a distributor was null and void, since it brought about a division of the market between exclusive distributors and since it created absolute territorial protection which limited or controlled production volume, sales/purchase volume, and the provision/use of services.[667] The Competition Agency held that since the parties agreed on passive territorial protection, this was prohibited per se.

405. In another case, an exclusive distribution agreement contained no hardcore restrictions, but contained a non-competition clause whereby the exclusive distributor could not sell any other competing products in the authorized territory for the duration of the agreement and three years thereafter. This was considered as a restrictive clause prohibited pursuant to Article 10(1)(a) and (b) of the BER on Vertical Agreements.[668] Invoking §152 of the EU Vertical Restraints

664. Decision of the Croatian Competition Agency of 9 November 2020, *Competition Agency v. Croatia osiguranje d.d.*, UP/I-034-03/20-01/015.
665. *See* Art. 10(2)(1) and (4) CA, Art. 3 of the Regulation on Block Exemptions and Vertical Agreements, and Art. 13 of the Motor Vehicles Distribution Regulation.
666. Article 3(2) of the BER on Vertical Agreements.
667. Decision of the Croatian Competition Agency of 3 April 2008, *Pliva farmaceutska industrija d.d. i Infai*, UP/I-030-03/2002-01/44.
668. Decision of the Croatian Competition Agency of 12 July 2012, *Competition Agency v. Primalab d.o.o.*, UP/I-034-03/2012-01/003. For a similar case, resolved however by a commitments decision, *see* decision of the Croatian Competition Agency of 29 December 2020, *Competition Agency v. Zagrebačka pivovara*, UP/I-034-03/20-01/002.

Guidelines,[669] the Competition Agency held that the exemption was not applicable in this case, since the duration of the agreement was indefinite, and thus the duty not to compete was also indefinite.

B. Exclusive Dealing

406. An exclusive dealing agreement is defined as a vertical agreement whereby the buyer is obliged directly or indirectly to purchase products which are the object of the agreement only from a specific supplier.[670]

407. In a single branding case, *PZ Auto*, the Competition Agency found a restrictive agreement by object in a situation where the authorized importer of several brands of motor vehicles for Croatia (PZ Auto) obliged its authorized distributors and repairers to purchase mechanical security locks for vehicles only from one supplier.[671] The importer established a quantitative selective distribution system which included a number of authorized distributors and repairers, which stipulated that authorized distributors and repairers would be financially rewarded if they purchased and distributed mechanical locks from a specific supplier (Kolnoa). This had the effect that the distributors and repairers stopped purchasing mechanical locks from a competing supplier (Magnat), which alerted the Competition Agency to initiate proceedings in this case. The Competition Agency held that the authorized distributors and repairers were indeed free to purchase the equipment from Kolnoa, and not from its competitors, but of their free will, and not because this was directly or indirectly imposed upon them by PZ Auto. The Competition Agency held that neither individual nor block exemption was available, the agreement being restrictive by object, with the aim of eliminating a significant part of competition from the relevant market. Despite the fact that the Competition Agency noted that no proof of actual anticompetitive effects was needed, since the aim of the agreement was to restrict competition, it still pointed to the fact that there was a steady fall of Magnat's market share after the conclusion of the agreement between PZ Auto and Kolnoa.

408. In 2018, a commitments decision was adopted by the Competition Agency in the *Coca-Cola* case, in which Coca-Cola HBC Hrvatska undertook to change its

669. EU Guidelines on Vertical Restraints, para. 152. Conditions under para. 152 require that a non-compete obligation is limited to five years, even if combined with other (non-hardcore) vertical restrictions, provided that the market share of the supplier and the market share of the buyer do not exceed 30%.

670. Article 3(4) of the BER on Vertical Agreements.

671. Decision of the Croatian Competition Agency of 4 October 2005, *Kolnoa d.o.o. i P.Z. Auto d.o.o.*, UP/I-030-02/2004-01/38; confirmed: Judgment of the Administrative Court of the Republic of Croatia of 21 May 2008, *P.Z. Auto d.o.o* i *Kolnoa d.o.o. v. Competition Agency*, Us-10247/2005-9.

HoReCa distribution agreements which contained exclusive purchase clauses.[672] For this purpose, the dominant firm in the cola drinks market committed to conclude separate distribution agreements for its carbonated non-alcoholic drinks assortment, where its dominance lay, and for its non-carbonated (non)alcoholic drinks, where it was not dominant. The agency held that the former were not to contain exclusive purchase clauses, while the latter may contain such clauses provided the buyer was free to choose between exclusively purchasing selected Coca-Cola products and offering both Coca-Cola and competing products in its assortment. Shortly after the opening of the Croatian case, the Slovenian competition authority also started proceedings against Coca-Cola, which ended in identical commitments taken over by the company.[673]

C. Selective Distribution

409. A selective distribution agreement is defined as a vertical agreement whereby a supplier is obliged to sell directly or indirectly products which are the object of the agreement only to distributors selected on the basis of transparent, specific criteria, and the distributors are obliged not to sell those products to unauthorized distributors.[674]

410. No restriction of competition was found by the Competition Agency in a case where the exclusive importer of Yamaha products (motorcycles, scooters, rubber boats, etc.) for Croatia established a selective distribution network pursuant to Article 3(3) of the BER on Vertical Agreements.[675] The importer's market share in all relevant markets was below 30%. A non-competition clause, prohibiting the distributor from selling or repairing competing products, was not found to be in breach of the BER on Vertical Agreements,[676] since the duration of the distribution agreement was less than five years, and since it was not geared to specific competitors, but was generally drafted (exclusion of competition with any competitors). As regards prices, no breach of the BER on Vertical Agreements was found,[677] since they were formulated as recommended prices.

411. In another case, focusing on the issue of fixed promotional prices, the Competition Agency held that the exclusive importer of Citroen motor vehicles for Croatia, which established a mixed qualitative-quantitative selective distribution

---

672. Decision of the Croatian Competition Agency of 29 November 2019, *Competition Agency v. Coca-Cola HBC Hrvatska d.o.o.*, UP/I-034-03/19-01/005. For a similar case *see* decision of the Croatian Competition Agency of 29 December 2020, *Competition Agency v. Zagrebačka pivovara*, UP/I-034-03/20-01/002.
673. Annual Report 2019, Croatian Competition Agency, pp. 21-22, https://www.aztn.hr/godisnja-izvjesca/ (accessed 19 January 2022).
674. Article 3(3) of the BER on Vertical Agreements.
675. Decision of the Croatian Competition Agency of 16 June 2011, *Competition Agency v. TM Zagreb d.o.o.*, UP/I-030-02/2010-01/017.
676. Article 10(1)(a) and (c) of the BER on Vertical Agreements.
677. Article 9(1)(a) of the BER on Vertical Agreements.

network, did not restrict competition.[678] The Competition Agency held that promotions, organized by the exclusive importer, whereby the importer would fix the minimum amount of discount per vehicle which would be granted by the distributor to end customers, were not in breach of competition rules. In practice, the price per vehicle paid by the distributor to the importer was greater than the price paid by the end customer to the distributor, but after selling the vehicle the distributor would be compensated by the importer for this difference ('participation'). The distributors that initiated the proceedings before the Competition Agency argued that this amounted to indirect RPM, i.e., indirect (resale) price-fixing. However, the Competition Agency held that this form of promotion was not in breach of competition rules, unlike limiting distributors' freedom to determine their price which was hardcore restriction. The Competition Agency noted that authorized distributors have the possibility of charging various prices when selling cars in promotions organized by the importer, and that indeed some of the distributors granted even bigger discounts than set by the importer. Thus, the Competition Agency held that intra-brand competition was not harmed. The Competition Agency considered that since the importer fixed the maximum resale price for the duration of the promotional sales, and since the possibility remained for the distributors to compete below the maximum price level, there was no restriction of competition in the relevant market for the distribution of new motor vehicles in Croatia. It was also evident that the market share of the importer in the relevant market was below 10%, that the relevant market was not concentrated and was open to competition. Moreover, the Competition Agency held that promotional sales with the aim of increasing the market share of a certain brand of vehicles were not only beneficial in terms of inter-brand competition, but they were also beneficial to consumers in terms of lower prices.

412. In a case where the parties requested an individual exemption, it was found that (exclusive and non-exclusive) quantitative selective distribution agreements between the exclusive importer of Piaggio motorcycles for Croatia and its distributors contained some vertical restraints. However, after analysing the effects of the agreements on the relevant market, the exemption could be granted provided the provisions that were found to be restrictive were deleted or amended.[679] There were three vertical restraints at issue in the exclusive agreements: (1) restriction of active sales; (2) a non-compete obligation; and (3) the obligation of non-disclosure of know-how for the duration of five years. As regards active sales, where authorized resellers were obliged not to actively search for potential customers outside their territory without the written permission of the importer, and not to actively sell to certain categories of buyers explicitly reserved for the importer, the Competition Agency held that, since the prohibition of active (and passive) sales for authorized

678. Decision of the Croatian Competition Agency of 17 December 2008, *Competition Agency v. Citroen Hrvatska d.o.o.*, UP/I-030-02/2006-01/80; confirmed: Judgment of the High Administrative Court of the Republic of Croatia of 22 February 2012, *Sanabilils d.o.o. v. Competition Agency*, Us-1774/2009-12.

679. Decision of the Croatian Competition Agency of 13 January 2006, *Piaggio Hrvatska d.o.o.*, UP/I-030-02/2005-01/002.

resellers to end buyers in selective distribution agreements was a hardcore restriction,[680] this had to be deleted. As regards the non-compete clause, whereby authorized resellers were not to sell competing products, directly or indirectly, for the duration of the agreement, the Competition Agency held that this was not a hardcore restriction of competition, but that block exemption rules were not applicable since they were in breach of Article 10(1)(c) of the Regulation on Vertical Restraints. However, it held that an individual exemption may be granted, provided that 20% of the distribution channel was left open to other competing brands, and taking into account that the non-compete clause had no negative effect on competition: the market share of the importer was falling, the market was not mature, and there was intense competition from other brands. Finally, the non-disclosure of know-how clause for five years after the termination of the agreement was held by the Competition Agency to be restrictive of competition, suggesting that a duration of one year would be acceptable.

413. The Competition Agency held that the non-exclusive distribution agreement had all the features of a single branding agreement (e.g., investing in the marketing of Piaggio products, a minimum volume of sales condition, spare parts to be supplied by the importer only, servicing according to Piaggio standards).[681] Since the restrictive provisions were the same as in the exclusive agreements, the Competition Agency held that all its findings applied to the non-exclusive agreements. The clauses on recommended and maximum resale prices, as well as rebates granted by the importer to the distributors, were found to be not restrictive of competition.

414. Granting the individual exemption, provided that the clauses identified as restrictive were deleted and/or amended, the Competition Agency held that the four conditions for exemption were met: (1), better distribution and a higher quality of service as the effects of the distribution agreement; (2) benefits for consumers in terms of a higher quality of service which surpass the restrictive effects; (3) as regards vertical restraints which were not indispensable for achieving the aims of the contract (restriction of active sales, non-competition clause, non-disclosure of know-how for five years), the economic and legal analysis showed that they had no negative effect on competition, since the market share of the importer was shrinking, there were many competitors and also dynamic competition in the market, and the duration of the agreement was only one year; (4) the non-competition clause may have the effect of eliminating a significant part of competition in the relevant market, but, if it was deleted or 20% of the market was left for competing brands, this would not amount to a prohibited agreement since there was strong inter-brand competition in the relevant market.[682] In total, the analysis of effects showed that while two positive conditions for exemption were met, the two negative conditions were not. However, the Competition Agency's economic and legal analysis showed no negative effects in the market, since the importer's market share was falling,

680. Pursuant to Art. 9(1)(c) of the Regulation on Vertical Agreements.
681. Decision of the Croatian Competition Agency of 13 January 2006, *Piaggio Hrvatska d.o.o.*, UP/I-030-02/2005-01/002.
682. *Ibid.*

there were many competitors, so competition was dynamic in the market, and the agreements were concluded for one year only.

415. In another *Piaggio* case, this one involving a dawn raid, the Competition Agency found no direct or indirect evidence that the supplier of Piaggio motorcycles and scooters, under a selective distribution system, restricted its authorized dealers by using recommended prices to impose a fixed (minimum) resale price, or that it imposed any pressure or incentive to fix (minimum) resale prices, or that it restricted the territory on which its authorized dealers may sell the goods.[683] The Competition Agency noted that although the supplier may recommend prices, recommendations as to the price may not become binding. In fact, actions of the dealer which are in compliance with the supplier's recommendations must not result from pressure or an incentive on the side of the supplier, but must reflect the dealer's free will in achieving its own economic interests. In the first step, the distribution contracts were analysed to find any anticompetitive clauses. In the second step, the Competition Agency undertook to 'interpret the provisions within a wider context to determine the manner in which the contracts were implemented in practice'. Despite some circumstantial evidence to the contrary, the Competition Agency held that to find a restrictive agreement in the concrete case it was 'necessary to obtain direct evidence, not only regarding the concordance of wills, but also regarding threat, coercion, a system of control, intimidation by warnings, punishment, etc.'.[684] The Competition Agency concluded that in this case dealers were free to create their commercial policy on resale prices, as well as on the territory for the sale of goods, and that they 'freely and independently obeyed the recommended price lists'.[685]

416. In another motor vehicles case, the Competition Agency found that the authorized importer and distributor of Mitsubishi vehicles in Croatia restricted competition by concluding prohibited agreements in the relevant markets of: (a) the distribution of new motor vehicles; (b) the servicing of Mitsubishi Motors vehicles; and (c) the distribution of spare parts for Mitsubishi Motors vehicles.[686] The Competition Agency held that the importer failed to apply equal conditions to equal

683. Decision of the Croatian Competition Agency of 17 December 2015, *Competition Agency v. Piaggio Hrvatska d.o.o.*, UP/I-034-03/2014-01/022.

684. Decision of the Croatian Competition Agency of 17 December 2015, *Competition Agency v. Piaggio Hrvatska d.o.o.*, UP/I-034-03/2014-01/022. For this purpose, the Competition Agency invoked Commission Directive 330/2010 on the application of Art. 101(3) to categories of vertical agreements, Vertical Restraints Guidelines of 2010, Guidelines for the application of Art. 81(3) and several ECJ judgments (Case C-338/00 P *Volkswagen v. Commission* ECLI:EU:C:2003:473; Case T-208/01 *Volkswagen v. Commission* ECLI:EU:T:2003:326; Case C-107/82 AEG-*Telefunken v. Commission* ECLI:EU:C:1983:293; Case C-25/84 and 26/84 *Ford Werke AG and Ford of Europe Inc v. Commission* ECLI:EU:C:1985:340); and a Commission decision (COMP/37.975 PO/Yamaha).

685. Decision of the Croatian Competition Agency of 17 December 2015, *Competition Agency v. Piaggio Hrvatska d.o.o.*, UP/I-034-03/2014-01/022.

686. Decision of the Croatian Competition Agency of 13 October 2011, *Auto Teskera et al.*, Official Gazette no. 145/2011.

transactions with different undertakings: on the occasion of establishing its distribution network, it restricted access to the market for the distribution of new motor vehicles (a qualitative-quantitative system of selective distribution) for two car dealers by not supplying them with its qualitative and quantitative criteria for admission into its distribution network, thereby placing them at a competitive disadvantage. This was in breach of Article 9(1)(4) of the CA, and Article 3(5) and (6) of the BER on Motor Vehicles. Exemption, individual or block, was not available in this case. In addition, a clause in the distribution contract limiting the duration of the contract to one year was found to be in breach of Article 9(1)(a) of the BER on Motor Vehicles.

417. In the *Monte v. Hyundai* case, the Competition Agency held that the authorized distributor of new motor vehicles and spare parts for the Hyundai brand in Croatia restricted competition in the relevant market of distribution of new motor vehicles in Croatia.[687] Both authorized car dealers agreements and authorized repairers agreements contained restrictive clauses. As regards the dealers' agreements, the following clauses were found to be restrictive: the distributor's approval necessary to open additional dealer stores or distribution points, the restriction of the transfer of dealers' rights and obligations to another authorized seller, and the restriction of the duration of the contract to six months. As regards the repairers' agreements, the following clauses were found to be restrictive: the repairers could not freely decide on the location of their business premises, or to open additional repair locations; Hyundai original spare parts only for the provision of 'other repair services'; manufacturers' authorization (Hyundai Motor Company) for the transfer of rights and obligations to another authorized repairer; and the restriction of the duration of the contract to six months. The Competition Agency held that these were ancillary restraints which restrict intra-brand competition, where the conclusion of the agreement is conditional on accepting provisions which are contrary to mandatory competition rules or which are deemed as hardcore restrictions which restrict inter-brand competition. Exemption, individual or block, was not available in this case. The authorized distributor was ordered by the Competition Agency to delete the restrictive provisions from the agreements.

418. In the *KMAG* case, the Competition Agency held that the authorized distributor of new motor vehicles for the KIA brand in Croatia restricted competition in the relevant market of the sale of spare parts and servicing of KIA motor vehicles in Croatia.[688] Both authorized car dealer agreements and authorized repairers agreements contained restrictive clauses. The restrictive clauses in contracts with authorized repairers were as follows: for any repairs, both under warranty and outside of

687. In breach of Art. 9(1) and (4), Art. 12(1)(d), Art. 14(4)(b) and Art. 14(5) of the Regulation on Motor Vehicles, and Art. 9(1) points 2, 3, 4, 5 CA, Decision of the Croatian Competition Agency of 8 April 2010, *Competition Agency v. Hyundai Auto Zagreb d.o.o.*, UP/I-030-02/2008-01/36.

688. In breach of Art. 9(1), Art. 12(1)(d) of the Regulation on Motor Vehicles, and Art. 9(1)(5) CA, Decision of the Croatian Competition Agency of 2 December 2010, *Competition Agency v. KMAG d.o.o.*, UP/I-030-02/010-01/015 (decision on the existence of a restrictive agreement); confirmed: Judgment of the High Administrative Court of the Republic of Croatia of 29 March 2012, *KMAG d.o.o v. Competition Agency*, Us-524/2011-6; Decision of the Croatian Competition Agency of 13

warranty, repairers must only use spare parts supplied by the distributor, and the duration of the contract was restricted to twelve months. The Competition Agency held that no individual or block exemption was available since the agreements contained hardcore restrictions and ordered the authorized distributor to delete the restrictive provisions from the contracts.

419. In the *Tomić/Šimatić* case, the Competition Agency held that by eliminating one of its authorized car dealers and repairers from the BMW network of authorized distributors and repairers, the authorized distributor did not infringe competition rules.[689] The Competition Agency held that since the car dealer banned from the network was selling BMW vehicles to third persons, resellers, thereby breaching the basic principles which protect the system of selective distribution established by the supplier, its elimination from the network was not contrary to competition rules. Besides, since the authorized car dealer and repairer did not obey the rules on registering for the training programme, unlike other authorized repairers, the Competition Agency held there was no breach of competition rules in denying it access to the training programme.

420. In the *Adria Lada* case, the Competition Agency held that the authorized distributor and repairer of LADA motor vehicles failed to organize a network of authorized distributors and repairers of LADA motor vehicles in compliance with the BER on Motor Vehicles, thereby restricting competition in the relevant markets for the repair and maintenance of motor vehicles and supply of spare parts.[690] In addition, the contracts concluded with car dealers contained clauses restricting access to relevant markets, directly fixing resale prices (RPM), and applying dissimilar conditions to equal transactions with different undertakings, thereby placing them in a disadvantaged position in relation to their competitors (no repair services of vehicles from other brands without written permission from Adria Lada;[691] all spare parts for LADA vehicles to be purchased from Adria Lada only;[692] the fixed price of an hour for repair of vehicles under guarantee;[693] limiting the duration of the contract to one year;[694] in the case of servicing other vehicles or using non-original spare parts, or spare parts from other suppliers, Adria Lada can unilaterally terminate the contract;[695] authorized repairers must use original spare parts only for

---

May 2013, *Competition Agency v. KMAG d.o.o.*, UP/I-034-03/12-03/004 (decision on fine); annulled: Judgment of the High Administrative Court of the Republic of Croatia of 27 February 2014, *KMAG d.o.o v. Competition Agency*, UsII-60/2013-8.

689. Decision of the Croatian Competition Agency of 3 November 2009, *Tomić and Co d.o.o. i Šimatić d.o.o.*, UP/I-030-02/2008-01/52; confirmed: Judgment of the Administrative Court of the Republic of Croatia of 3 February 2010, *Tomić and Co d.o.o. v. Competition Agency*, Us-13954/2009-4.

690. In breach of Art. 3(5) of the Regulation on Motor Vehicles – it did not make publicly available criteria for admission into the qualitative system of servicing LADA motor vehicles, and/or applied those criteria in a discriminatory manner, Decision of the Croatian Competition Agency of 24 September 2009, *Competition Agency v. Adria Lada d.o.o.*, UP/I-030-02/2008-01/67.

691. In breach of Art. 14(1)(c) of the Regulation on Motor Vehicles.

692. In breach of Art. 12(1)(d) of the Regulation on Motor Vehicles.

693. In breach of Art. 10(1)(a) of the Regulation on Motor Vehicles.

694. In breach of Art. 9(1)(a) of the Regulation on Motor Vehicles.

695. In breach of Art. 14(1)(c) of the Regulation on Motor Vehicles.

servicing vehicles outside the guarantee).[696] No block exemption was available since the agreements contained hardcore clauses.

D. *Franchising*

421. A franchising agreement is defined as a vertical agreement by which one undertaking (franchisor) provides to another undertaking (franchisee), for a direct or indirect financial reward, the right to use the franchise, i.e., a package of industrial or intellectual property rights for the purpose of selling a specific kind of product. The package of industrial or intellectual property rights relates to a trademark, know-how, models, design, copyright, technological knowledge, or patents to be used for the subsequent sale of products which are the object of the agreement to end users.[697]

II. Technology Licensing

422. Technology licensing is regulated by the BER on Technology Transfer.[698]

A. *Patent Licensing*

423. For patent licensing, the BER on technology transfer is applicable.[699]

B. *Trademark Licensing*

424. For trademark licensing, the BER on Technology Transfer is applicable.[700]

C. *Know-How and Trade Secret Licensing*

425. For know-how and trade secret licensing, the BER on Technology Transfer is applicable.[701]

426. In one of the last individual exemption cases before the system of individual exemptions was abandoned after the new CA came into force on 1 October 2010, shifting the burden of proof onto contractual parties to make sure contract provisions were not contrary to the CA, individual exemption was granted in a case

696. In breach of Art. 12(1)(d) of the Regulation on Motor Vehicles.
697. Article 3(6) of the BER on Vertical Agreements.
698. Official Gazette no. 9/2011, Uredba o skupnom izuzeću sporazuma o prijenosu tehnologije.
699. BER on Technology Transfer.
700. *Ibid.*
701. *Ibid.*

where the transfer of assets, employees, and know-how occurred between companies in the market for international courier services.[702] Invoking the Commission Notice on restrictions directly related and necessary to concentrations of 2001,[703] the Competition Agency held that a non-competition clause may last up to three years in contracts which involve the transfer of assets of undertakings, including the transfer of IP (in particular, goodwill and know-how). The Competition Agency held that, pursuant to Article 10(4) of the BER on Vertical Agreements, there is no restriction of competition if the duration of the obligation of the buyer is limited to one year after the termination of the agreement, and the restriction relates to competing products at the business premises and in the country in which the buyer was located for the duration of the agreements, and is deemed indispensable for the protection of know-how which was transferred by the supplier to the buyer. However, use, transfer, or disclosure of know-how may be of unlimited duration if the know-how is secret, significant, and recognizable.[704]

702. Decision of the Croatian Competition Agency of 16 December 2010, *UPS Intereuropa sajam*, UP/I-030-02/2010-01/019, Official Gazette no. 15/2011.

703. Commission Notice on restrictions directly related and necessary to concentrations of 2001.

704. Pursuant to Art. 10(5) of the Regulation on Vertical Agreements.

Chapter 2. Prohibited Practices of Dominant Undertakings

§1. Exploitative Practices

I. Excessive/Unfair Pricing

427. Article 13 point 1 of the CA prohibits 'directly or indirectly imposing unfair purchase or selling prices or other unfair trading conditions'.[705]

428. The practice of the Competition Agency, when it comes to dealing with the abuse of a dominant position, abounds in cases dealing with excessive/unfair pricing. Here are some examples.

429. In the case *Grad Rab v. Konzum*, the Town of Rab complained to the Competition Agency that a major retail chain (Konzum) charged during the summer season 20% higher prices, and that this amounted to abuse of dominance by way of excessive pricing.[706] The Competition Agency rejected the request to start proceedings. Not only did it establish that Konzum neither had a dominant position on the Island of Rab, nor in the Town of Rab, and that thus no investigation into abuse was possible, but it also held that Konzum was exposed to strong competition on the relevant market, which meant that consumers had choice. The Competition Agency noted that its task was not to regulate prices, but to ensure free interplay of market mechanisms, intervening where appropriate to stop anticompetitive use of market power, of which in this case it held no indication existed.

430. In another case, *Croatia Airlines v. Zračna luka Zagreb and Zračna luka Zagreb – Ugostiteljstvo*, the Competition Agency found that prices imposed by dominant undertakings were both unfair and discriminatory.[707] Here, the Competition Agency found that Zračna luka Zagreb and Zračna luka Zagreb – Ugostiteljstvo abused their dominant position in the relevant market by directly imposing prices on users of its catering handling services for aeroplanes at Pleso Airport that were unfair.[708] The Competition Agency found that the abusive conduct had negative effects not only on direct users of their services (Croatia Airlines), but also on final users.

431. The Competition Agency ordered that the dominant undertaking which abused its position (Zračna luka Zagreb – Ugostiteljstvo) vis-à-vis Croatia Airlines

705. *See* Ch. 3 §2 Dominant Undertakings, §5 Tests of Illegality, Ch. 4 §3 Market Power/Dominant Position, §6 Monopolization and Abuse of Dominance, *supra*.
706. Decision of the Croatian Competition Agency of 28 September 2015, *Competition Agency v. Konzum d.o.o.*, UP/I-034-03/2015-01/021.
707. Decision of the Croatian Competition Agency of 30 December 2008, *Croatia Airlines v. Zračna luka Zagreb d.o.o and Zračna luka Zagreb – Ugostiteljstvo d.o.o.*, UP/I-030-02/2007-01/15, Official Gazette no. 66/2009; confirmed: Judgment of the Administrative Court of the Republic of Croatia of 18 October 2012, Us-4027/2009-14.
708. Within the meaning of Art. 16(1) and (2)(1) CA.

must change its prices within a certain time frame, so that the prices are clear, transparent, and non-discriminatory, and also that the prices must be in correlation with the real cost to the undertaking for providing the catering handling services and that the prices must also not be dependent on the location of the premises within Pleso Airport from which this service is provided. This intervention as regards prices was justified according to the Competition Agency since the relevant market was in the course of being liberalized in Croatia but that the EU rules were still not fully applicable. Thus, the Competition Agency held that, pending liberalization of the market, the control of prices for 'catering handling services' by an authorized state body was necessary.

432. On the contrary, the Competition Agency found no unfair pricing abuse in the market for the supply of food for aeroplanes (prices were increased by 62% by its current supplier Zračna luka Zagreb – Ugostiteljstvo d.o.o.), since access to this market was fully open, and Croatia Airlines was free to choose any other supplier of food which would compete with Zračna luka Zagreb – Ugostiteljstvo.

433. In the *Ponikve* case, the Competition Agency held that the company supplying running water to households on the island of Krk, as a natural monopolist having a dominant position in the relevant market, abused its dominant position by imposing unfair selling prices.[709] The dominant undertaking divided consumers into thirty-two categories, each paying a different price depending on their annual water consumption. The Competition Agency held that this categorization was based on no linear or logical correlation between water consumption and the set price, and that certain categories of consumers but also consumers within certain categories were put in an unequal position in relation to other consumers. The Competition Agency found that consumers were not incentivized to consume water sustainably or according to their own needs, but that they achieved financial gain if they consumed water non-sustainably since they were to pay less if they consumed more water. The Competition Agency ordered the company to change its prices within a certain time, provided that the tariff model imposed no unfair selling prices leading to the unequal position of consumers, and that it ensures the efficient functioning of the water supply system, and the preservation of water as a very important natural resource for the Republic of Croatia. In particular, it was held that any tariff whereby a fixed fee would be included in a volume-based fee would not be acceptable since it would lead to placing consumers in an unequal position. The Competition Agency said that this model (a fixed fee included in a volume-based fee) was not accepted anywhere in the EU.

434. No abuse of dominance by charging excessive prices was found in a case where the Competition Agency refused to initiate proceedings against a company that was allegedly the only supplier of natural gas for motor vehicles in Zagreb, and which was purportedly charging an abusive price, making Croatia allegedly the only

709. In breach of Art. 16(1) and (2) point 1 CA, Decision of the Croatian Competition Agency of 20 October 2005, *Competition Agency v. Ponikve d.o.o.*, UP/I-030-02/2004-01/066.

country in Europe where natural gas was more expensive than gasoline.[710] The Competition Agency found that prices in Croatia were comparable with the EU average price, and that a negligible number of vehicles in Croatia were running on natural gas, and that each vehicle running on natural gas had an alternative gasoline motor which made a switch possible if the gas price went higher than the gasoline price. This, concluded the Competition Agency, made it impossible to create any abuse by imposing too high a price and gaining additional profit.

435. In another case where no abuse of dominance by charging unfair prices was found, the Competition Agency acted on a complaint from a competitor of a large local newspaper publisher which claimed that, by including its previously separately sold classified ads publication into its newspaper and not increasing the price of the newspaper itself, the large publisher abused its dominant position.[711] The competitor published its own classified ads publication. The Competition Agency held that it was very common for newspaper publishers to include in their publications smaller topic-specific add-ons, which did not amount to a breach of competition rules. The Competition Agency went on to emphasize that, with the welfare of consumers being one of the driving forces of competition policy, separate smaller add-ons contributed to the newspaper content, and thus were of benefit to consumers. Therefore, the inclusion of a free add-on in the newspaper had no negative effects for end consumers. Indeed, this allows consumers to derive benefits from the free market system in which undertakings satisfy the demand of consumers by producing higher quality goods and services, with lower prices, with the ultimate goal of efficiency and increased consumer welfare.

436. In an interesting case, which started off as a case against the biggest bank in Croatia for an alleged abuse of dominant position by charging excessive prices for its late payment notices to debtors with mortgage loans before the Croatian National Bank, and where later, due to a change in legislation, the case was transferred to the Competition Agency for adjudication, the Competition Agency held that there were no grounds for the continuation of proceedings since the question of the high late payment fees was in the domain of courts, and competition rules were not applicable.[712] Most crucially, the Competition Agency held that there was no separate relevant market for late payment notices, which meant that there was no dominant position, and thus no abuse. However, the issue of the high cost for consumers/debtors was to be dealt with from the contractual law point of view, and from the point of view of consumer protection rules.

710. Decision of the Croatian Competition Agency of 14 May 2015, *Competition Agency v. Gradska plinara Zagreb-Opskrba d.o.o.*, UP/I-034-03/2015-01/002.
711. Decision of the Croatian Competition Agency of 16 June 2015, *Competition Agency v. Novi list d.d.*, UP/I-034-03/2015-01/004.
712. Decision of the Croatian Competition Agency of 6 March 2014, *Competition Agency v. Zagrebačka Banka d.d.*, UP/I-034-03/2013-02/028, confirmed judgment of the High Administrative Court of the Republic of Croatia of 27 August 2015, *Croatian National Bank v. Competition Agency*, UsII-43/14-10.

437. When it comes to unfair trading conditions as a form of abuse of dominance, the following case illustrates the reluctance of the Competition Agency to protect smaller/weaker competitors against stronger, vertically integrated opponents. In this case, the Competition Agency found no evidence that Blitz and Duplicato Media (vertically integrated movie distribution and movie theatres companies) abused their dominant position in the market of movie distribution in Croatia by directly or indirectly imposing unfair trade conditions within the meaning of Article 16(2)(1) of the CA against their competitor in the Town of Zadar, which had previously enjoyed a dominant position in Zadar and its local area, before a new modern cinema complex was opened by the new, vertically integrated entrant.[713] As already mentioned above,[714] despite the fact that no abuse was found in this case, the Competition Agency warned the dominant firm and its subsidiaries which have dominance in the market for movie distribution in Croatia that they had special responsibility 'to treat equally all movie theatre firms, to secure on time a sufficient number of copies of a movie title, and, if it is their assessment that the movie will not be financially profitable, to offer a minimum guarantee based exclusively on the amount of the unit cost of the additional movie copy, and not on some other unreliable criteria'. The Competition Agency emphasized that it would continue to follow closely the highly concentrated market of movie distribution and the market for the public screening of movies in Croatia, since consolidation in this sector was not subject to any sector rules.

438. Another form of exploitative behaviour is found under Article 13 point 2 of the CA ('limiting production, markets or technical development to the prejudice of consumers'). In an interesting case, the Competition Agency looked at whether a dominant firm in the market for the public transport of passengers in a local market (Krapina-Zagorje County, where it had a market share of 90–100%) was using its dominant position in this market to spill over its market power to a neighbouring market (the market for bus station services in the Town of Krapina where it had a market share of 50%), thereby abusing its position by limiting production, markets or technical development to the prejudice of consumers within the meaning of Articles 16(1) and 16(2)(2) of the CA.[715] At issue was whether the opening of a new bus station by the firm dominant in the market for the public transport of passengers, and starting to compete in the neighbouring market for bus station services, where it was not previously active as a competitor (it only used an existing bus station), amounted to an abuse of dominance. The Competition Agency held that, in general, vertical integration even by a dominant firm was permissible, although not always desirable. It held that such vertical integration did not lead to a significant distortion of competition, as long as access to any bus station was allowed under equal conditions to any public line transport services firm.

713. Decision of the Croatian Competition Agency of 24 February 2011, *Kino Zadar Film d.d. v. Blitz d.o.o. and Duplicato Media d.o.o.*, UP/I-030-02/2008-01/080.

714. Chapter 3, §2 Dominant Undertaking.

715. Decision of the Croatian Competition Agency of 19 December 2006, *Branko Kunštek and Fanika Vešligaj v. Presečki grupa d.o.o.*, UP/I-030-02/2006-02/5, Official Gazette no. 142/2006, confirmed: Judgment of the Administrative Court of the Republic of Croatia of 21 January 2010, Us-13887/2006-10.

439. After obtaining the opinion of the Ministry of Sea, Tourism, Transport and Development, which confirmed there were no legal obstacles for building a new bus station in Krapina, the Competition Agency held that bus transport companies had an equal opportunity of access either to the bus station of the Presečki grupa or to the bus station of Autotransporti Kunštek Krapina, and that it was their own business decision which bus station to use. The Competition Agency continued to explain that vertical integration would have a beneficial effect on end consumers because the vertically integrated firm would be able to avoid double costs (of stopping at both bus stations), and lower its prices or maintain prices at the same level.

440. The Competition Agency held that it was up to the state body allowing the opening of a new (second) bus station to assess if in this way public interest was being served, and not the Competition Agency. However, the Competition Agency considered, because this was a public service of general interest, that the primary criteria should be a significant advancement in the quality of bus services and lower prices of those services, and only secondarily the competition between firms providing those services.

441. In another case, the Competition Agency held that the conduct of jointly dominant firms did not amount to abuse by charging unfair prices (within the meaning of Article 16(2)(1) of the CA), by influencing the retail price of general-information dailies by linking the distribution cost with the retail price, since the effect on the retail price was only indirect and since the publishers were free to set the retail price.[716] The Competition Agency invoked the position of the European Commission to state that, exceptionally, the uniform price of books, newspapers, and some medical equipment was exempted from competition rules, provided there was no effect on interstate trade.

II. Discrimination

442. Discrimination as a form of abuse of a dominant position is regulated by Article 13 point 3 of the CA: it is prohibited to apply dissimilar conditions to equivalent transactions with other undertakings, thereby placing them at a competitive disadvantage.

443. In a case already mentioned above, the Competition Agency found that the dominant undertakings were imposing discriminatory prices (within the meaning of Article 16(1) and (2) point 3 of the CA): they were imposing different prices for the same services without any justification based on the cost differential arising from

716. Decision of the Croatian Competition Agency of 30 June 2010, *Media-ideja d.o.o. v. Tisak d.d. and Distri-Press d.o.o.*, UP/I-030-02/2005-01/43; confirmed: Judgment of the Administrative Court of the Republic of Croatia of 30 June 2010, *Distri-Press d.o.o. v. Competition Agency*, Us-12765/2007 and Judgment of the Administrative Court of the Republic of Croatia of 17 February 2011 *Tisak d.d.*, U-III-4082/2010.

the provision of those services.[717] It was found that the difference in the price between the 'handling 1 service' and 'handling 2 service' was not justified by the difference between the transport costs and other variable costs, i.e., that the distance between the storage areas used by Zračna luka Zagreb – Ugostiteljstvo and any other storage area within Pleso Airport did not justify the difference in price, since the services provided from any storage area within Pleso Airport were deemed as equivalent transactions. Thus, the Competition Agency held that the difference in price based exclusively on the criterion of the location of the storage area was discriminatory, i.e., that the undertakings abused their dominant position.

444. In another case, already discussed above, the Competition Agency found that the only national body for collective rights management abused its dominant position by granting a more favourable discount for the payment of its reproduction and use fees to members of one association of companies – importers of IT goods, and a less favourable discount to another association, thereby placing it at a competitive disadvantage.[718] The Competition Agency held that those discounts were discriminatory, and that there was no objective justification based on the costs for such treatment. The Competition Agency held that the rules on discounts had the effect of distorting competition in the secondary market, i.e., the market for the sale of products for which a reproduction and use fee was levied, as the firms which were granted a higher discount were able to be more competitive in terms of its final price for end consumers, thereby placing firms which had to pay higher fees at a competitive disadvantage. As already mentioned, the Competition Agency held that the dominant undertaking did not act in accordance with its particular responsibility to preserve effective competition, as expected from a dominant undertaking. Such a firm has a special responsibility not to act in a way that weakens the level of competition existing in the market, since it can significantly influence the level and development of effective competition in the relevant market. The Competition Agency noted that because of its status regulated by law, HDS-ZAMP was an economically stronger party since it was in a position to enforce its conditions in the relevant market.

445. In an unusually economic heavy-case analysis, due primarily to the efforts of a party harmed by market conduct to advance its arguments before the Competition Agency, the joint dominance of two companies (Tisak and Distri-Press) was found to exist in the relevant market of the wholesale distribution of general-information newspapers in Croatia (within the meaning of Article 15(1), (2) and (4) of the CA).[719] Discussing the oligopolistic market conditions present in this case,

717. Decision of the Croatian Competition Agency of 30 December 2008, *Croatia Airlines v. Zračna luka Zagreb d.o.o and Zračna luka Zagreb – Ugostiteljstvo d.o.o.*, UP/I-030-02/2007-01/15, Official Gazette no. 66/2009; confirmed: Judgment of the Administrative Court of the Republic of Croatia of 18 October 2012, Us-4027/2009-14.

718. Decision of the Croatian Competition Agency of 3 November 2009, *HUVEL v. HDS-ZAMP*, UP/I-030-02/2008-01/041; confirmed: Judgment of the High Administrative Court of the Republic of Croatia of 20 April 2012, *Hrvatsko društvo skladatelja v. Competition Agency*, Us-14370/2009-13.

719. Decision of the Croatian Competition Agency of 30 June 2010, *Media-ideja d.o.o. v. Tisak d.d. and Distri-Press d.o.o.*, UP/I-030-02/2005-01/43; confirmed: Judgment of the Administrative Court of

the Competition Agency noted that in an oligopolistic market it occurs frequently that there is 'a certain mutual interdependence between oligopolists regarding strategic decisions'. In the concrete case, there was a 'symmetric duopoly' in the relevant market: two main providers of the same services, with a more or less equal costs structure, and thus equal interests in the relevant market. Their smaller competitors, which have negligible market power and a regional character, must constantly align their market behaviours with the dominant suppliers. The Competition Agency noted that due to the nature of the relevant market, the firms can adopt the same or almost the same terms as regards prices and other trade conditions without the need for an explicit agreement. It was found that the dominant parties' general terms and conditions were identical. They both had the same distribution fee calculation method, and the same rebate (27%) for general-information newspapers which cost HRK 6.00 a copy (the price of most general-information newspapers), and the same distribution fee and rebate calculation method for the general-information newspaper which initiated the proceedings at hand (whose price was HRK 3.00).

446. However, in the neighbouring market of the intercity transport of general-information newspapers, the Competition Agency found no joint dominance since the publishers were able to organize intercity transport by themselves, and also use other transport services providers. Still, the Competition Agency accepted the claim of the plaintiff that it was easier and more cost effective for the publisher to use the same supplier for micro- and macro-distribution services.

447. The Competition Agency found that Tisak and Distri-Press abused their jointly dominant position by having a different monthly distribution fee calculation method for two different sets of general-information newspaper publishers: for those whose newspaper price was HRK 6.00, the distribution costs were predictable (they amounted to 27% of the net selling price, and the number of copies which were not sold was not relevant); on the contrary, for the only newspaper whose price was HRK 3.00, the distribution costs were difficult to predict since the calculation method not only took account of the net selling price per copy but also the number of unsold copies. In effect, the first category of publishers had a fixed fee, irrespective of the number of copies sold, and for the other category the fee was variable. Despite the fact that for some newspapers in the first category the number of unsold copies was very high (up to 80%), there was no additional fee for unsold copies. This placed Media-ideja d.o.o. (with a level of unsold copies at around 40%) at a competitive disadvantage. Indeed, the Competition Agency found that no general-information daily managed to cover the minimum distribution costs per copy, contrary to the claims by the jointly dominant undertakings that tried to justify the difference in treatment by explaining that the cheaper daily did not manage to cover its distribution costs. Moreover, it was held that the provisions of their general terms

---

the Republic of Croatia of 30 June 2010, *Distri-Press d.o.o. v. Competition Agency*, Us-12765/2007 and Judgment of the Administrative Court of the Republic of Croatia of 17 February 2011 *Tisak d.d.*, U-III-4082/2010. For a detailed discussion on the factors relevant for joint dominance, *see* Ch. 3 §2, *supra*.

and conditions were non-transparent and unclear, with the parties advancing contradictory information and arguments during the proceedings. Thus, the Competition Agency found the abuse to result from the non-transparent and unclear content of the provisions regulating the calculation of the distribution fee, allowing for various interpretations which placed Media-ideja d.o.o. at a competitive disadvantage.

448. The Competition Agency found that there were spill-over effects of the abuse on the neighbouring market of general-information dailies: foreclosure of the market and the potentially more difficult entry for new participants which seek to sell their daily general-information newspapers at a lower price. Indeed, since 2000 there have been no new market participants offering a price below HRK 6.00 (except one which exited very soon). It was held that this could also harm consumers who were unable to get lower-priced products.

449. The Competition Agency rejected the request of Media-ideja d.o.o. to determine the financial loss that it suffered due to the abusive conduct of the jointly dominant firms, since it found that in absolute terms Media-ideja d.o.o. paid a lower distribution price per copy in comparison to its competing publishers. Indeed, the Competition Agency held that because of its lower retail price the publisher would always suffer from a higher financial burden in terms of distribution, and there is no liability of the distributors in this part since the publisher is free to set its retail price and bear any commercial risks arising therefrom.

450. To conclude, the Competition Agency stated that it took into account the specificities of the relevant market, and the need for the distributors to cover their costs, but it held that the negative effects arising from unequal treatment regarding the distribution fee calculation method were still there. In this regard, it was in particular relevant that the two firms held a jointly dominant position in the relevant market, that they had no significant competitors, and that there was an effect on the neighbouring market where Media-Ideja d.o.o.'s daily '24 sata' was the only newspaper sold at a lower price.

451. In another case, the Competition Agency held that INA d.d., the only supplier of jet fuel (JET A-1) in Croatia and thus an indispensable business partner for Dubrovnik Airline d.o.o., abused its dominant position by applying different criteria for setting the price of fuel for Dubrovnik Airline when compared to the criteria applied to other (foreign) buyers, thereby placing Dubrovnik Airline d.o.o. at a competitive disadvantage.[720] The Competition Agency noted, though, that discounts linked exclusively to the volume of goods or services supplied from the same supplier were not prohibited, and were not to be regarded as the application of dissimilar conditions to equivalent transactions.

---

720. Decision of the Croatian Competition Agency of 19 May 2011, *Competition Agency v. INA d.o.o.,*, UP/I-030-02/2009-01/035, Official Gazette 79/2011, confirmed: Judgment of the High Administrative Court of the Republic of Croatia of 9 February 2012, *INA Industrija nafte d.d. v. Competition Agency*, Us-7153/2011-8.

§2. Exclusionary Practices

I. Predation

452. Telecom cases have been particularly prone to predation allegations, usually coupled with allegations of margin squeeze. In one of these cases, the Competition Agency examined the market for leased electronic communication cables and the market for the transmission of TV programmes to end users in Croatia, concluding that there was no abuse.[721] As regards the first claim, that of a margin squeeze, the Competition Agency considered both the upstream market for wholesale lease of electronic communications cables, and the downstream market for the transmission of TV programmes to end users. The Competition Agency held that one of the conditions for a margin squeeze was that the input of an upstream dominant firm was indispensable for its downstream competitors to compete in the downstream market. It found that the former incumbent's (Hrvatski Telekom, HT) cables were not indispensable to compete downstream, since there were substitutes for its network, since other firms besides HT were leasing their electronic communications cables, and some downstream firms did not use the HT network to provide their services. As regards the second claim, that of predatory pricing on the relevant market for the transmission of TV programmes to end users, the Competition Agency found that in this market HT was not dominant in the period from 2007 to 2009, only reaching more than 40% of the market in 2009, which is not a long enough period to indicate a stable market share. This conclusion on the issue of dominance was also reached after taking into account the position and market share of competitors, the fact that the market was fast growing and dynamic, and taking into account market trends. Even if HT did have a dominant position, the Competition Agency found that the facts did not allow for the conclusion that the price of HT's product downstream (MAXtv) was predatory, since it was higher than the average variable cost (in compliance with the ECJ test on predation). The Competition Agency noted that the fact that there had been no exit from this market (TV programmes), and that several firms had entered it, pointed to the conclusion that there was effective competition in that market. In addition, there were regulatory non-discrimination obligations imposed by the sector regulator whose goal was to ensure non-discriminatory access to the market.

453. In another telecom predation case, the Competition Agency tackled the concept of predation.[722] It held that predation, as a form of abuse of the dominant position of an undertaking in the relevant market, manifests itself in selling for a limited time goods or services for prices which are below the appropriate costs, with the aim of eliminating from the market its competitors or of preventing them to access the market. The consequence of such conduct is usually the strengthening of

721. Decision of the Croatian Competition Agency of 31 August 2010, *B.net Hrvatska v. Hrvatski telekom d.d.*, Official Gazette no. 115/2010.

722. Decision of the Croatian Competition Agency of 12 July 2012, *Competition Agency v. Hrvatski Telekom d.d. and Iskon Internet d.d.*, UP/I-030-02/2009-01/11, Official Gazette no. 114/2012; confirmed: Judgment of the High Administrative Court of the Republic of Croatia of 14 December 2016, *Amis telekom d.o.o. v. Competition Agency*, UsII-32/15-12.

the market power of the dominant undertaking and harm for end consumers. Further, it held that a predation strategy is rational if the dominant undertaking succeeds in making competitors exit the market and/or prevents potential competitors from entering the market, only to increase its price to the level before the predation or even to a higher level, thereby achieving additional profit which it would not have been able to achieve in a competitive context; such conduct results in direct harm to consumers.

454. In order to assess if in this case there was an abuse by predation, invoking EU competition law criteria, the Competition Agency noted that it must determine the short-term renouncing of profits, the possible elimination of competitors from the market, the possible recoupment of costs, and the intention of the dominant firm to exclude competitors from the market. It held that the recoupment of cost, in accordance with EU law, was not necessary to prove predation, but it was an additional factor which may point to a predation strategy. It also held that the criteria for predation must be cumulatively met: the short-term renouncing of profits, the elimination of competitors from the market and market foreclosure, the intention to exclude, and harm for end consumers. The Competition Agency found that the cumulative criteria for predation were not met in this case: in particular, the elimination of competitors from the market and market foreclosure, the recoupment of cost, the existence of the intention to eliminate competitors, and also that no negative effects for end consumers were found.

455. It found dominance in the relevant market for broadband access to the Internet for private users in Croatia (90–100% market share in 2007, 70–80% market share in 2011), but it found no direct evidence of elimination of competitors.

456. The average revenue per user for Iskon.DUO in 2007 and 2008 and Iskon.TRIO in 2009 was below the average total cost. In 2007, Iskon lowered its prices after Amis significantly reduced its prices for comparable services, thus Iskon matched its prices with its smaller competitor which entered the market and offered lower prices. In this regard, the Competition Agency held (invoking ECJ case law: United Brands, Case 27/76, paragraph 189, BPB Industries, Case T-65/89, paragraph 69, Irish Sugar, T-228/97, paragraph 112) that a dominant firm cannot be denied the right to defend its own commercial and economic interests if under threat. However, the Competition Agency emphasized that the dominant firm must take account the fact that the protection of its own commercial interests must be proportional to the conduct of other competitors and must take account of their economic power. In addition, the protection of its own commercial and economic interests must not lead to the further strengthening of dominance. In this regard, the Competition Agency held that lowering prices after a competitor had entered the market and reduced its prices could be considered as a 'reasonable adaptation to new market conditions'. The Competition Agency observed that this was not a short-term lowering of prices by Iskon, but a response to a new competitor who offered lower prices, and that prior to its entry prices were relatively high as compared to other markets. The Competition Agency held that this was directly beneficial to consumers in Croatia, including Iskon's consumers.

457. It was also relevant, in terms of any possible elimination of competitors from the market, that from 2007 to 2011 most operators had an increase in the number of users. Hence, the Competition Agency considered it was clear that a predatory strategy by the dominant firm would not be economically rational or successful.

458. As regards recoupment, the Competition Agency found that the prices of the Iskon.DUO service, after falling in 2007, did not in the short-term return to their previous level, which led to the conclusion that the lowering of the prices of the Iskon.DUO service in 2007 was a corollary of the entry into the market of new competitors.

459. No direct short-term harm for consumers was found by the Competition Agency, since the Iskon.DUO prices did not return to their previous level, and competing operators were becoming stronger. Indeed, the Competition Agency held that it was reasonable to conclude that the lowering of the price of Iskon.DUO had a positive effect on end consumers.

460. Finally, the Competition Agency held that Iskon's actions on the market alone, taking into account the structure of the relevant market, its trends and Iskon's share in the growth of the T-HT Grupa during the time in question were not able to significantly affect the effective competitive structure of the market.

461. In another predation case, the Competition Agency held that an undertaking which was going through bankruptcy proceedings not only could not be deemed dominant, but that it could not be deemed able to engage in predatory pricing strategy since it had insufficient financial resources.[723] The claimant here (Promet d.o.o.) asked the Competition Agency for protection from unfair competition. The Competition Agency pointed to another body which was competent for unfair competition (the State Inspection Office), and to the Trade Act which regulates the notion of unfair competition. The Competition Agency held that lowering prices might result from competition in the market, where firms satisfy consumer demand through the higher quality of their goods and services and with lower prices, eliminating thereby less efficient competitors from the market.

462. No predation was found in a case where a dominant undertaking was not able to engage in a predation strategy for the duration of a contract (two years) won in a public tender, since it could not unilaterally change its prices for the duration of the agreement.[724] The Competition Agency held that other competitors were not excluded from the market since they could submit a bid in other public tenders.

463. In another predation case, the claim of predation was not accepted, since the plaintiff's prices were still lower than those of the respondent, even after the

723. Decision of the Croatian Competition Agency of 6 May 2011, *Competition Agency v. Croatia bus d.d. u stečaju*, UP/I-030-02/2011-01/017.

724. Decision of the Croatian Competition Agency of 21 May 2015, *Competition Agency v. Presečki grupa d.o.o.*, UP/I-034-03/2015-01/005.

respondent had lowered its prices.[725] The Competition Agency held that 'price alignment with a competitor' was a legitimate strategy, even for a dominant undertaking.

II. Tying

464. Article 13(4) of the CA prohibits, as a form of abuse of a dominant position, making the conclusion of contracts subject to acceptance by the other parties of supplementary obligations which, by their nature or according to commercial usage, have no connection with the subject of such contracts.

465. In the *Croatia Airlines v. Zračna luka Zagreb and Zračna luka Zagreb – Ugostiteljstvo* case, the Competition Agency found that the dominant undertakings abused their position by ceasing to supply Croatia Airlines with catering handling services, at the same time making the continuation of this service conditional on the purchasing of some additional catering services from Zračna luka Zagreb – Ugostiteljstvo d.o.o., thereby breaching Article 13(4) of the CA.[726] In the concrete case, Croatia Airlines switched to other food suppliers. This prompted the dominant provider of handling services at Pleso Airport, whose daughter company used to supply food to Croatia Airlines before the switch, to cease the provision of services in which it was the dominant and only provider at Pleso Airport and to make the continuation of this essential service conditional on Croatia Airlines' willingness to continue to purchase food products from its daughter company.

466. In the *VIPnet v. HT-Hrvatske telekomunikacije d.d. and T-Mobile Hrvatska* case, the Competition Agency found that HT and its subsidiary T-Mobile abused their dominant position by concluding contracts on the provision of telecom services with twenty-three companies which contained supplementary obligations which, by their nature or according to commercial usage, have no connection with the subject of such contract.[727] The following clauses were found as hardcore restrictions:

(1) clauses whereby the user of telecom services must notify HT and T-Mobile if any other competitor offers the user any new services (not covered by the contract with HT and T-Mobile), and that in such a case the user must accept HT

---

725. Decision of the Croatian Competition Agency of 24 February 2011, *Kino Zadar Film d.d. v. Blitz d.o.o. and Duplicato Media d.o.o.*, UP/I-030-02/2008-01/080, Official Gazette no. 88/2011.

726. Decision of the Croatian Competition Agency of 30 December 2008, *Croatia Airlines v. Zračna luka Zagreb d.o.o and Zračna luka Zagreb – Ugostiteljstvo d.o.o.*, UP/I-030-02/2007-01/15, Official Gazette no. 66/2009; confirmed: Judgment of the Administrative Court of the Republic of Croatia of 18 October 2012, Us-4027/2009-14.

727. Decision of the Croatian Competition Agency of 12 July 2007, *Competition Agency v. HT-Hrvatske telekomunikacije d.d. i T-Mobile Hrvatska d.o.o.*, UP/I-030-02/2005-01/50, Official Gazette no. 100/2007; confirmed: Judgment of the Administrative Court of the Republic of Croatia of 9 September 2010, *HT-Hrvatske telekomunikacije d.d. i T-Mobile Hrvatska d.o.o. v. Competition Agency,* Us-8992/2007-8.

and T-Mobile's offer if the price offered by HT and T-Mobile is equal or less than the price offered by their competitor, and if the quality of the service offered by HT and T-Mobile is equal or better than the quality offered by their competitor;

(2) clauses whereby the user must request from HT and T-Mobile any substitute new services which are offered by a competitor, and the user can accept the competitor's offer only if HT and T-Mobile fail to offer the same substitute new service, notwithstanding the price and quality; the user must pay the difference between the full price and the discounted price that was granted in the case of termination;

(3) the user is allowed to use, without any consequences, the existing telecom services of their competitors only for commercial or security reasons, meaning services for which the competitor's revenue from the user does not go above a certain percentage earned by HT and T-Mobile during the previous year for each telecom service, and not more than a certain percentage paid by the user for all telecom services in a certain year;

(4) fourth, the user must notify HT and T-Mobile about the percentage of telecom services supplied to the user by their competitors;

(5) fifth, the user is offered additional discounts if the user switches to HT/T-Mobile for telecom services which at the time of signing the contract with HT/T-Mobile are supplied by their competitors; and

(6) sixth, the user must use any telecom services offered by HT/T-Mobile in the market, and the ones that are offered by them.

467. The Competition Agency held that the object of the contract, and consequently its effect, was to strengthen/maintain the present market share, and to eliminate/restrict competition, whereby HT/T-Mobile abused their dominant position. The Competition Agency held that in a situation where they already had an extremely high market share, HT/T-Mobile were obliged to act in such a manner as not to distort competition. Although a dominant position is not prohibited per se, by concluding those contracts the dominant firms did not behave with special responsibility to preserve effective competition which is a level of care demanded of dominant firms.

468. Furthermore, the Competition Agency held that in applying Article 16 of the CA, it was not relevant if anticompetitive effects were actually achieved. The Competition Agency also held that abuse of dominance is determined in an objective manner, notwithstanding the intention of dominant firms.

469. The Competition Agency found that HT and T-Mobile, acting as a single economic entity, were engaged in spilling over their market power and using their comparative advantages from the markets in which they could to a significant extent behave independently of their competitors, consumers, buyers, or suppliers to those markets where they could not have behaved in such a manner.

470. It was also particularly relevant that the parties with whom the contracts were concluded were all very large companies, in fact the most significant users of telecom services. The Competition Agency held that, although HT and T-Mobile had the right to protect their business interests, such clauses as found in the contracts containing hardcore restraints cannot be deemed as suitable for protecting their business interests.

471. Regarding consumer sales promotions as a potential form of abuse of dominance, in an interesting case the agency looked at the conduct of the former incumbent telecom operator (HT), following the raising of possible competition concerns by one of its competitors.[728] The Competition Agency held that in principle consumer sales promotions, provided they are not targeted at specific categories of buyers or consumers, have a positive impact on consumers because they allow for a more affordable buying experience through certain benefits which are directly or indirectly translated into lower prices. From the point of view of competition rules, sales promotions are not prohibited per se. However, the Competition Agency held that lower prices achieved through sales promotions may be scrutinized if anticompetitive effects are more significant than the positive effects on end consumers.

472. After a quantitative analysis, the Competition Agency did not see in this case any indicators relating to the relevant market of broadband Internet for private users and the transmission of TV programmes to private end consumers that would point to the conclusion that there was foreclosure or elimination of competitors from the market, since there was the continuous entry of new operators in this market, and almost all operators had seen an increase of users from year to year, and despite its promotional activities HT's market share was diminishing. This was beneficial in alleviating the previously existing asymmetry in the broadband Internet market.

473. The Competition Agency noted that, although it was HT which first entered the market for innovative services (broadband Internet, Internet Protocol Television (IPTV)), thus securing a large base of customers, offering promotions to its existing and potential end consumers after new competitors entered the market did not result in market foreclosure, but, on the contrary, in intensifying competition for the benefit of consumers.

474. The Competition Agency differentiated between competition-neutral sales promotions (because of the off-setting regulatory obligations), and sales promotions which were not accompanied by relevant regulatory rules. The first were sales promotions during which HT also had to offer, under its regulatory obligations, promotions to other buyers at the wholesale level, so that other operators could replicate the same promotional activity. The second were sales promotions where buyers would obtain a certain device for a symbolic price for concluding a contract for using a certain service.

475. The Competition Agency stated that no correlation was found between sales promotions and growth in the number of new consumers. Having assessed all

728. Decision of the Croatian Competition Agency of 15 December 2011, *Competition Agency v. Hrvatski Telekom d.d.*, UP/I-030-02/2009-01/034.

the circumstances, the Competition Agency concluded there were no conditions for initiating infringement proceedings in this case.

III. Rebates

476. Discounts linked exclusively to the volume of goods or services supplied from the same supplier are not prohibited, and are not to be regarded as the application of dissimilar conditions to equivalent transactions.[729]

477. After a thorough economic and legal analysis in the *Adris grupa and TDR* case, the Competition Agency found that Adris and its subsidiary TDR abused their dominant position by implementing a strategy for creating a network of exclusive buyers of their cigarettes in Croatia, and that they eliminated competitors from the relevant market and restricted access to competitors to the relevant market by concluding with their buyers agreements where an additional obligation was imposed on them to satisfy all or the majority of their needs for cigarettes within a certain period from TDR.[730] The supplier, TDR, financially incentivized such buying by granting prohibited, conditioned retroactive rebates, that is, loyalty rebates. Buyers which bought from TDR in quantitative terms more cigarettes were not granted higher rebates, but the right to additional/subsequent rebates was made conditional on loyalty towards TDR, depending on how much of their total needs for cigarettes they met by buying exclusively from TDR. Therefore, the Competition Agency found the dominant undertakings applied unequal conditions to equal transactions, placing some buyers at a competitive disadvantage, and made the conclusion of contracts conditional on the buyers' acceptance of additional obligations which by their nature or by trade usage were not connected with the object of the agreement.

478. The Competition Agency renounced its initial legal qualification of the anticompetitive behaviour in this case which was 'restrictive agreements', taking into account the recent practice of the Commission and the ECJ. Since Adris and TDR held a dominant position and had very significant market power within the period under consideration (higher than 70%), and that the agreements that were concluded were an instrument whereby their sales policy was being executed, the Competition Agency held that the case had to be resolved as a case of the abuse of dominance within the meaning of Article 16 of the CA, which has 'identical content as Article 102 TFEU'.

729. Decision of the Croatian Competition Agency of 19 May 2011, *Competition Agency v. INA d.o.o.*, UP/I-030-02/2009-01/035, Official Gazette no. 79/2011, confirmed: Judgment of the High Administrative Court of the Republic of Croatia of 9 February 2012, *INA Industrija nafte d.d. v. Competition Agency*, Us-7153/2011-8.

730. Decision of the Croatian Competition Agency of 16 June 2011, *Competition Agency v. Adris grupa d.d. and TDR d.o.o.*, UP/I-030-02/2006-01/082, Official Gazette no. 103/2011; confirmed: Judgment of the High Administrative Court of the Republic of Croatia of 22 April 2015, *TDR d.o.o. i Adris grupa d.d. v. Competition Agency*, UsII-9222/2011-4.

479. The Competition Agency held that Adris and TDR incentivized their buyers to buy exclusively from them, whereby making access to the relevant market harder for TDR's competitors. The Competition Agency invoked the case law of the Court of Justice of the EU and the General Court to state that, within the meaning of Article 102 TFEU, the strategy of excluding competitors from the market has as its goal to prevent market access to competitors, and to prevent competitors' access to buyers.[731]

480. The Competition Agency invoked the position of the ECJ to state that the conduct of a dominant firm whereby its buyers are tied by agreements, even if this is demanded by buyers, to satisfy all or the majority of its needs for a certain product from the dominant firm, and in return they are granted a reward in the form of rebates, is an abuse of a dominant position pursuant to Article 102 TFEU.[732]

481. In another case, following a detailed legal and economic analysis, the Competition Agency found two forms of abuse: (1) a discriminatory rebate policy (Article 16(2)(3) of the CA); and (2) additional unfair trade conditions (Article 16(2)(1) of the CA).[733]

482. As regards the first form of abuse, the Competition Agency held that Proplin abused its dominant position in the market for the sale of liquefied gas in Croatia by enforcing a non-transparent and discriminatory rebate policy towards its buyers, thus applying dissimilar conditions to similar transactions with different undertakings, placing them thereby at a competitive disadvantage within the meaning of Article 16(1) and (2)(3) of the CA.

483. Proplin's rebate policy was not transparent: its rebate policy rules were not in the usual fashion accessible to its buyers, it was not publicly available, and it was not submitted to all buyers on the conclusion of the supply contract. The buyers were informed of the rebate policy orally, and only a selected number of them were informed: this depended on the state of the market, the supplied quantity, and if the buyer belonged to one of categories determined by Proplin's internal decision on the rebate policy. Some buyers had no information that rebates were available. Other buyers which were granted rebates were not able to check if the rebates granted were in accordance with Proplin's internal rules on rebates, and as a result there were some which were granted less rebate, and some which were granted more

731. Case 85/76 *Hoffmann La Roche v. Commission* ECLI:EU:C:1979:36, para. 91; Case C-62/86 AKZO *Chemie BV v. Commission* ECLI:EU:C:1991:286, para. 69; Case T-228/97 *Irish Sugar v. Commission* ECLI:EU:T:1999:246, para. 111.

732. Here several ECJ/CFI judgments were invoked: Case 85/76 *Hoffmann La Roche v. Commission* ECLI:EU:C:1979:36, para. 89; Case T-155/06 *Tomra Systems ASA et al. v. Commission* ECLI: EU:T:2010:370, para. 208.

733. Decision of the Croatian Competition Agency of 30 December 2009, *Sedam plin d.o.o. and Brala – trade d.o.o. v. Proplin d.o.o.*, UP/I-030-02/2006-01/41, Official Gazette no. 62/2009; confirmed: Judgment of the High Administrative Court of the Republic of Croatia of 19 December 2012, *Proplin d.o.o. v. Competition Agency*, Us-5086/2009-4, Official Gazette no. 11/2013.

rebate than stipulated in Proplin's internal rules, thereby resulting in dissimilar conditions regarding equal transactions with different firms.

484. The Competition Agency rejected Proplin's arguments that some buyers were denied a rebate due to non-compliance with a certain set of criteria; on the contrary, the Competition Agency found that some buyers were granted rebates without any regard to the set criteria, which was found to indicate that there was no uniform application of the rebate policy to all buyers.

485. The Competition Agency also found as discriminatory Proplin's rule whereby the company CEO was allowed to grant a special rebate to certain buyers, without any regard to the quantities purchased, in particular because its main goal was to prevent buyers switching to its competitors. This in effect meant that its purpose was to tie those buyers, that it has an impermissible restrictive effect on competition, and that it cannot be objectively justified since Proplin had other legal means at its disposal to protect its interests.

486. In addition, the Competition Agency found that the rule whereby Proplin could exceptionally grant a rebate to buyers of strategic importance, or if the quantities purchased went significantly above those determined by Proplin's internal rules, further contributed to the non-transparency of its rebate policy. It was neither clear what the notion of strategic importance meant, nor was the right to be granted special rebates or the concept of significantly large quantities clearly regulated.

487. The Competition Agency held that it is the right of any firm to try to gain as many buyers as possible through its actions, as well as to keep its existing buyers. Equally so, the dominant supplier has the right to protect its position in the market. However, because of its position in the market and its economic power, the dominant firm has special responsibility not to cause a distortion of competition by its conduct. In the same manner, the Competition Agency held that Proplin has the right to grant quantitative rebates or discounts to its buyers, but they have to be transparent and be available to any buyer, and/or any firm in the relevant market, under equal conditions. This obligation arises from its dominance in the relevant market, since the stronger the market position and the greater its economic strength, the bigger the danger that it will distort competition in that market.

488. Furthermore, the Competition Agency held that Proplin abused its dominant position in the relevant market by directly imposing unfair trade conditions on one of its buyers, which was additionally obliged to buy liquefied gas only from Proplin, otherwise its contract would be terminated. The Competition Agency held that this was a hardcore restriction of competition since the dominant supplier is not allowed to conclude a contract with an exclusivity element, i.e., oblige the buyer to buy exclusively from the dominant supplier and for the supplier in return to grant rebates as a reward. In this manner the buyer was limited in its choice of supply sources, and at the same time access to the market was prevented for Proplin's competitors.

489. In a case initiated by a transport truck company, a long-time user of Jadrolinija's maritime shipping services on its Split-Ancona route, the Competition Agency looked at Jadrolinija's pricing/discount schemes, and held that the initiative to start proceedings for abuse of dominance must be dismissed because its categorization of buyers for the purpose of granting discounts was not against competition rules and was grounded on objective criteria.[734]

490. The Competition Agency held that categorization of buyers or users was part of usual commercial practice within the framework of a rebate policy to compete on prices with competitors and to attract buyers and users of its products and/or services. Quantitative discounts were in general in compliance with competition rules, for their justification was in reducing production or distribution costs, and they resulted from savings arising from larger orders.

491. In the case at hand, Jadrolinija granted transport companies using their Split-Ancona route discounts as a certain percentage of the price. The right to a discount was not conditional, and all transport companies were granted discounts in the same manner in accordance with clearly set criteria, based on the frequency of journeys. Not all transport companies have the same need to use Jadrolinija's services on the Split-Ancona route, which was reflected in the cost Jadrolinija has to bear in providing this service to a particular company on this route. The higher the number of journeys, the higher the discount.

492. The Competition Agency cited the ECJ's judgment in *Portugal v. Commission* to state that 'it is in the essence of the quantitative discounts system that bigger buyers of a certain product or users of a service have the right to lower average unit price or higher average discounts than those offered to smaller buyers or users'.[735]

493. The Competition Agency found that another criterion for granting discounts – the payment method – was also justified by objective grounds, since the payment of a ticket in cash, by credit card or bank transfer, is executed within twenty-four hours of booking, and if payment is conducted by means of an order form, payment is made within fifteen days of an invoice being issued. Thus, the Competition Agency found a lower discount for payment with an order form to be reasonable because in such a case the risk concerning payment was greater.

494. In the *HUVEL v. HDS-ZAMP* case, the Competition Agency held that the discounts granted were discriminatory and that they had a negative effect on competition in the downstream market for the sale of products for which a reproduction fee for private or other own use was levied.[736] No evidence was submitted showing

734. Decision of the Croatian Competition Agency of 13 February 2014, *Competition Agency v. Jadrolinija*, UP/I-034-03/2013-01/045.

735. Case C-163/99 *Portugal v. Commission* ECLI:EU:C:2001:189.

736. Decision of the Croatian Competition Agency of 3 November 2009, *HUVEL v. HDS-ZAMP*, UP/I-030-02/2008-01/041, Official Gazette no. 9/2010, confirmed: Judgment of the High Administrative Court of the Republic of Croatia of 20 April 2012, *Hrvatsko društvo skladatelja v. Competition Agency*, Us-14370/2009-13.

also took into consideration that according to HAKOM, HT was processing regulatory decisions in a timely manner and was being proactive in dealing with a clogged up system for granting wholesale access.

501. Holding that the Competition Agency was not right to suspend the case and was obliged to adopt a substantive decision in this case, the High Administrative Court, apparently relying on an erroneous translation of Article 5(2) of the Regulation 1/2003, annulled the decision of the Agency in the *HT/H1* case.[741] The subsequent decision of the Competition Agency was annulled again with the High Administrative Court ordering retrial.[742] Finally, in its 2018 decision, the Competition Agency decided that HT did not breach Article 13 of the CA while deciding the proceedings against HT on the basis of Article 102 TFEU to be suspended.[743]

502. In the *AKD* case, the Competition Agency decided that the only undertaking in Croatia authorized to manufacture official national electronic ID cards and issue relevant certificates did not abuse its dominant position by refusing to supply the Singer.exe component of the middleware.[744] Relying on the Commission's Guidance on Enforcement Priorities in assessing whether all necessary criteria for finding an abusive refusal to deal were satisfied, the agency held that the supply of the refused input was not objectively necessary for operators to be able to compete effectively on the downstream market for intermediation in application of qualified electronic signatures, thus allowing the finding of no abusive conduct.

V. Price Squeeze

503. In the *B.net Hrvatska v. Hrvatski Telekom* case, the competitor of HT in the retail market claimed there was an abuse of a dominant position by a price squeeze, i.e., that HT, as a vertically integrated operator, was squeezing B.net's and other firms' profits in the downstream market by charging very high prices for leasing lines in the upstream market.[745]

504. B.net claimed that HT had a market share of around 90% in the upstream market, and that, because of the high prices of leasing county connection lines from

741. Judgment of the High Administrative Court of the Republic of Croatia of 16 October 2014, *H1 Telekom d.d. v. Competition Agency*, UsII-65/2014-9. For a more detailed discussion see *supra* para 221 *et seq*.
742. Decision of the Croatian Competition Agency of 17 December 2014, *Competition Agency v. Hrvatski Telekom d.d.*, UP/I-034-03/2013-01/007; Judgment of the High Administrative Court of the Republic of Croatia of 29 October 2015, *H1 Telekom d.d. v. Competition Agency*, UsII-8/15-10.
743. Decision of the Croatian Competition Agency of 14 November 2018, *Competition Agency v. Hrvatski Telekom d.d.*, UP/I-034-03/2013-01/007. For substantive points the Competition Agency largely relied on the decision of the European Commission of 22 June 2011 in the case Telekomunikacja Polska, COMP/39.525.
744. Decision of the Croatian Competition Agency of 3 March 2021, *Agencija za komercijalnu djelatnost*, UP/I-034-03/63-2021/023.
745. Decision of the Croatian Competition Agency of 31 August 2010, *B.net Hrvatska d.o.o. v. Hrvatski telekom d.d.*, Official Gazette no. 115/2010.

HT, it was forced to build an expensive 'head-end' station in each town in which it was providing its retail service. So, it never used HT's infrastructure in the first place, but in each town in which it provided its retail service (cable TV) it built a central station, since the cost was lower than the cost of leasing SDH and Metro-Ethernet lines; thus, there was no need to use HT's leased lines, and it only used that service to a very limited extent from other providers.

505. The Competition Agency rejected this claim, finding no abuse, and finding that the input for the provision of services in the downstream market, which was obtainable upstream, was not indispensable. The evidence for this was the fact that some competitors in the retail market were not leasing lines from HT for the provision of their service, and that apart from HT there were other firms leasing the lines, and that there were substitutes for the service of HT leased lines. Thus, the Competition Agency decided that leasing lines from HT was not an indispensable input to compete in the downstream market.

506. The agency concluded that B.net did not use HT's leased lines, but its own infrastructure. The same applied to most of its other competitors in the retail market; they used mainly their own infrastructure. However, those using leased lines were able to choose from several operators (HT, Odašiljači i veze, HEP, HŽ, and others). Thus, the Competition Agency held that all the criteria for finding a price squeeze were not met, since leased lines from HT were not an indispensable input for the provision of B.net's retail services in the downstream market.

Chapter 3. Concentrations

507. It is commonly known that mergers can be either horizontal or non-horizontal. In Croatia, there is no specialized secondary legislation distinguishing between these two types of mergers. However, it is generally recognized that horizontal mergers are those between actual or potential competitors,[746] while non-horizontal mergers appear in two main forms. They can be vertical mergers or conglomerate mergers. The distinction between vertical mergers and conglomerate mergers can be subtle.[747] Moreover, in practice, mergers may entail both horizontal and non-horizontal effects. This happens when the merging firms are not only in a vertical or conglomerate relationship but are also actual or potential competitors of each other in one or more of the relevant markets.[748]

508. Horizontal mergers generally create most competitive concerns since they involve actual or potential competitors. However, in a horizontal merger it is usually easier to demonstrate the likely anticompetitive effects linked to a horizontal merger because horizontal mergers result in the immediate removal of competitive constraint.[749] In this sense, a merger assessment in vertical and conglomerate mergers may be more challenging than the assessment of horizontal mergers because the competition authority must take into consideration not only the immediate anticompetitive effects, but also those operations which may produce anticompetitive impacts in the near or further future, such as the foreclosure of actual rivals or the possibility to engage in certain conduct, etc.

509. However, regardless of whether a merger is horizontal or is of another type, the equal assessment standard applies to all types of merger. In any case, the Competition Agency assesses whether the proposed concentration would significantly impede effective competition in the market and whether it is likely that a concentration would create or strengthen the dominant position of the undertakings involved. Differences in assessment with regard to horizontal and non-horizontal concentration may occur with regard to the level, quality, and type of evidence to prove the anticompetitive effect of a merger,[750] although the CA itself does not formally suggest any such difference.

746. Guidelines on the assessment of horizontal mergers under the Council regulation on the control of concentrations between undertakings, OJ C 31, 5.2.2004, 2, para. 5.
747. For instance, products may be supplied by some companies with the inputs already integrated (a vertical relationship), whereas other producers leave it to the customers to select and assemble the inputs themselves (a conglomerate relationship). Guidelines on the assessment of horizontal mergers under the Council regulation on the control of concentrations between undertakings, OJ C 31, 5.2.2004, 1, footnote 5.
748. Guidelines on the assessment of horizontal mergers under the Council regulation on the control of concentrations between undertakings, OJ C 31, 5.2.2004, 1, para. 7.
749. C.E. Mosso, *Non-horizontal Mergers: A European Perspective*, 31 Fordham International Law Journal, 1442, 1446 (2007).
750. For more, *see* ibid. *See also* E. Gippini Fournier & F. Castillo de La Torre, *Evidence, Proof and Judicial Review in EU Competition Law* (Elgar Competition Law and Practice, Cheltenham, UK, Northampton, USA, 2017).

§1. Horizontal Mergers

510. Most merger notifications in Croatia relate to horizontal mergers. Most are cleared in Phase I. Only a small number of horizontal mergers assessed by the Competition Agency have raised serious competition concerns and even those mergers were conditionally approved after the parties had agreed to take on commitments. So far, only one merger has been prohibited.[751] In that particular case, the Competition Agency first prohibited a concentration because of the significant increase of market share of the undertakings concerned. However, later it conditionally approved it, imposing a set of structural and behavioural remedies.[752]

511. Probably one of the most complex horizontal mergers in the Competition Agency's practice was the merger between Agrokor and Mercator.[753] Before the merger, both companies held retail networks on the whole territory of the Republic of Croatia. Already prior to the merger, Agrokor was the biggest Croatian retail company and the implementation of this concentration resulted in strengthening Agrokor's already strong market position in the territory of Croatia. Prior to the concentration, Agrokor, and its leading vertically integrated retail company Konzum, already had a market share of between 20–30% at the national level, with a market share of around 50% in Zagreb. It was expected that following the concentration Konzum's market share would increase by an additional 5–10%. Besides, the Competition Agency was particularly concerned about the increased asymmetry of the market as a consequence of the merger and the increase in purchasing power of Konzum towards suppliers. Therefore, in order to remove the negative effect of the concentration on the competition, the Competition Agency conditionally approved the proposed concentrations, obliging Agrokor to comply with very strict and comprehensive measures and conditions.[754]

512. Another factually complex and problematic concentration in the Competition Agency's practice was the proposed merger between Europapress Holding and Slobodna Dalmacija.[755] The assessment of this concentration was specific for a number of reasons. It was the first assessment of a concentration carried out by the Competition Agency in the privatization process.[756] The Competition Agency in this

751. Decision of the Croatian Competition Agency of 11 September 2001, *Zagrebačka banka d.d., UniCredito Italian S.p.A and Alianz d.d.*, UP/I-030-02/2001-01/87.

752. Decision of the Croatian Competition Agency of 30 October 2001, *Zagrebačka banka d.d., UniCredito Italian S.p.A and Alianz d.d.*, UP/I-030-02/01-01/87.

753. Decision of the Croatian Competition Agency of 24 March 2014, *Agrokor d.d. Zagreb and Mercator d.d. Ljubljana*, UP/I-034-03/2013-02/2008.

754. *See also* Competition Agency Press Release, *Concentration between Agrokor and Mercator Conditionally Approved* http://www.aztn.hr/koncentracija-agrokor-mercator-dobila-uvjetno-odobrenje/ (accessed 2 May 2018).

755. Competition Agency's case summary, *Europapress Holding d.o.o. Zagreb and Slobodna Dalmacija d.d. Split*, http://www.aztn.hr/uploads/documents/eng/documents/decision/TN/UPI-030-022004-01033.pdf (accessed 11 May 2018). For more details, *see* V. Butorac Malnar & J. Pecotić Kaufman, *Ocjena koncentracija poduzetnika po kriteriju opadajućeg poslovanja u doba recesije*, 61 Zbornik Pravnog fakulteta u Zagrebu 1253 (2011).

756. *Ibid.*

between Agrokor and Tisak.[765] Prior to the concentration, Tisak already had a dominant position in the wholesale press market on the territory of the Republic of Croatia and in the retail press market on the territories of the relevant countries, and it was a significant competitor in the markets for the wholesale and retail of tobacco products with a strong network of retail outlets.[766] Agrokor, on the contrary, was an undertaking in a dominant position with significant financial power. It had access to resources, connections with other undertakings, the ability to dictate market conditions from the demand and supply side, and the ability to exclude other competitors from the market, particularly due to the strong market power of Konzum, which it owned.[767] Prior to the concentration, Agrokor's market share in the retail press market was insignificant; however, based on the conducted analysis, the Competition Agency concluded that the proposed concentration would enable the Agrokor Group to include in its retail network kiosks as a new form of retail outlet, stretching its retail business to a new market segment. In this way, Agrokor would hold all forms of retail outlets, from small kiosks to big hypermarkets which would ultimately lead to the strengthening of the position of an already very strong undertaking. Thus, the concentration was declared conditionally compatible and a set of measures was imposed on Agrokor to eliminate the negative effects of the concentration.[768]

§3. Market/Product Extension Mergers

518. A market extension merger and a product extension merger do not have a standard definition but it is generally taken that a market extension merger involves firms that sell the same products but in separate markets, while a product extension merger concerns a merger between companies whose products are related to each other and that operate on the same market.[769] Companies involved in this type of merger are actually trying to gain product or market extension through the merger. A merger review in this area is controversial, as commentators and enforcement agencies disagree on the extent to which one can predict competitive harm resulting from such mergers.[770] An example of a market extension merger assessed by the Competition Agency was the merger between the Adria Media Group d.o.o. Belgrade from the Republic of Serbia which gained control over the undertaking Adria Media Zagreb d.o.o., originally a Croatian company. Both companies, prior to the concentration, were selling the same products, although in different geographic markets. With this merger, the undertaking Adria Media Group d.o.o. from the Republic of Serbia expanded its activity to the Croatian market.

---

765. Decision of the Croatian Competition Agency of 15 March 2007, *Agrokor d.d. Zagreb and Tisak d.d. Zagreb*, UP/I-030-02/2006-02/33.
766. *Agrokor d.d. Zagreb and Tisak d.d. Zagreb*, the Competition Agency's case summary, http://www.aztn.hr/uploads/documents/eng/documents/decision/TN/UPI-030-022006-02033.pdf (accessed 5 Jun. 2018).
767. *Ibid.*
768. *Ibid.*
769. ICN, Merger Guidelines Workbook, 12, para. 3.10 (2006) http://www.internationalcompetitionnetwork.org/uploads/library/doc321.pdf (accessed 18 May 2018).
770. *Ibid.*

§4. Pure Conglomerate Mergers

519. A pure conglomerate merger is a merger between firms that neither compete in the same market nor operate at different levels of the supply chain.[771] Thus, within this type of merger, it is not likely that there will be a significant increase of market share of the involved undertakings. However, this does not mean that it is not possible for a conglomerate merger to create anticompetitive effects by means of, for example, tying and bundling strategies.

520. A pure conglomerate merger assessed by the Competition Agency was the merger between Adris d.d. and Croatia osiguranje.[772] Given the fact that before the concentration Adris d.d. was not present in the insurance market at all and that there were no overlapping activities between Adris d.d. and Croatia osiguranje, the Competition Agency cleared the proposed concentration without opening Phase II, since the concentration in question did not raise any competition concern.

521. Another example is the concentration between Irikon d.o.o. and Radio Drava d.o.o., whereby Irikon d.o.o., a company whose main business activity is business consulting, gained control over Radio Drava d.o.o, a company whose main activity relates to radio broadcasting.[773]

§5. Joint Ventures

522. The regulatory framework for joint ventures has already been analysed in Part 1, Chapter 4, §8. As previously explained, the CA which is currently in force provides for an explicit distinction between a full function and partial function joint venture in the same way as is done in EU law. However, the rules on joint ventures in Croatian legislation have been changing in line with the merger control reform in the EU. Until 2013, the CA distinguished between concentrative and cooperative joint ventures. Only concentrative joint ventures constituted concentration, while cooperative joint ventures were considered as agreements between undertakings. Legislative changes by the CA 2009 introduced a new division of joint ventures, distinguishing between full function and non-full function joint ventures.[774]

523. The Competition Agency has assessed only a few joint ventures altogether.

771. Non-Horizontal Guidelines, para. 97.

772. Decision of the Croatian Competition Agency of 6 February 2014 *Adris grupa d.d., Rovinj and Croatia osiguranje d.d. Zagreb*, UP/I-034-03/2013-02/017.

773. Decision of the Croatian Competition Agency of 24 January 2013, *Irikon d.o.o., Koprivnica and Radio Drava d.o.o., Koprivnica*, UP/I-034-03/12-02/003.

774. The 2009 CA was aligned with the EU acquis, and joint ventures with coordinative effects are still deemed as concentrations of undertakings, but their coordination effects are analysed under the rules on restrictive agreements.

524. In one of these cases, Viro Tvornica šećera d.d. and Pfeifer & Langen KG,[775] the Competition Agency analysed if this was a concentrative or a coordinative joint venture. The parties claimed that the joint venture would be a fully functional entity in the market, it would be free to engage in trade with competitors, to buy sugar in the open market and sell it to other firms in the market, it would have its own management and staff, it would have its own means for performing its activities, it would also sell and distribute its parent companies' products in certain geographic markets, but that it would also sell and distribute products manufactured by other producers. Moreover, the parties claimed that it would be free to decide on issues relevant to its business, and would independently decide on its prices, business plans, quantities of products for sale and distribution, middle management appointments, etc. However, since the activities of the joint venture were mostly restricted to distributing or selling products manufactured by the parent companies, i.e., since the joint venture was to perform only one function of its parents (distribution, not manufacturing), the Competition Agency held that it was not a full function joint venture. In other words, the Competition Agency held that the joint venture was to 'coordinate distribution and other important business activities of its parents which manufacture the same products' and assessed it as an agreement between undertakings.

525. Following the above conclusion, the Competition Agency further analysed if the conditions for an exemption would be met. It held that the first two conditions prescribed by Article 8(2) of the CA had been met (technological development, benefits for consumers), but that the second two conditions were not met (first, the agreement contained restrictions which were not necessary to achieve its purpose, resulting in market division and price-fixing, and, second, the agreement resulted in the elimination of a significant part of the competition in the relevant market, notably, after two years Viro would not be able to independently sell its products either in the EU or in Croatia, and would be eliminated as a competitor to Pfeifer & Langen). Therefore, the Competition Agency held that the cumulative conditions for exemption had not been met.

526. As a result, the Competition Agency should have declared the agreement in this case null and void. However, the Competition Agency held that, since the start of the application of the agreement had been halted, pending the end of the antitrust proceedings, the individual exemption might be granted, subject to certain remedies and conditions. The undertakings agreed to delete hardcore restrictions from the agreement, following which the exemption was granted for a period of three years.[776]

775. Decision of the Croatian Competition Agency of 14 February 2008, *Viro Tvornica šećera d.d. and Pfeifer & Langen KG*, UP/I-030-02/2006-01/40, Official Gazette no. 43/2008, decision on individual exemption of an agreement, available at http://www.aztn.hr/odluke_arhiva.asp (accessed 16 Mar. 2018).

776. *See* the Annual Report of the Croatian Competition Agency for 2008, 8 (July 2008), http://www.aztn.hr/uploads/documents/eng/documents/AR/Annual_Report_of_the_Croatian_Competition_Agency_for_2008.pdf (accessed 25 Sep. 2018).

527. However, only a year and a half after the exemption decision, the Competition Agency revoked its exemption due to the changed circumstances in the market.[777] The circumstances were changed due to a merger between one of the joint venture parents (Viro d.d.) and another Croatian competitor and sugar manufacturer (Sladorana d.d.), which was allowed by the Competition Agency. One of the reasons for granting the individual exemption was the fact that the market share of Viro d.d. was falling, and the market share of Sladorana d.d., its competitor, was rising. However, since post-merger those two firms would have 40–50% of the market share in the relevant market of the sale of sugar, the Competition Agency held that the implementation of the merger might lead to the strengthening of the dominant position of Viro as regards its competitors, with potential negative effects on competition, since pursuant to the exempted agreement Viro would have an exclusive right to import sugar produced by Pfeifer & Langen, one of the leading German sugar manufacturers.

528. In 2010, the Competition Agency cleared the joint venture between Recro Ulaganja d.o.o. and M SAN ulaganja d.o.o.[778] which resulted in the creation of a new undertaking MR Servis d.o.o. which was under the joint control of the above undertakings. In this particular case, the Competition Agency held that the joint venture constituted a concentration. The Competition Council approved the concentration without initiating Phase II of the investigation. As a justification for the clearance decision, the Competition Agency said that the creation of a new economic operator in the market in the servicing of computer equipment, consumer electronics, and mobile phones would contribute to the strengthening of competition, the better positioning of service providers, and the lower prices of service providers.[779] More recently, in 2019 Competition Agency cleared the concentration where Viro Grupa and Tvornica šećera Osijek created and jointly controlled a new undertaking NewCo for the wholesales and for the production of white sugar.[780]

---

777. Case *Viro tvornica šećera d.d. Virovitica and Pfeifer & Langen, Germany*, no. UP/I-030-02/2006-01/40, annulment of individual exemption.
778. Decision of the Croatian Competition Agency of 25 March 2010, *Recro Ulaganja d.o.o. and M SAN ulaganja d.o.o.*, UP/I-030-02/2009-02/11.
779. *Ibid.*
780. Decision of the Croatian Competition Agency of 5 March 2019, *Viro Tvornica Šećera d.d., Zagreb i Tvornica Šećera Osijek d.o.o.*, UP/I 034-03/19-02/001.; See also, OECD, *Annual Report on Competition Policy Developments in Croatia,* DAF/COMP/AR(2020)43, 10 - 12 June 2019, available at https://one.oecd.org/document/DAF/COMP/AR(2020)43/en/pdf. (accessed 14 March 2022).

Part III. Administrative Procedure

Chapter 1. Administrative Investigations Before the Antitrust Authority

§1. Initiative

I. General Sector Inquiries

529. According to the CA, there are two types of sector inquires depending on their purpose. The first one, termed preliminary market investigation, is an investigative tool used by the Competition Agency with the aim of determining whether sufficient competition concerns exist in order to formally open infringement proceedings against a particular undertaking.[781] This type of inquiry is preceded by an initiative to open proceedings against a particular undertaking, which may be submitted by either a legal or natural person.[782] The preliminary market investigation performed by the Competition Agency serves as a basis for opening the infringement proceedings. Under Article 32(1) of the CA, the Competition Agency is empowered for that purpose to collect data and information from any person that may have certain knowledge contributing to the investigation. These may include legal and natural persons, professional associations or economic interest groups, associations of undertakings, consumers' associations, public administration authorities and local and regional self-government units.

530. Besides this preliminary market investigation, the Competition Agency regularly performs general sector inquires, i.e., 'market studies as research projects with the purpose of gaining an in-depth understanding of how particular sectors or markets work'.[783] This power of the Competition Agency is regulated by Article 32(14) of the CA, which does not specify any other related details. Sometimes, the results obtained during the sector inquiry may trigger the opening of a formal investigation against a particular undertaking. It may be observed that the Competition

781. Article 32(1).
782. Article 37(1).
783. Annual Report for 2016, 12, available at http://www.aztn.hr/ea/wp-content/uploads/2015/05/Summary-GI-2016-ENG.pdf (accessed 30 May 2018).

Agency regularly and successfully conducts sector inquiries. Depending on the structure and the competitive circumstance of particular markets, some inquiries are conducted on an ad hoc basis, while others are conducted on an annual basis. This is usual in dynamic and sensitive markets, such as retail groceries markets,[784] which have been monitored by the Competition Agency through sector inquiries for more than a decade.[785] In 2019, in addition to the mentioned grocery markets, the Competition Agency successfully performed a sector inquiry into the press publishing market, the insurance market, and the market inquiry into the provision of online hotel booking services in the Republic of Croatia.[786]

II. Ex Officio Investigations

531. Under the Croatian CA, every proceeding is conducted ex officio by the Competition Agency,[787] save a merger control proceeding, which is initiated by the parties through the notification procedure.[788] The Competition Agency may decide to open proceedings based on a formal complaint submitted by an undertaking,[789] on the ground of a preliminary market or sector inquiry, or any other information pointing to a potential competitive concern.[790] In all these cases, the Competition Agency has the power to decide whether or not to proceed with the formal opening of a procedure, the criteria being the likely impact on the market or the enforcement priorities of the Competition Agency. Because the proceeding conducted by the Competition Agency must be in the public interest, where the Competition Agency considers that the competitive concern does not significantly distort competition in the relevant market or where it finds that the case does not fall within its enforcement priorities, it may decide not to open proceedings.[791]

784. For a detailed analysis of the grocery retail market in Croatia, *see* J. Pecotić Kaufman, *Control of Mergers in the Grocery Retail Market in Croatia*, in *Challenges for the Trade of Central and Southeast Europe*, 95 (S. Renko, B. Knežević, eds., Emerald Group Publishing Limited, 2013).
785. Annual Report for 2020, English version, 12.
786. *Ibid*, 12.
787. Article 38 CA.
788. Article 38(3) CA. In the wording of this article, the Competition Agency may act on its own initiative where the parties to the concentration fail to notify the concentration, in the case of the withdrawal of or amendments to the decision on the concentration, and where it decides on the adoption of necessary measures after the implementation of the prohibited concentration.
789. Article 37 CA.
790. An excellent example of a proceeding being opened on account of information published in the daily press is the Decision of the Croatian Competition Agency of 17 March 2015, *Competition Agency v. Sokol Marić d.o.o. et al.*, UP/I-034-03/2014-01/002, confirmed: Judgment of the High Administrative Court of the Republic of Croatia of 22 April 2016, *Sokol Marić d.o.o. v. Competition Agency*, UsII-40/15-10 (and other cases), annulled: Judgment of the Constitutional Court of the Republic of Croatia of 1 February 2018, *Sokol Marić d.o.o.*, U-III-2791/2016 (and other cases).
791. Article 38(4) CA.

III. Complaints

532. Any legal or natural person[792] may initiate the opening of proceedings in writing in the form of either a request, proposal, notice or a complaint.[793] This is a formal initiative conferring certain procedural rights to the applicants, such as the right to request the delivery of the short form of the Statement of Objections,[794] the right to submit objections to it,[795] the right to be heard as a witness to the proceedings,[796] and, finally, the right to institute proceedings before the High Administrative Court against the Competition Agency if the latter decides not to open proceedings or renders a non-infringement decision.[797] The person submitting such a request must identify itself and substantiate the initiative by providing information on the basis of which it may be established against whom the initiative is being made: the facts of the case, the practice or circumstances which have led to the initiative, the relevant data and documents, and other evidence proving the allegations.[798]

533. The fact that an initiative has been submitted does not automatically mean that the Competition Agency will indeed open the proceedings. The decision of the Competition Agency depends on its assessment whether the conditions for formally initiating the infringement proceedings have been met and whether conducting such proceedings is in the public interest.[799] In order to decide, upon receipt of the initiative, the Competition Agency carries out a preliminary market inquiry by collecting information and notifications from the undertakings operating in that market.[800] If based on the information provided by the person who initiated the opening of proceedings and the data collected during the preliminary market inquiry the Competition Agency finds sufficient circumstantial evidence raising competition concerns that might have a substantial impact on the market, it will formally decide to open proceedings against the undertakings concerned.

534. The initiative may be submitted for the opening of proceedings for the alleged breach of both the CA and Articles 101 and 102 TFEU. In both cases, if the Competition Agency decides that there are no grounds for opening proceedings,[801] it is required to render a formal decision to that effect which may not be appealed,

792. Article 37(1) CA superfluously makes the precision that such an initiative is granted also to a professional association or an economic interest group, an association of undertakings, a consumers' association, the Government of the Republic of Croatia, central administration authorities, and local and regional self-government units.
793. Article 37(1) CA.
794. Article 37(4) CA.
795. Article 48(4) CA.
796. Article 37(4) CA.
797. Articles 38(8) and 47(5) CA.
798. Article 37(2) CA.
799. Article 38(4) and (5) CA.
800. Article 38(5) CA.
801. For example, where the European Commission or any competent national competition authority of the EU Member State carries out the proceeding in the same case or has already closed the proceeding in the same case (Art. 38(7) CA).

although the interested party may initiate an administrative dispute against the Competition Agency before the High Administrative Court of Croatia.[802]

535. In very specific cases, such as the one related to the initiative to start infringement proceedings against the Croatian Bar Association on account of its decision to impose an allegedly discriminatory entry fee for in-house lawyers, judges, etc. wanting to be admitted to the Bar, unlike trainees for the Bar which paid no fee, the Competition Agency held that it must dismiss any initiative if the body against which the initiative is submitted was authorized by law to self-regulate the profession.[803]

§2. Powers

I. Requests for Information

536. The right of the Competition Agency to request information, i.e., collect data, refers to all activities performed by the Competition Agency within the ambit of competition law, but is mostly exercised for the purposes of sector inquiries and individual infringement proceedings. The collection of data encompasses gathering all necessary information in the form of written and oral statements and documentation.[804] The submission of data may be requested from all interested persons – parties to the proceedings as well as any other undertaking, be it a legal or a natural person active on the market, including consumers' and professional associations, economic interest groups or associations of undertakings. Where necessary, data may be requested from public administration bodies and local or regional self-government units.[805] When requested for the submission of information, the addressees have to be informed in writing on the legal ground and the purpose of the request with a specified time limit for submission and the penalty clause in the case of non-compliance.[806] The request for information must be proportionate and not compel the parties to self-incrimination. [807]

537. When it comes to the parties to the proceedings, the Competition Agency has additional investigative tools to obtain data. The Competition Agency may request the parties to the proceedings to enable the inspection of:

802. Article 38(8) CA.
803. Decision of the Croatian Competition Agency of 11 February 2021, *Competition Agency v. Croatian Bar Association*, UP/I-034-03/20-01/020. However, the agency stated that it will publish in due course a new opinion, having in mind also the regulation in other EU Member States, on the conditions for exercising lawyers' services, especially the conditions for entry into the profession. The decision of the Agency in this case was confirmed by the judgment of the High Administrative Court of the Republic of Croatia of 16 June 2021, *Anonymous v. Competition Agency*, UsII-132/21-5.
804. Article 41(1)1 CA.
805. *Ibid.*
806. Article 41(2) CA.
807. Article 41 (3) CA.

- business premises;
- immovable and movable assets;
- business books;
- data bases; and
- other documentation.[808]

In addition, the Competition Agency may request the parties to carry out any other fact-finding activities.[809] This additional tool is very broadly worded so as to encompass any activity that the Competition Agency deems relevant and necessary to establish the facts of the case. This right gives wide discretionary power to the Competition Agency in determining fact-finding activities, while not jeopardizing the rights of the parties which are safeguarded by the general rules on administrative procedure.

538. In the cases of the above-listed announced inspections and data requests, the Competition Agency is not required to obtain a court order, which does not imply that the collaboration of the parties is voluntary. Quite the contrary, non-compliance represents an administrative offence subject to a fine, and the right of the Competition Agency to draw inferences from it.[810] The penalty for the failure to comply with any of the described requests of the Competition Agency differs significantly depending on whether it was committed by the parties to the proceedings or other persons, the penalty for the former case being much more rigorous. In the case of non-compliance with a request by the Competition Agency, parties to the proceedings may be fined up to 1% of their turnover in the preceding financial year,[811] while third persons may be fined from HRK 10,000 to a maximum of HRK 100,000 for non-compliance.[812]

539. The sanctioning takes place within the 'fines procedure' specifically opened and conducted in order to establish whether the grounds for imposing the fine have been met. The fines procedure resembles the infringement proceedings; it includes the issuing of a Statement of Objections and an oral hearing safeguarding the rights of the parties and the establishment of facts.[813] The parties may not appeal the decision imposing the fine; however, they may take actions against the Competition Agency before the High Administrative Court of the Republic of Croatia.[814]

Besides collecting data through written requests, the Competition Agency is empowered to conduct interviews to that end as well. By way of new Article 41.a CA the Competition Agency may summon for an interview any person who may possess information relevant for the infringement proceedings before it and may do so already in the investigative phase or after the formal opening of the infringement

808. Article 41(1)2 CA.
809. Article 41(1)3 CA.
810. Article 41(8) CA.
811. Article 62 CA.
812. Article 63 CA.
813. Article 41 (4) CA.
814. Article 41(5) CA.

proceeding. [815] It is important to stress out the proportionality requirement of the interview and the prohibition to compel the interviewees to admit an antitrust infringement.[816]

II. Investigating and Search Powers

540. Certainly the most effective and broad investigative power of the Competition Agency in the enforcement of national and EU competition rules is the right to conduct dawn raids and seize documents. The Competition Agency's competence to carry out dawn raids was introduced in as early as 2003; however, this valuable tool had not been used up until 2014 when the Competition Agency finally managed to obtain the necessary digital forensic equipment and train its staff to use it.[817]

541. A dawn raid is an exceptional investigative tool authorizing the Competition Agency to conduct unannounced on-the-spot inspections of business premises, land, and means of transport, to seal any business premises or records and to temporarily seize the evidence related to a competition law infringement found there. More specifically, as long as they obey the proportionality requirement and do not force to self-incrimination,[818] authorized persons are empowered to:

- enter and inspect any premises, land, and means of transport in any location where the undertaking under investigation performs its business activities,[819] including private premises of the members of the board and staff or third persons, in which case two witnesses must be present;[820] and
- examine the business books and other business records and take or obtain copies thereof irrespective of the means by which they are stored (such as computers, servers, telephone equipment, etc.). [821]

With the IT forensic unit and equipment, the Competition Agency may download content on the spot, or may perform more detailed analysis upon seizure:

- temporarily seize the necessary documentation;
- seal any premises, books or records during the inspection;
- ask any representative or member of staff of the undertaking concerned for oral or written explanations about fact or documents related to the dawn raid; and

815. Article 41.a (1) CA.
816. Article 41.a (2) CA.
817. Summary of the Annual Report of the Croatian Competition Agency for 2014, available at http://www.aztn.hr/ea/wp-content/uploads/2015/05/Annual-Report-of-the-Croatian-Competition-Agency-for-2014.pdf (accessed 20 Jul. 2017).
818. Article 42 (9) CA.
819. Article 42 (6) CA.
820. Article 44 CA.
821. Article 42 (6) CA.

– perform any other actions in accordance with the purpose of the inspection.[822]

Here again, just as it is the case with the announced inspections, the broad wording gives the Competition Agency room for accommodating the needs of the inspection as it sees fit.

542. It is important to stress that written communication with legal representatives are exempted from the investigation to the extent they constitute confidential or privileged information. The CA neither defines what constitutes privileged or confidential information nor does it delimit its scope. Instead, it refers to legal acts regulating the duty of legal professional confidentiality, i.e., the Legal Profession Act[823] which contains only one, very wide and general rule on the duty of legal professional confidentiality. Article 13 provides that an attorney is obliged to keep confidential any information he or she was entrusted with by his or her client or has otherwise learned in the course of representing the client. While this duty extends to all employees of the law firm, it does not cover in-house lawyers, which is very important when it comes to dawn raids. The same situation applies under the autonomous interpretation of the principle of legal professional privilege given by the ECJ in *Akzo* [824] concerning investigations conducted by the Commission under Regulation 1/2003.

543. From the perspective of the Legal Profession Act, it is irrelevant whether the information obtained is confidential or not, as all the information learned in the course of representing a client is covered by the duty of confidentiality, and an attorney may use it only for the benefit of his or her client.[825] However, from the perspective of the CA, it is the confidential nature of the information that qualifies it for exemption from seizure. According to Article 45(2) and (3) of the CA, when the undertaking concerned or its legal representative refuses to hand down documents on the ground that it contains confidential or privileged information, the Competition Agency is allowed to inspect the document and if it disagrees, the documents must be sealed and signed by the parties and their representatives. The privileged character of a such documents is decided upon later, by the application of the General Administrative Procedure Act related to prejudicial questions.[826] This legislative solution is problematic when it comes to documents indeed containing privileged information. Even though such information will not be admissible as evidence in the proceedings, the fact remains that the authorized person from the Competition Agency came to know of such information and may be influenced by its content. However, this should be seen as a necessary collateral meant to prevent the misuse of exemption from the inspection of confidential and privileged information.

822. Article 42(6) CA.
823. Legal Profession Act, Official Gazette nos 9/1994, 117/2008, 50/2009, 75/2009, 18/2011, 126/21.
824. Case C-550/07 P *Akzo Nobel Chemicals Ltd and Akcros Chemicals Ltd v. European Commission* ECLI:EU:C:2010:512.
825. Article 7 (2) of the Legal Profession Act.
826. Article 45 CA.

544. The Competition Agency interprets very strictly the rules on the protection of privileged information. According to the interpretation of the Competition Agency in the case *Gorenje*,[827] this provision can come into play only when there is an actual disagreement between the parties and Competition Agency officials related to the confidential nature of a particular document.[828] The request for the protection of privileged information of a general nature covering any correspondence, notices, and other communication with an attorney, as made by Gorenje, was found inadequate for that purpose.[829] This approach applied irrespective of the fact that during the dawn raid the entire hard disc of computers was copied and seized for later analysis and thus the parties submitted a general request for the protection of privileged information. The fact that the parties did not object to this type of document harvesting and neither specified pieces of documents they considered to be covered by attorney-client privilege at the moment of seizure nor in subsequent objections to the inspection report, was interpreted as no disagreement triggering the procedure foreseen by Article 45(2) and (3) of the CA.[830]

545. Dawn raids may be performed only in situations when it may be reasonably assumed that the evidence related to the investigated competition law infringement is kept there and may be destroyed, concealed, replaced, or altered.[831] Unlike announced inspections, dawn raids may be performed only upon a court order of the High Administrative Court of the Republic of Croatia, which may not be appealed.[832] Given that the premises subject to dawn raids may be located in jurisdictional areas of different administrative courts, the exclusive jurisdiction of the High Administrative Court over such orders is consistent with the principle of procedural economic efficiency and urgency, especially given the shortness of time for decision-making.[833] In fact, the High Administrative Court must react very quickly upon receiving the request from the Competition Agency in order not to jeopardize the planned inspection. Article 42(2) of the CA specifies that the decision on whether to grant the order must be rendered within two days from the receipt of the request. If granted, the court order must specify the legal ground for the inspection, the authorized persons, and the time limit of its performance.[834] Here again, a valuable interpretation was given in the *Gorenje* case, where the Competition Agency

827. Decision of the Croatian Competition Agency of 20 December 2016, *Competition Agency v. Gorenje Zagreb*, UP/I-034-03/13-01/035.
828. Article 46(4) CA reads: 'The parties to the proceedings and persons who were subject to the inspection may provide their written comments on the inspection report within fifteen days from the day of the receipt of the inspection report.'
829. The concrete request for privileged information of Gorenje covered 'all letters, notices, and other forms of communication, including but not limited to emails, no matter in which field ("from", "to", "cc" or "bcc") the address of any of the party's lawyers is indicated; attachments to email messages, documents stored in digital form and originating from or intended for the lawyers of Gorenje Zagreb'.
830. Decision of the Croatian Competition Agency of 20 December 2016, *Competition Agency v. Gorenje*, UP/I-034-03/13-01/035, Official Gazette no. 26/2017.
831. Article 42(1) CA.
832. Article 42 CA.
833. L. Rostaš-Beroš, *Nadležnost upravnih sudova u zaštiti tržišnog natjecanja*, 35 Zbornik Pravnog fakulteta Sveučilišta u Rijeci 345, 351 (2014).
834. Article 42(2)(2) CA.

explained that the deadline specified in the court order relates to carrying out the inspection, i.e., seizing and/or copying the documentation, and not to reviewing the documents seized. The latter is not time restricted, either by some statutory deadline or by the order itself.[835]

546. The same procedure applies when the dawn raid is planned upon the request of the Commission or a competition authority from another Member State, in which case they are assisted by designated persons from the Competition Agency. In either situation, if the dawn raid is resisted, the authorized persons may be assisted by the police in order to perform the inspection.[836] Beyond these rules contained in the CA, the procedure and extent of the investigating powers of the Commission are regulated by Regulation 1/2003 directly applicable in the Croatian legal order.

547. The CA fails to specify the extent of court review in deciding on the requests for a dawn raid made by the Competition Agency. However, it is our opinion that being a full jurisdiction court, the High Administrative Court is competent to review both the legality and the proportionality of the request for a dawn raid. Its review is, however, much more limited when the court order for a dawn raid is requested on behalf of the EU Commission. In that situation, the High Administrative Court would not be competent to review the legality of the request, as only EU courts are eligible to decide on the legality of Commission decisions. According to Article 20(8) of Regulation 1/2003, the High Administrative Court, as a nationally appointed competent court, could only control whether the Commission decision:

> is authentic and that the coercive measures envisaged are neither arbitrary nor excessive having regard to the subject matter of the inspection. In its control of the proportionality of the coercive measures, the national judicial authority may ask the Commission, directly or through the Member State competition authority, for detailed explanations in particular on the grounds the Commission has for suspecting infringement of Arts 81 and 82 of the Treaty, as well as on the seriousness of the suspected infringement and on the nature of the involvement of the undertaking concerned. However, the national judicial authority may not call into question the necessity for the inspection nor demand that it be provided with the information in the Commission's file. The lawfulness of the Commission decision shall be subject to review only by the Court of Justice.[837]

548. If either the party to the proceeding or a third party obstructs the enforcement of the dawn raid court order, they may be fined up to 1% of their turnover in the preceding financial year.[838]

---

835. Decision of the Croatian Competition Agency of 20 December 2016, *Competition Agency v. Gorenje*, UP/I-034-03/13-01/035, Official Gazette no. 26/2017.
836. Article 42(4) CA.
837. Article 20(8) of Regulation 1/2003.
838. Article 62(4) CA.

III. Cooperation with Other State Institutions

549. In the course of its activities, the Competition Agency regularly cooperates with competent judicial, regulatory, and other authorities.[839] For instance, upon the written request of the Competition Agency, the police will, free of charge, assist it in the conduct of dawn raids and seizure of objects.[840] Likewise, any state institution or authority will upon the written request of the Competition Agency provide it with all requested data and documentation.[841] Cooperation with commercial courts is also of relevance, as those are the courts competent to apply Articles 101 and 102 TFEU. In order to preserve the uniformity of application of EU rules, whenever commercial courts conduct such proceedings they are obliged to inform the Competition Agency of them and to share any opinion obtained by the EU Commission during such proceedings.[842] The Competition Agency also has the right to submit non-binding opinions to the competent courts in relation to the competition law matters before it, and such opinions have to be shared with the parties.[843] The cooperation described is intense and very important for the efficient enforcement of competition rules.

550. The cooperation with other bodies extends to competition authorities of other EU Member States as well. As a means of assisting them with their investigative measures, the Competition Agency is allowed to carry out an inspection or other fact-finding measures, such as interviews or collection of data on their behalf.[844] For that purpose, the CA envisages mutual exchange of information which may be later used as evidence.[845] In addition, the Competition Agency upon request of another NCA helps notifying the undertakings concerned on relevant procedural aspects related to the application of Article 101 and/or 102 TFEU.[846]

§3. Right of Defence

551. The proceedings before the Competition Agency are regulated by the CA as *lex specialis*, the general rules of the General Administrative Procedure Act as *lex generalis*,. The right to defence is secured through the application of these acts and may take various forms, as discussed below. The extent of the procedural rights granted depends on the procedural status of the person concerned. Article 36 of the CA stipulates that parties to the proceedings are only the persons against whom the Competition Agency is carrying out a proceeding within its competence. This does not imply that other interested parties do not have any procedural rights. On the contrary, besides the parties who have the widest procedural rights, the Competition

839. Article 66(1) CA.
840. Article 66(2) CA.
841. Article 66(3) CA.
842. Article 66a (1) and (2) CA.
843. Article 66a (4) and (5) CA.
844. Article 66 (4) CA.
845. Article 66 (5) CA.
846. Article 66 (6) CA.

Agency recognizes an entire list of procedural rights for a person upon whose initiative the proceeding has been formally opened, as well as other persons whose rights and interests are being decided upon by the Competition Agency.[847]

I. Content and Notification of Opening Decisions

552. Before formally initiating proceedings, the Competition Agency conducts a preliminary market investigation or takes other measures necessary to establish if it is in the public interest to carry out proceedings. Once the Competition Agency is sufficiently satisfied that the identified competition concerns may substantially distort competition, the Competition Agency is obliged to render a procedural order by which it officially initiates proceedings against one or more undertakings. Such an order must contain at least the following information:

- reference to the case;
- the legal ground (under the CA or Articles 101 and 102 TFEU);
- a description of the facts, practices, or circumstances which led to the initiation of the proceedings; and
- a request for the delivery of data and documentation.[848]

553. The described procedural order is final; it may neither be appealed nor may an administrative dispute be initiated against it before the High Administrative Court.[849] The party to the infringement proceedings is provided with a copy of the procedural order,[850] while the initiator of the proceedings is informed about it by way of a written notification.[851]

II. Proceedings: Hearings, Access to File, Briefs

554. The right of defence of the parties is secured throughout the competition proceedings. At the very opening of the proceedings, prior to the issuing of the Statement of Objections, the parties are notified about the facts which led to the opening of proceedings and are given the opportunity to respond. In fact, by the wording of Article 40 of the CA, once the proceedings start, the Competition Agency sets a time limit, which may range from eight to a maximum of thirty days,[852] for the party to the proceedings to respond and deliver the requested data and documents.[853] In order to secure compliance with the request for the delivery of data, the CA envisages that whenever a party fails to act in a timely manner upon

847. Article 36 CA.
848. Article 39(1) CA.
849. Article 39(2) CA.
850. Article 40(1) CA.
851. Article 40(6) CA.
852. On the ground of Art. 40(4), this deadline may exceptionally, for justified reasons, be extended by the Competition Agency upon the request by the party for up to an additional thirty days.
853. Article 40(2) and (3) CA.

such a request, the Competition Agency has the right to establish the facts and circumstances of the case on its own initiative, based on its own findings, the available data, and documentation. In such a case, the Competition Agency issues the Statement of Objections without delay and sets the oral hearing.[854]

555. At this initial stage of the proceedings, prior to the issuing of the Statement of Objections, the parties are allowed to propose commitments aimed at restoring healthy competition in the market.[855] Should this be the case, the parties will submit a written brief to that effect, upon which it is likely that they will continue to communicate in a less formal way with the Competition Agency in order to achieve the best possible result.

556. In order to be able to defend themselves properly, the parties must have access to the file of the Competition Agency. The right of access to the file is regulated by Article 47 of the CA, which sets the basic rule that parties to the proceedings have the right to access the file upon their written request, after the receipt of the Statement of Objections.[856] Access to the file is usually granted within fifteen days of the request[857] and covers the entire material contained therein except the internal documents of the Competition Agency, such as drafts of decisions, official statements and notes, correspondence and information exchanges with the EU Commission or other NCAs. The latter may not be copied or inspected. [858]

557. As mentioned earlier, the right of access to the file is not limited to the parties to the proceedings. Under certain, more restrictive circumstances, such a right is granted to persons who initiated the opening of the antitrust proceedings and to other interested persons who have been granted the same status.[859] They may be granted access to the file in situations only where the Competition Agency has reached a decision not to open proceedings, or where it has reached a non-infringement decision.

CA amendments from 2021 introduced detailed rules on the right to access leniency statements and settlement submissions. In principle, those documents are shielded from discovery save at the request of the parties to whom these documents relate and only insofar as they are necessary for them to exercise their right to defence either in that proceedings[860] or in proceedings before the High Administrative Court related to the allocation of fine between cartelists, or the review of the Competition Agency's decision.[861] This regulatory solution is extremely important in order to preserve the efficiency of the leniency programme and settlement procedure as the main procedural means in the fight against cartels. For that reason, even if obtained by the party, some information is temporarily prevented from being

854. Article 40(5) CA.
855. Article 49 (1) CA.
856. Article 47(1) and (2) CA.
857. Article 47(3) CA.
858. Article 47(4) CA.
859. Under Art. 36(3) CA.
860. Article 47.a (1) CA.
861. Article 47.a (2) CA.

used in proceedings before the High Administrative Court if this may jeopardize the ongoing proceeding before the Competition Agency. The former relates particular to information prepared for the purpose of the proceedings before the Competition Agency by persons other than the parties; information drawn up and in the course of proceedings by the Competition Agency; and withdrawn settlement submissions.[862] Finally, any exchange of information contained in leniency statements and settlement submissions may be exchanged between the competition authorities only in accordance with rules set out in Article 12 of the Regulation 1/2003.[863]

III. Statement of Objections

558. The Statement of Objections comes half way through the proceedings, where the Competition Agency informs the parties about the facts that it has preliminarily established, for the purpose of giving them the right to express their views on all the relevant facts and circumstances of the case even before the oral hearing has been set.[864]

559. At this stage of proceedings, the parties are allowed to submit written replies[865] in which they may present additional evidence and propose other witnesses.[866] The time limits for replies to the Statement of Objection is set at thirty days,[867] which is considered adequate to guarantee the parties sufficient time to prepare their defence. As mentioned earlier, even the applicants upon whose initiative the procedure has been opened and interested persons granted the same status receive the short, non-confidential version of the Statement of Objection, against which they may submit written replies as well.[868]

560. It is very important to stress that after issuing the Statement of Objections and receiving the replies from the parties, the Competition Agency may decide to carry out new analyses and establish new facts or examine evidence. In this case, the Competition Agency is obliged to issue a new Statement of Objections and notify the parties about it, which triggers another sequence of replies.[869] This mechanism is very effective in safeguarding the right of defence of the parties, representing an expression of the statutory rule according to which the Competition Agency may not base its decisions on facts and circumstances in respect of which the parties to the proceedings have not been granted the right of defence.[870]

862. Article 47.a (3) CA.
863. Article 47.a (4) CA.
864. Article 48(1) CA.
865. Article 48(2) CA.
866. Article 48(3) CA.
867. Article 48(2) CA.
868. Article 48(4) and (5) CA.
869. Article 48(6) CA.
870. Article 48(7) CA.

561. The CA regulates the mandatory content of the Statement of objections which is very important for the achievement of legal certainty of the parties involved and the exercise of their right to defence. Besides the elementary information about the persons involved in the infringement and the preliminary defined relevant market, the Statement of objections must include as well the time, place, and the duration of the suspected infringement and the detailed description of the facts that led to that conclusion. In addition, the Statement of objections must specify which competition rule is thought to be thereby violated and indicate the relevant provision for the calculation of the fine. Most important, as already stated, the parties must be invited to present any additional evidence and witnesses and submit their defence. The latter may be done in writing within a month from the receipt of the Statement of Objections.[871]

IV. Final Hearing and Decision

562. The final, oral hearing is the central procedural mechanism before the Competition Agency securing the right of defence. As mentioned earlier, prior to the 2021 amendments to the CA, its former + Article 35, specified that the form and content of the notice of the hearing, the course of the main hearing, the appearance of the parties and third persons at the main hearing, and the minutes of the main hearing were regulated by the rules of the Misdemeanour Act.

563. This combined legislative solution was derived from the fact that for a long time competition law infringements were considered to be misdemeanour offences and were sanctioned by the competent misdemeanour court. Once the Competition Agency has gained power to fine infringing undertakings, it was considered necessary to retain the rules on the oral hearing related to misdemeanour offences in order to preserve and safeguard the right of defence of the parties. This regulatory setting changed with the 2021 amendments to the CA, which no longer references the Misdemeanour Act. This change however did not negatively reflect upon the rights of the parties, as will be described below.

564. As a rule, the oral hearing is closed to the public in order to protect business secrets and other confidential information.[872] During proceedings, besides the parties, the person who initiated the proceedings may be summoned to the oral hearing either on his or her own request or by a decision of the Competition Agency.[873]

565. The Competition Agency sets the oral hearing upon the expiry of the deadline for the written defence in response to the Statement of objections, so as to ensure that the parties have the opportunity to present evidence and that all relevant circumstances are taken into account, such as mitigating and aggravating circumstances concerning the infringement, and other criteria necessary for setting a

871. Article 48 (8) CA.
872. Article 50(1) CA.
873. Article 50(2) CA.

fine.[874] Following the experiences with the pandemic, the CA introduced the possibility to conduct the oral hearing electronically in case of extraordinary circumstances.[875]

566. The oral hearing may be rescheduled once in cases where the summoned parties or their lawyers fail to appear. However, this right is granted only once. If the same happens in the rescheduled hearing, it will not be postponed again, but instead the Competition Agency will conduct it with the parties who are present and make its decision on the basis of its own findings and the available data and information.[876] Once the final hearing is closed, the Council of the Competition Agency deliberates and reaches its decision on the merits and the appropriate fine or/and the daily penalty.[877] Pursuant to the decision of the Council, the Competition Agency closes the proceeding by issuing a single decision on the merits and the fine[878] with specified deadlines and methods of enforcement if applicable.[879]

874. Article 52(1) CA.
875. Article 52 (2) and (3) CA.
876. Article 50(3) CA.
877. Article 52 (4) CA.
878. Article 52 85) CA.
879. Within the meaning of Article 30 (1)CA.

Chapter 2. Voluntary Notifications and Clearance Decision & Merger Control

567. The control of mergers is one of the basic pillars of the competition law system, along with antitrust rules and abuse of dominance.[880] Generally, there are two basic models of merger control systems, *ex ante,* which is based on mandatory pre-merger notification, and *ex post*, or a voluntary merger control regime which allows parties to implement the transaction in advance of having applied for and received merger clearance.[881] Croatia, like the majority of other merger jurisdictions in Europe, has an *ex ante* mandatory merger control system.[882]

§1. Preliminary Filing Obligations

568. A mandatory pre-merger notification (prior notification) system was introduced in Croatia with the first CA in 1995. Accordingly, parties of a merger are obliged to notify the Competition Agency about the planned transactions. There is no specific deadline for making a filing. Notification must be submitted before the implementation of the concentration in question, following the conclusion of a contract on the basis of which control or a decisive influence has been acquired by the controlling undertaking, or following the publication of the invitation to tender which gives rise to a change in control or decisive influence over undertaking or of a part of it.[883] All undertaking parties to the concentration submit one joint notification. However, in the case where control or a decisive influence is acquired over a whole or part of one or more undertakings by another undertaking, it is the duty of the controlling undertaking to submit the prior notification to the Competition Agency.[884]

569. The CA also provides for the possibility of prior notification. Prior notification is permitted if the undertakings that are parties to the concentration, bona fide, provide evidence to the Competition Agency of the proposed conclusion of the contract or announce an invitation to tender which will give rise to control over previously independent undertaking or a part of it.[885] Prior notification is possible for a simplified procedure and for a regular assessment procedure.[886]

880. UNCTAD, Trade and Development Board, Challenges in design of merger control regime for young and small competition authorities, 26 April 2017, Geneva, TD/B/C.I/CLP/45 http://unctad.org/meetings/en/SessionalDocuments/ciclpd45_en.pdf (accessed 25 Sep. 2018).
881. *Ibid.*
882. Articles 15–24 of the Competition Act 2009. The UK, for example, has a voluntary merger control system.
883. Article 19(3) CA.
884. Article 19(2) CA.
885. Article 6(2) of the Regulation on the Notification and Assessment of Concentrations.
886. Articles 4 and 6 of the Regulation on the Notification and Assessment of Concentrations.

570. However, unlike EU law, Croatian legislation does not explicitly regulate the pre-notification process,[887] but it is the practice of the agency to allow pre-notification meetings provided a written claim of the parties to the concentration has been submitted to the Competition Agency.

571. Notification must be made on the Notification Form which is a constituent part of the Regulation on Notification and Assessment of Concentrations,[888] and it should be submitted in Croatian. Along with the Notification Form, undertakings must submit the following documents: (1) the original or a certified copy of the document, or a certified translation, showing the legal grounds for the concentration if the original official text is not originally written in Croatian; (2) annual financial statements of the parties to the concentration for the financial year preceding the concentration; (3) other documents and data which the Competition Agency finds necessary for the assessment of the effects of the concentration concerned.[889]

572. Apart from this compulsory content of the notification, the notifying party or parties may submit to the Competition Agency any data or document which they find relevant for the assessment of the concentration. This particularly refers to those documents which support the parties' statement about the positive effects of the proposed concentration for competition since the burden of proof of the positive effects of the concentration lies with the parties to the concentration.[890] On the contrary, upon the request of the parties to the concentration, the Competition Agency may in particularly justified cases release the parties of the concentration from submitting some documents if it finds that the documents or information in question are not necessary for the assessment of the concentration concerned.[891]

573. Where the parties to the concentration fail to notify the concentration to the Competition Agency, the Competition Agency may act on its own and initiate an assessment procedure.[892]

574. The CA also provides rules on a simplified procedure for situations where it is unlikely that the concentration will raise competition concerns. In such cases, the parties to the concentration can submit a short-form notification.

575. A simplified procedure is introduced in the merger control system in Croatia by the CA 2009. A short-form notification and the so-called simplified procedure may be used if at least one of the following conditions are met:

887. DG Competition Best Practices on the Conduct of EC Merger Control Proceedings, available at http://ec.europa.eu/competition/mergers/legislation/proceedings.pdf (accessed 25 Sep. 2018).
888. Regulation on Notification and Assessment of Concentrations. Appendix 1, Standard Notification Form, 12-26.
889. Article 20 CA and Art. 5(6) of the Regulation on Notification and Assessment of Concentrations.
890. Article 5(6) of the Regulation on Notification and Assessment of Concentrations.
891. Article 20(2) CA.
892. Article 38(2) CA.

(1) if there is no horizontal overlap between the parties to the concentration and if there is no vertical relationship between the parties to the concentration in the market which is upstream or downstream of a market in which another party to the concentration is engaged;
(2) if two or more of the parties to the concentration are engaged in business activities in the same relevant product and geographic market (horizontal relationship), provided that their combined market share is less than 20%, and/or when one or more of the parties to the concentration are engaged in business activities in a relevant product market which is upstream or downstream of a product market in which any party to the concentration is engaged (vertical relationship), provided that none of their individual or combined market share at either level is 30% or more;
(3) if a party to the concentration is to acquire sole control of an undertaking over which it already has joint control; or
(4) in the case where two or more undertakings acquire control over a joint venture, where the joint venture has no, or negligible, actual or foreseen activities within the Republic of Croatia.[893]

Notwithstanding the above, if the Competition Agency finds that there are substantial indications that the proposed concentration will raise competition concerns, it may decide that no simplified procedure treatment is applicable. In such a case, it may require that a full notification of the concentration be made.[894]

576. Notification of the concentration to the Competition Agency has a suspensive effect. The parties to the concentration are prohibited from implementing a concentration until a clearance decision by the Competition Agency is obtained.[895]

577. According to Article 19(5) and Article 22(1) of the CA, if the Competition Agency within thirty days does not open Phase II of the investigation, it will be considered that that concentration is cleared. On the contrary, if the Competition Agency within thirty days following the receipt of a complete notification initiates Phase II of the investigation procedure, the parties to the concentration cannot implement the concentration until the Competition Agency issues a decision allowing the notified concentration.[896]

578. Exceptionally, the Competition Agency may, in duly justified cases, on the request of the parties to the concentration, grant the implementation of certain operations relating to the implementation of the notified concentration before the expiry of thirty days or before the delivery of the decision by which the Competition Agency allows the implementation of the concentration.[897] Such a situation

893. Article 20(4) CA.
894. Article 20(5) CA.
895. Article 19(5) CA and Art. 7 of the Regulation on Notification and Assessment of Concentrations.
896. Article 20(4) CA.
897. Article 19(6) CA and Art. 7(2) of the Regulation on Notification and Assessment of Concentrations.

occurred in the concentration between Agrokor and Mlinar.[898] During the course of the assessment procedure, Agrokor came before the Competition Agency with the request to hold a Shareholders' General Assembly in order to appoint new members of the Supervisory Board. Since some members of the 'old' Supervisory Board resigned their position after Agrokor announced a public bid, the company in this case was prevented from functioning normally. Therefore, in order to ensure the normal functioning of Mlinar, the Competition Agency, despite the general prohibition to undertake any operation during the assessment procedure, approved this request, finding it justified and necessary.[899]

579. However, as noted above, the implementation of a concentration before a clearance decision happens only in rare and exceptional cases. If the parties to a concentration implement the concentration before the Competition Agency's decision, or if they implement the concentration contrary to the decision of the Competition Agency by which the concentration has been assessed as incompatible, or if they implement the concentration without notifying the Competition Agency, although the notification was obligatory, the Competition Agency will, ex officio, by means of a separate decision, propose all necessary measures, whether behavioural or structural, aimed at restoring efficient competition in the relevant market, and set the deadlines for their adoption.[900] The Competition Agency may in particular: (a) order the shares and interest acquired to be transferred or divested; (b) prohibit or restrict the exercise of voting rights related to the shares or interest in the undertakings that are parties to the concentration or impose a discontinuation of the joint venture.[901] In the same decision, the Competition Agency will also set an appropriate fine on the undertakings concerned for the committed infringements.[902]

I. Criteria and Thresholds

580. As in most other European jurisdictions, the CA prescribes two commonly used jurisdictional thresholds that determine whether any given transaction is subject to a merger review and notification requirements.[903] The first concerns the transactions that are subject to merger control.[904] The second concerns notification thresholds, which refer to the size of the transaction or the parties.[905]

898. Decision of the Croatian Competition Agency of 29 December 2009, *Agrokor d.d., Zagreb and Mlinar d.d. Križevci*, UP/I-030-02/2008-02/44.
899. *Ibid*, 9.
900. Article 24(1) CA.
901. Article 24(2) CA.
902. Article 24(3) CA.
903. Definition of Transaction for the Purpose of Merger Control Review, OECD, DAF/COMP(2013)25, 8, available at http://www.oecd.org/daf/competition/Merger-control-review-2013.pdf (accessed 13 Apr. 2018).
904. For more information, *see* Ch. 7, *infra*.
905. *Ibid*.

581. The optimal merger threshold for that particular jurisdiction is always a purely jurisdictional issue.[906] The Croatian CA prescribes that subject to notification are concentrations where:

(1) the combined aggregate worldwide turnover for all the undertakings concerned (arising from the sales of goods or services in the financial year preceding the concentration) is HRK 1 billion (approx. EUR 1,360,600,000), provided that at least one party to the concentration has a registered seat or a branch office in the Republic of Croatia – (the worldwide threshold test);[907] and
(2) the aggregate turnover of each of at least two parties to the concentration arising from the sales of goods or services on the market of the Republic of Croatia is of at least HRK 100 million (approx. EUR 13,600,000) – the national threshold test.[908]

Exceptionally, Competition Agency will have power to assess concentrations where undertakings concerned did not meet the turnover threshold set forth in the Article 17(1). The Article 19 (7) of the CA expressly provides that in case of a referral by the EU Commission to the CA, the CA will assess the referred concentration irrespective of whether the undertakings concerned meet the turnover threshold prescribed by Article 17(1) of the CA. In case of referral, undertakings concerned will have to notify the CA on the proposed concentration within thirty days from the day when CA received Commission's decision on referral.

II. Turnover Calculation

582. The CA provides for methods of calculating turnover. The methodology that is used is the standard methodology of the European Commission or other national European regulators. In Article 17(2), the CA prescribes that 'turnover should be calculated based on amounts derived from sale of products and the provision of services in the financial year preceding the concentration'.[909] So the basic parameter for calculating turnover is the amounts achieved through the sales of goods, products, and services in the normal course of business, meaning ordinary activities only for the last financial year preceding the concentration.

583. However, if the parties to the concentration are unable to deliver audit accounts for the financial year preceding the concentration, the CA prescribes that

906. With regard to the national threshold test, it should be emphasized that the Croatian CA contains a rule which is modelled on Article 1 of Regulation 139/04, and which differs from the rule prescribed in the CAs of comparable jurisdictions, such as the Slovenian, Polish, or German jurisdictions.
907. Article 17(1)(1) CA.
908. Article 17(1)(2) CA.
909. Article 17(2) CA.

in that case they are obliged to deliver accounts which relate to the closest financial year, and that is the last year for which the parties to the concentration have concluded their financial statement.[910]

584. The CA specifically states that intra-group transactions are excluded from turnover calculation.[911] In addition, where the concentration consists of the acquisition of part or several parts of one or more undertakings, the turnover of those business units which are not the subject of sale contract will be excluded.[912]

585. The CA does not provide any guidance on whether, for example, tax or sales rebates should be deducted from turnover or whether aid granted to undertakings by public bodies should be included in the calculations of turnover. In those calculations, the Competition Agency will use interpretations provided by the European Commission.

586. With regard to undertakings whose turnover is taken into account, Article 17(3) of the CA prescribes that the aggregate annual turnover should be calculated by adding together the respective turnover of the following:

- the undertaking party to the concentration;
- those undertakings in which the undertaking concerned, directly or indirectly, owns more than: half the shares or capital or business assets, or has the power to exercise more than half the shares or capital or business assets, or has the power to exercise more than half of the voting rights, or has the power to appoint more than half the members of the supervisory board, the administrative board or bodies legally representing the undertakings, or

  has the right to manage the undertakings' affairs.

- those undertakings which have in the undertaking party to the concentration the rights or powers listed in line 2 of this point;
- those undertakings in which an undertaking as referred to in line 3 of this point, have the rights or powers listed in line 2 of this point and,
- those undertakings in which two or more undertakings as referred to in lines 1 to 4 of this point, jointly have rights or powers listed in line 2 of this point.

587. The CA contains a special rule that applies for the calculation of the turnover of banks, financial institutions, and insurance companies.[913] For this category of undertakings, the total turnover should be calculated on the basis of the total turnover of their ordinary business operations in the financial year preceding the concentration.[914]

910. *Ibid.*
911. Article 17(3)(2) CA.
912. Article 17(4) CA.
913. Article 18 CA.
914. For more detail, *see* Art. 18 CA.

III. Market Share Calculation

588. The assessment procedure of the relevant market regularly involves a market share calculation. The CA explicitly states that in the course of the assessment, the CA should estimate, among other things, the market share of the undertakings concerned.[915] When calculating the market share, the Competition Agency will calculate the market share of the parties to the concentration and the market share of actual and potential competitors. In some cases, in the relevant market analysis, the Competition Agency uses the data of only those competitors whose market share exceeds 10%.[916] In other cases, the Competition Agency provides a very detailed analysis of the market share of all competitors, for all relevant product markets, before and after the concentration. When assessing a particular concentration, the Competition Agency also gives a general estimation of the total increase of the market share of the undertakings concerned following the concentration. Market share is calculated on the basis of the value of production and/or sales expressed in HRK or expressed in the number of units or other measure.[917] As a rule, market share is calculated for a one-year period. However, it may be defined as a shorter or longer period if necessary.[918] Where the assessment of the pre-and post-merger market share suggests that the concentration may weaken competition in the relevant market, the Competition Agency will examine in great detail the direct competitive constrains, and the notably unilateral and coordinated effect of the proposed concentration.

589. For the purpose of the calculation of market share, the Competition Agency uses the following estimates:

(a) estimates delivered by undertakings, including legal and natural persons that are not parties in the proceedings concerned (e.g., competitors);
(b) studies received from trade associations or employers' associations;
(c) data received from central administration authorities;
(d) data from independent institutions involved in market inquiry;
(e) data from local and regional self-government units;
(f) data from public authorities; and
(g) estimates of the Competition Agency.[919]

In relation to some particular markets, the Competition Agency can also use customers' surveys and/or undertakings' surveys for the calculation of market share.

915. Article 21 CA; Arts 13, and 14 of the Regulation on the Definition of Relevant Market.
916. *See*, for example, the Decision of the Croatian Competition Agency of 28 July 2004, *Europapress Holding d.o.o., Zagreb and Slobodna Dalmacija d.d. Split*, UP/I-030-03/2004-01/33.
917. Article 13 of the Regulation on the Definition of the Relevant Market, Official Gazette no. 9/2011.
918. *Ibid.*
919. Article 14(1) and (3) of the Regulation on the Definition of Relevant Market, Official Gazette no. 9/2011.

IV. Other Relevant Notions

590. The system of merger control in Croatia includes a mechanism for the direct notification of the concentration to the Commission, for re-attributing cases from the Commission to the Competition Agency, and for suspending proceedings if assessment proceedings have been opened by the Commission or another competent NCA.

591. With regard to notification to the Commission instead of to the Competition Agency, the CA states that: 'Exceptionally, parties to the concentration are not under the obligation to submit notification of the concentration to the Competition Agency if there is an obligation to submit notification of the concentration to the European Commission.'[920] Thus, notification to the Commission, and not to the agency, is mandatory when the concentration has a community dimension within the meaning of Council Regulation No. 139/04.

592. The European Commission assessed a concentration with a European dimension involving a Croatian undertaking in 2017. Although concentrations at the EU level are rarely prohibited, the EU Commission prohibited the proposed takeover of Cemex Croatia by Heidelberg Cement and Schwend because it had strong concerns that the takeover would significantly reduce competition in the grey cement markets and lead to increased prices in Croatia.[921] In October 2020 the General Court fully upholds Commission's prohibition decision. It confirmed that the Commission's decision was correct and that the takeover of Cemex Croatia, a leading cement producer in Croatia, would significantly reduce competition in relevant product market and that it would lead to higher prices for grey cement in Croatia. The court further concluded that the remedies offered by HeidelbergCement and Schwenk were insufficient.[922]

593. With regard to the case referral from the Commission to the Competition Agency, the relevant EU law is applicable, notably Article 4(4) and (5), Article 9, and Article 22 of Regulation 139/04 and Commission Notice on Case Referrals in respect of concentrations.[923] However, connected to this, the CA additionally states that where the Commission, following the notification, decides not to assess the notified concentration, it will assign the assessment of the concentration to the Competition Agency. Competition Agency has a power to assess concentration even if the proposed concentration does not meet the criteria for mandatory notification under Article 17(1) of the CA.[924] In such a case, the parties to the concentration

920. Article 17(7) CA.
921. European Commission: Press Release, *Commission Prohibits Heidelberg Cement and Schwenk's Proposed Takeover of Cemex Croatia*, Brussels, 5 April 2017, available at http://europa.eu/rapid/press-release_IP-17-883_en.htm (accessed 12 Jun. 2018).
922. Judgment of 5 October 2020, Case T-380/17 *Heidelberg Cement AG and Schwenk Zement KG v European Commission* ECLI:EU:T:2020:471.
923. Commission Notice on Case Referrals in Respect of Concentrations (2005/C 56/02).
924. Article 19(7) CA.

must submit notification to the Competition Agency within thirty days from the day of receipt of the relevant referral decision of the Commission.[925]

594. The CA also imposes an obligation on the parties of the concentration to notify the Competition Agency if an obligation exists for notification of the concentration to another competent merger control authority outside the territory of the Republic of Croatia or if they have already submitted such notification to some other competent merger control authority outside the Republic of Croatia.[926]

595. If the European Commission or another competent NCA has already started with the assessment procedure for concentration that is also notified to the Competition Agency, and if the Competition Agency has opened an assessment procedure, the Competition Agency will bring a decision on suspending the pending proceedings.[927]

§2. Structure of Proceedings

I. Preliminary Assessment and Full Investigation

596. The examination of a merger notification is divided into two phases: the initial investigation commonly referred to as the Phase I investigation and the in-depth investigation or the Phase II investigation. Articles 15 and 16 of the Regulation on Notification and Assessment of Concentration outline the merger review process in the Phase I and Phase II investigations.

A. *Initial Investigation: Phase I*

597. The Phase I investigation starts following the receipt of the Notification Form (or following the short-form Notification Form). Once the Competition Agency has received the notification of a concentration it will first examine the completeness of the notification. It will examine whether the notification has been submitted by the persons authorized, whether the notification has been submitted in the prescribed number of copies, whether the notification contains all the prescribed data and supporting documents and whether notification to the concentration is made to the Commission or any competent authority, or, in the case where the procedure under a previously submitted notification has been closed, whether the notifying party has submitted the decision of the authority in question to the Competition Agency.[928] Where the notifying party for a justifiable reason and despite efforts involved fails to collect certain data or documents which constitute the obligatory content of the notification, they are obliged to explain from whom

925. *Ibid.*
926. Article 5(5) of the Regulation on Notification and Assessment of Concentrations.
927. Article 30(3) CA.
928. Article 13 of the Regulation on Notification and Assessment of Concentrations.

and where they tried to collect the data concerned and the reasons why the relevant data could not be collected.[929] Formally, the Phase I assessment procedure opens on the day when the Competition Agency receives complete notification, upon which it will issue a receipt[930] to the notifying parties. This date is important since the time limit for assessment in Phase I starts from the day when the complete notification is submitted.

598. The Competition Agency's review in Phase I usually involves sending a detailed request for information to the parties, and to third parties, including public authority bodies, associations of undertakings, competitors, and customers. Besides, following the receipt of a complete notification, the Competition Agency on its website publishes a request to all interested parties to give their opinion and/or comments on the proposed concentration.[931] The deadline for the submission of the relevant comments may not be shorter than eight or longer than fifteen days.[932] The purpose of this invitation is to provide the Competition Agency with a better understanding of the players and the relevant market.[933]

599. The Phase I process ends in one of the following ways. The Competition Agency will either reach a clearance decision or initiate the Phase II investigation. It will bring a clearance decision if on the basis of the complete notification and other available information it finds that a notified concentration does not give rise to serious competition concerns.[934] In that case, the Competition Agency will without delay give the notifying party to the concentration a special notice on the compatibility of the concentration concerned. The notice will also be published on the website of the Competition Agency.[935]

600. On the contrary, if the notified concentration raises serious doubts as to its compatibility with the relevant market and, in particular, if the concentration may result in the strengthening of a dominant position or in the creation of a dominant position,[936] a more detailed investigation follows. In this event, the Competition Agency will issue a procedural order on the initiation of proceedings for the assessment of the compatibility of the concentration concerned.[937]

---

929. Article 13(2) of the Regulation on Notification and Assessment of Concentrations.
930. The receipt must contain the case (class) number and other general information of the parties to the concentration, the date of submission of the notification to Competition Agency, etc.
931. Article 21(5) CA.
932. Article 21(6)(4) CA.
933. Article 21(5) CA.
934. The term used in Art. 22(1) CA is 'not to be incompatible with the relevant market'.
935. Article 22(1) CA and Art. 15 of the Regulation on Notification and Assessment of Concentrations.
936. Article 22(3) CA.
937. *Ibid.*

B. In-Depth Investigation: Phase II

601. Phase II proceedings involve a detailed in-depth analysis of all relevant issues and the merger's effects on the competition. During Phase II, the Competition Agency typically becomes involved in gathering additional information on the proposed concentration. The Competition Agency, immediately after the issuance of a procedural order on the initiation of proceedings for the assessment of compatibility, on the basis of a case-by-case method, will set the applicable appraisal criteria.[938] The CA contains whole lists of criteria that the Competition Agency should take into account during the assessment procedure.[939] The first set of criteria include the following: the structure of the relevant market, actual and potential competitors in the relevant market, the supply and demand structure and its trends, and the technical, economic, and legal conditions necessary to enter or to withdraw from the relevant market. The second set of criteria include the following: market share, the market position and financial power, and the business activities of all the undertakings on the relevant market, the possible changes in business operations and the business plan of the parties to the concentration, and alternative sources of supply. The last set of criteria include the following: distribution channels, transportation costs, specialization in production, innovation in technology, and the lowering of prices and goods or services and other benefits for the other undertakings and/or consumers directly deriving from the implementation of the concentration. As already said, the Competition Agency has discretion in selecting the most appropriate criteria.

602. If, during further investigation, the Competition Agency still holds concerns with regard to the proposed concentration, and if it concludes that the proposed merger will likely impede effective competition, it will issue a Statement of Objections to the notifying parties.[940] In the Statement of Objections, the Competition Agency will inform the parties to the proceedings in writing about the preliminarily established facts for the purpose of enabling them to express their views on all relevant facts and circumstances on the case before the oral hearing. The parties to the proceedings have the right to respond to the Statement of Objections in writing within one month from the receipt of the Statement of Objections. They can propose structural or behavioural remedies in order to remove the negative effects of the concentration concerned.[941] They can also present evidence and propose witnesses to be heard.[942]

603. At this stage of the proceedings, the Competition Agency will also enable all interested parties to become involved in the process.[943] This primarily refers to the person who filed the initiative and thus informed the Competition Agency about

938. Article 21 CA; Article 15 of the Regulation on Notification and Assessment of Concentrations.
939. *Ibid.*
940. Articles 22 and 48 CA.
941. Article 22(4) CA.
942. Article 48(3) CA.
943. Article 48(1) CA.

a particular merger. Although the person who files the initiative is not a party to the proceedings, it enjoys certain procedural rights. For example, it may, by means of a written request, ask the Competition Agency for a copy of the Statement of Objections, and it can ask to be heard as a witness to the proceedings.[944]

II. Time Framework

604. The Competition Agency must reach a decision on Phase I within thirty days following the receipt of a complete notification.[945] In the case where the parties to the concentration fail to notify the concentration to the Competition Agency, the Competition Agency will on its own motion initiate an assessment procedure. In this case, the Competition Agency must also reach a Phase I decision within thirty days, but this date starts to run on the day when the procedural order on the initiation of proceedings is taken.[946] As a general rule, the Phase II decision must be reached within three months following the adoption of a procedural order on the initiation of proceedings.[947] However, there are a few exceptions to this rule. First, the Competition Agency may extend this deadline for three more months when it finds it necessary to carry out additional expertise or analyses.[948] It will inform the parties about that extension before the expiry of the prescribed deadline.[949] Then, when the concentration concerned is declared conditionally compatible and when the Competition Agency has issued a Statement of Objections, the three months deadline shall be suspended.[950] Parties to the concentration have one month, starting from the day of the receipt of the Statement of Objections, to propose adequate commitments and other conditions to remove the negative effects of the concentration concerned.[951] In this case, a decision on the commitments undertaken by the undertakings, as well as a decision on non-compliance with the set conditions and the obligations imposed by the Competition Agency, will be reached within three months from the day on which all the facts relevant from the adoption of a decision are established.[952]

III. Right of Defence

605. Apart from the rights to judicial protection against a Competition Agency decision,[953] parties to the concentration, during the Phase I investigation, but mostly during the Phase II investigation, are granted a number of fundamental procedural

944. Article 37(4) CA.
945. Article 22(1) CA.
946. Article 38(3) CA.
947. Article 57(2) CA.
948. Article 57(6) CA.
949. *Ibid.*
950. Article 22(9) CA.
951. Article 22(4) CA.
952. Article 57(5) CA.
953. *See* Part III, Ch. 3, *infra*.

rights whose purpose is to protect the parties' right of defence. They have the right to access the file after the Competition Agency has issued a Statement of Objections,[954] to propose witnesses, and to present additional evidence.[955] They also have the right to be heard before the Competition Agency brings a final decision affecting their interests.[956] And last, they have the right to a written reply in relation to the Statement of Objections within a month from the receipt of the Statement of Objection.[957] Apart from the above rights, the parties to the concentration enjoy all other procedural rights prescribed by the CA and the General Administrative Procedure Act, just as in cartel and abuse of dominance proceedings.[958]

§3. Clearance and Conditional Clearance

606. Following the Phase II investigation, the Competition Agency may reach one of the following decisions: (1) it may unconditionally clear the proposed concentration; (2) it may prohibit the concentration; or (3) it may approve the concentration subject to remedies. A concentration will be cleared if following a detailed Phase II assessment procedure the Competition Agency concludes that the concentration would not significantly impede effective competition in the relevant market. A concentration will be prohibited if during the assessment procedure the Competition Agency proves that the concentration would impede effective competition in the market, in particular where such a concentration would create or strengthen a dominant position. In this sense, the Competition Agency must prove causality between the proposed merger and any deterioration of the competitive conditions in the market.[959] And last, the Competition Agency may approve the concentration subject to remedies (conditions and obligations).

I. Conditions and Undertakings

A. *Content*

607. Article 22 of the CA authorizes the Competition Agency to approve a concentration subject to conditions and obligations. Generally, it is for the parties to the concentration to propose suitable remedies. They can propose commitments before the initiation of proceedings, in notification, and after the initiation of proceedings, within a time period not exceeding one month following the issuance of the Statement of Objections by the Competition Agency.[960] The Competition Agency may

954. Article 47 CA.
955. Article 48(3) CA.
956. Article 50 CA.
957. Article 48(2) CA.
958. *See* Part III, Ch. 1, §3.
959. For more, *see* Guidelines on the Assessment of Horizontal Mergers under the Council Regulation on the Control of Concentrations between Undertakings, OJ C 31, 5.2.2004, 5–18.
960. Article 22(3) and (4) CA and Art. 17 of the Regulation on Notification and Assessment of Concentrations.

fully or partially accept the proposed remedies.[961] The Competition Agency may also order any remedy necessary to remove the competition concerns.[962] However, in practice, the Competition Agency and the parties to the concentration always negotiate the most suitable remedy. when the parties to the concentration propose commitments (remedies), they should make the proposals on the Remedies Form which is a constituent part of the Regulation on Notification and Assessment of Concentrations.[963]

608. With regard to the type of remedies, the Regulation of Notification and Assessment of Concentration expressly mentions two types of remedies: structural and behavioural remedies.[964] However, it neither provides any further guidance on or explanation of which remedy is structural and which remedy is behavioural, and nor does it provide guidance on the deadlines for fulfilling the obligations and commitments, which can be considered as a certain legislative gap. In order to bridge this legislative gap, the Competition Agency in practice relies on relevant EU case law and the Commission Notice on Remedies.[965] Besides, over time, the Competition Agency has also created some internal practices and procedures. There are a certain number of published Competition Agency decisions where remedies have been imposed, which enables academics, practitioners, and undertakings to gain useful insight into the remedy policies of the Competition Agency. Hence, this can be of some help to undertakings, since a suitable remedy is always examined and negotiated on a case-by-case basis.

For example, in the concentration between Agrokor and Mercator,[966] Agrokor committed itself to implementing a whole set of strict and comprehensive measures, both structural and behavioural. First, it took on the obligation to divest ninety-six stores from the combined network of Konzum and Mercator whose total revenue made up 60% of the revenue of Mercator-H in 2012. This structural remedy to divest was primarily aimed at the City of Zagreb where Konzum used to be the market leader.[967] In this particular case, divestiture meant the sale, the termination of lease contracts, or the lease of stores for at least ten years. Agrokor also committed itself to start searching for an upfront buyer ready to take over the stores before it acquired control over Mercator. With regard to a suitable buyer, it was

961. Article 17 of the Regulation on Notification and Assessment of Concentrations.

962. Article 22(4) CA and Art. 17(4) of the Regulation on Notification and Assessment of Concentrations.

963. For more details, *see* Regulation on Notification and Assessment of Concentrations, Appendix 4, 35.

964. Article 17 of the Regulation on Notification and Assessment of Concentrations.

965. Commission notice on remedies acceptable under Council Regulation (EC) no. 139/2004 and under Commission Regulation (EC) nos 802/2004; 2008/C, 267/01.

966. Decision of the Croatian Competition Agency of 24 March 2014, *Agrokor d.d. Zagreb and Mercator d.d. Ljubljana*, UP/I-034-03/2013-02/2008; *see also* Competition Agency Press Release, *Agrokor-Mercator Merger Conditionally Approved*, available at http://www.aztn.hr/en/agrokor-mercator-merger-conditionally-approved/. *See also* http://www.aztn.hr/uploads/documents/eng/documents/decision/TN/UPI-030-022011-02009.pdf (accessed 23 Jun. 2018).

967. *See also* Competition Agency Press Release: *Agrokor-Mercator Merger Conditionally Approved* 3, available at http://www.aztn.hr/en/agrokor-mercator-merger-conditionally-approved/; *see also* http://www.aztn.hr/uploads/documents/eng/documents/decision/TN/UPI-030-022011-02009.pdf (accessed 23 Jun. 2018).

agreed that the buyer could not be a person connected with Agrokor or Mercator or with their board members and that it must have sufficient financial means to provide reasonable assurance that it would be able to operate in the market. The stores that Agrokor failed to divest within six months following taking control over Mercator had to be offered for sale or lease by means of a public tender published in at least one national daily or weekly publication. As a final measure, all stores that were not sold or leased had either to be closed or used for a purpose other than retail business. Concerning behavioural remedies, they were primarily aimed at protecting Mercator-H's suppliers and the entry and/or expansion of competition on Konzum's shelves in relation to key product categories from producers that were part of the group.[968] So, in this regard, Agrokor agreed that it would enable each of the five biggest Mercator-H's suppliers to sell three of their best-selling products in Konzum for three years following the acquisition of control over Mercator under conditions that were not worse than the conditions that Konzum approved for their competitors in its own sales network. Besides this, Agrokor also took on the obligation to allow at least three of its competitors to display their products on 30% of Konzum's shelves under conditions that were no worse than those approved for companies that belong to the Agrokor group.[969]

609. In another conditionally approved concentration also involving Agrokor, notably a concentration between Agrokor and Tisak,[970] Agrokor agreed not to transform the retail outlets of the undertaking Tisak into retail store for groceries. It further undertook the obligation that Tisak would display on its shelves at least 25% of substitutes for Agrokor's products, meaning 25% of products of Agrokor's competitors. Agrokor also agreed that all the agreements concluded between Tisak and its suppliers prior to the concentration would stay in force under the same conditions and for at least one year from the delivery of the Competition Agency decision to the parties. Last, Agrokor was prohibited from selling brands of the undertaking Konzum, such as K plus or Rial, in the retail outlets of the undertaking Tisak. An independent auditor was appointed for three years to oversee the implementation of the measures and to inform the Competition Agency about compliance with the commitments.[971]

610. In the concentration between the undertaking Europapress Holding and Slobodna Dalmacija,[972] and more recently in the concentration between HT and

968. *See also* the Competition Agency Press Release: *Agrokor-Mercator Merger Conditionally Approved* 4, available at http://www.aztn.hr/en/agrokor-mercator-merger-conditionally-approved/; *see also* http://www.aztn.hr/uploads/documents/eng/documents/decision/TN/UPI-030-022011-02009.pdf (accessed 23 Jun. 2018).

969. *Ibid.*

970. Decision of the Croatian Competition Agency of 15 March 2007, *AGROKOR d.d. Zagreb and TISAK d.d.*, UP/I-030-02/2006-02/33.

971. *Ibid.*

972. Decision of the Croatian Competition Agency of 28 June 2004, *Europapress Holding d.o.o., Zagreb and Slobodna Dalmacija d.d. Split*, UP/I-030-02/2004-01/33, Official Gazette no. 111/2004; summary of the decision: http://www.aztn.hr/uploads/documents/eng/documents/decision/TN/UPI-030-022004-01033.pdf (accessed 25 Sep. 2018).

Optima,[973] the Competition Agency conditionally approved both proposed concentrations and imposed a set of commitments despite the fact that in both cases the parties to the concentration invoked the 'failing firm defence'. The CA does not explicitly endorse the failing firm defence. However, where it is likely that despite the strengthening of a dominant position in the market a concentration involving an undertaking facing financial troubles will enhance the general welfare by preserving jobs or will increase the efficiency of existing capacity, the Competition Agency will accept the parties' 'failing firm' arguments and will weigh the general positive impact against the negative impact that a merger might have on the market structure and market competition.

611. In the Europapress Holding and Slobodna Dalmacija merger, following a detailed assessment procedure, the Competition Agency concluded that the concentration in question would significantly impede effective competition in one of the affected relevant markets, notably in the press distribution market, particularly relating to its wholesale part. In addition, it also came to the conclusion that the implementation of the concentration would result in higher barriers to entry to the press distribution market and that market foreclosure following the concentration would be more probable, etc. However, the Competition Agency approved the concentration subject to a number of conditions and obligations, mainly because it considered that in this way Slobodna Dalmacija, as a local brand newspaper, would be maintained and that the know-how of the journalists who are acquainted with their readers' needs and customs would be preserved. The Competition Agency also assessed that a 'financial injection' would enable Slobodna Dalmacija to 'survive' in the market. In this regard, the Competition Agency stated that 'although this argument cannot be given priority in respect of competition rules, it will at least contribute to job maintenance'.[974]

612. In the concentration between HT and Optima, HT acquired control over Optima in a pre-bankruptcy settlement. So, in this case, too, the conditions for a 'failing firm defence' were satisfied. In this regard, the Competition Agency concluded that it could be expected that without a merger Optima would exit the market. The Competition Agency approved this concentration, imposing comprehensive commitments.

First, the Competition Agency for the first time in its practice limited the duration of the concentration to a period of four years without the possibility of extension. Second, as part of a deal with the Competition Agency, the parties to the concentration agreed not to perform any function in the management or supervisory board of the merging companies, including all HT affiliated companies. The parties to the concentration also agreed on special rules to prevent an information exchange

973. Decision of the Croatian Competition Agency of 9 June 2017, *H1Telekom d.d. Split and OT-Optima Telekom d.d. Zagreb*, UP/I-034-03/2016-02/006; Decision of the Croatian Competition Agency of 19 March 2014, *H1Telekom d.d. Split and OT-Optima Telekom d.d. Zagreb*, UP/I-034-03/13-02/007; Decision of the Croatian Competition Agency of 9 June 2017, *Hrvatski Telekom d.d./OT-Optima Telekom d.d.*, UP/I-034-03/2013-02/007.

974. Decision of the Croatian Competition Agency of 28 June 2004, *Europapress Holding d.o.o., Zagreb and Slobodna Dalmacija d.d. Split*, UP/I-030-02/2004-01/33, Official Gazette no. 111/2004.

between the parties (so-called Chinese walls). HT also agreed not to employ key Optima employees, to protect the confidentiality of Optima's user database, to refrain from any action that would impact on Optima's sales activity, etc. Since, due to some circumstances that could not have been predicated or avoided, the parties to the concentration could not fulfil certain commitments within the prescribed deadlines, the Competition Agency, on the request of the parties, partially repealed its decision of 19 March 2014. In a new decision, the Competition Agency defined new measures, conditions, and deadlines. In the new decision, Optima undertook to allow the use of free colocation space for the duration of the concentration on all its colocations existing prior to the merger with H1 Telekom. Optima also committed itself to lease or sell to a suitable buyer emptied H1 colocations from which H1 would move to Optima's colocations, etc.

613. However, the most important aspect of this case concerns the fact that the Competition Agency changed its decision with regard to the duration of the concentration and it approved a prolongation for an additional three years, until 2021,[975] mostly because it believed that during this time Optima would be able to achieve a significant improvement in business efficiency and thus would be able to fulfil the financial obligations arising from the pre-bankruptcy settlement.[976] According to the Competition Agency decision, the concentration between HT and Optima would cease as of 10 July 2021 irrespective of the closing of the transaction of the sale of shares. The process of the sale of the Optima's shares started in January 2020. Company Telmach expressed its interest in buying Optima's shares from HT. SharePurchase Agreement between HT, Zagrebačka banka and Telemach was signed in January 2022.

614. When proposing commitments, parties to a concentration have to propose a trustee to oversee the parties' compliance with the commitments. Although the appointment of a trustee is regular practice,[977] the CA and the Regulation on the Notification and Assessment of a Concentration are completely silent on that issue.

615. While Article 22 of the CA deals with commitments proposed by undertakings and negotiated with the Competition Agency, Article 24 of the CA regulates situations where the Competition Agency can ex officio impose behavioural or structural measures. The Competition Agency is entitled to impose any appropriate measure in the cases where: (1) the concentration has been implemented contrary to the decision of the Competition Agency by which the concentration was prohibited; and (2) the concentration has been implemented without obligatory prior notification.[978]

975. Decision of the Croatian Competition Agency of 9 June 2017, *Hrvatski Telekom d.d./OT-Optima Telekom d.d.*, UP/I-034-03/2013-02/007.

976. Decision of the Croatian Competition Agency of 9 June 2017, *H1Telekom d.d. Split and OT-Optima Telekom d.d. Zagreb*, UP/I-034-03/2016-02/006; Decision of the Croatian Competition Agency of 19 March, *H1Telekom d.d. Split and OT-Optima Telekom d.d. Zagreb*, UP/I-034-03/13-02/007.

977. *See*, for example, *Optima/H1* merger, *HT/Optima* merger, *Agrokor/Mercator* merger.

978. Article 24(1) CA.

In these cases, the Competition Agency may, by means of a separate decision, in particular:

(1) order that the shares or interest acquired be transferred or divested; and
(2) prohibit or restrict the exercise of voting rights related to shares or interest in the undertakings that are parties to the concentration, and order the joint venture or any other form of control by which a prohibited concentration has been put into effect be removed.[979]

B. Timing

616. Parties to a concentration may propose measures as early as in the prior notification.[980] They can propose measures within thirty days from the day of the receipt of the Statement of Objections.[981] In the event that the Competition Agency does not accept or just partly accepts the remedies proposed by the parties to the concentration, the Competition Agency may impose any other measure which it finds appropriate for the restoration of effective competition in the market.[982] In this case, the Competition Agency determines the deadline in which the parties to the concentration have to fulfil obligations and commitments. The Competition Agency must reach a final decision on whether the concentration is conditionally compatible within six months from the date of the adoption of the procedural order.[983] However, it should be emphasized that the above deadline does not run from the day of receipt of the procedural order until the day of receipt of the proposed commitments.[984]

§4. Relations with Other Merger Control Authorities

I. Other Authorities Within Local Jurisdiction

617. Examination of a concentration is exclusively performed by the Competition Agency. However, the Competition Agency closely cooperates with several sectoral regulators. Such cooperation is established with the HAKOM for concentrations in network industries, such as postal services, railway services, etc., the AEM for concentrations in media and electronic media, the Croatian National Bank for concentrations in the banking sector, and the HERA for concentrations in the energy sector.[985]

979. Article 22(2) CA.
980. Article 22(5) CA.
981. Article 22(4) CA.
982. *Ibid.*
983. Article 57(2) and (6) CA.
984. Article 22(6) CA.
985. For more, *see* para. 58, *supra.*

618. The CA further imposes mandatory cooperation with the Competition Agency on all public administration authorities such as local authorities, and regional and self-government bodies. Upon the written request of the Competition Agency, they are obliged to submit to the Competition Agency, free of charge, any requested data and documentation, including documentation covered by the business secrecy obligation.[986]

II. International Coordination

619. With regard to international coordination, the CA explicitly, with several provisions, prescribes mandatory cooperation between the Competition Agency and the European Commission, and the Competition Agency and national competition authorities of the Member States.[987] In principle, these rules apply not only to the control of concentrations but also in connection to the application of Articles 101 and 102 TFEU. It should be emphasized that in merger cases EU rules on the referral system apply automatically and these rules are legally binding for the Competition Agency. Moreover, it is important to point out that the Competition Agency is a member of the ECN and, in line with the ECN mission, the Competition Agency cooperates with other national competition authorities. In all cases that relate to a merger transaction that is reviewable in more than one EU Member State, the Competition Agency should inform other national competition authorities by means of the existing European Competition Authorities Notice system, which involves an exchange of basic non-confidential case information, after notification in such a multi-jurisdictional merger case has been received.[988] The legal basis for the actions mentioned stems from Article 53(7) of the CA. The Competition Agency is also a member of the ICN, and within this network it cooperates with competition authorities outside the EU.

986. Article 66 CA.
987. Articles 26(2), 30(12), and 32(11) CA.
988. Best Practices Cooperation between EU National Competition Authorities in Merger Review, November 2001, available at http://ec.europa.eu/competition/ecn/nca_best_practices_merger_review_en.pdf (accessed 13 Jun. 2018).

Chapter 3. Challenging of the Administrative Decision

§1. Competent Courts

620. The decisions of the Competition Agency are subject to the judicial review of the High Administrative Court. The High Administrative Court is the highest judicial instance in administrative matters in Croatia.[989] In administrative matters, the High Administrative Court usually adjudicates as an appellate court, although in competition cases it acts as a first instance court. The challenge procedure against Competition Agency decisions before the High Administrative Court is regulated by the CA, with the Administrative Dispute Act being applied subsidiarily. The central provisions governing the principles of judicial review in competition cases are Articles 67 and 68 of the CA. Article 67 of the CA provides for the following: the review court, types of legal remedies against a Competition Agency decision, grounds for review, composition of the judicial panel, time limits for lodging a claim before the High Administrative Court, and those who can bring an action against a Competition Agency decision before the High Administrative Court (*locus standi*).

621. With regard to the type of remedies against a Competition Agency decision, Article 67 of the CA prescribes that there is no appeal against Competition Agency decisions. A Competition Agency decision can only be challenged by lodging a lawsuit initiating administrative dispute proceedings directly to the High Administrative Court. The legal grounds for a lawsuit are the following:

(1) misapplication or erroneous application of the substantive provisions of competition law;
(2) manifest errors in the application of procedural provisions;
(3) incorrect or incomplete facts of the case; and
(4) inappropriate fine and other issues contained in the decision of the Competition Agency.[990]

622. However, it should be emphasized that not all Competition Agency acts can be challenged. A lawsuit cannot be lodged and therefore an administrative dispute cannot be opened against procedural orders (conclusions).[991] So, for example, if the Competition Agency opens ex officio an assessment procedure and issues a procedural order on the initiation of proceedings for an assessment of a concentration, no

989. D. Aksamovic, *Judicial Review in EU and Croatian Competition Cases: The Procedure and Intensity of Judicial Review*, in *EU Competition and State Aid Rules* 80 (V. Tomljenovic, et al., eds., Springer, Berlin, Germany, 2018).
990. Article 67(1) CA.
991. Article 67(3) CA.

lawsuit can be brought against such a decision. A procedural order can be challenged when the Competition Agency reaches a final decision on the merits of a claim.[992] Moreover, no appeal is allowed against a warrant to carry out a dawn raid.[993]

623. As a general rule, a claim against a decision of the Competition Agency cannot suspend proceedings, except in the part of the decision which relates to fines.[994]

624. With regard to the question of who has active legal capacity or who can file a lawsuit with the High Administrative Court, the CA is quite precise and strict. A claim against a Competition Agency decision establishing an infringement can be filed only by the injured party (parties to the proceedings),[995] whereas a claim against a decision that no infringement of competition rules has been committed and a decision on the basis of which the proceedings are terminated can be submitted by a person who filed the initiative[996] and a person who has been granted the same procedural rights.[997]

625. Other procedural aspects of a dispute, such as the content of a lawsuit, court decisions, the content of a judgment, and legal remedies against High Administrative Court decisions, are regulated by the Administrative Disputes Act,[998] which in competition cases applies as *lex generalis.*

626. All claims in competition cases are decided by a panel of three judges. When deciding on a claim, the High Administrative Court can bring one of the following decisions: it can dismiss the claim if it finds that the claim is incomplete,[999] it can reject the claim if it establishes that it is unfounded,[1000] or it can accept the claim.[1001] The High Administrative Court will accept the claim if it establishes that a particular decision is unlawful. In this case, it will nullify the decision and can either resolve the matter itself or remand the decision to the Competition Agency and order action.[1002]

---

992. *Ibid.*
993. Article 67(6) CA.
994. Article 67(4) CA.
995. According to Art. 36 CA, parties to the proceedings are undertakings against which proceedings have been carried out by the Competition Agency and undertakings that are party to the concentration.
996. According to Art. 37 CA the initiative for initiating proceedings before the Competition Agency can be submitted in writing by any legal or natural person, professional association, economic interest group, association of undertakings, consumer association, the Government of the Republic of Croatia, central administration authorities, and local and regional self-government units.
997. Article 67(5) CA.
998. Administrative Disputes Act, Official Gazette nos 20/10, 143/12, 152/14, 94/16, 29/17.
999. Article 29(2) of the Administrative Disputes Act.
1000. Article 57 of the Administrative Disputes Act.
1001. Article 58 of the Administrative Disputes Act.
1002. Article 58(1) of the Administrative Disputes Act.

627. The percentage of rejected claims against a Competition Agency decision is relatively high. According to the most recent data, in the five-year period, from 2014 until January 2020, the CCA brought 322 decisions related to competition law enforcement; out of them, plaintiffs brought 82 claims before the HACRC.[1003] Out of the aforementioned eighty-two claims, fourteen claims were successful, while sixty-three claims were dismissed. There were five (other) decisions where the HACRC dismissed the action (lawsuit) as incomplete or as lacking in jurisdiction. A little more than 17% of the successful claims, compared to almost 77% of unsuccessful claims, shows that the chance to win a case before the HACRC against the CCA is pretty low. The reasons for the low success rate are difficult to detect, but we can assume that they include unfounded claims, poor or insufficient evidence and others.[1004]

628. Here are examples of some successful claims before the High Administrative Court. For example, in the judgment of the High Administrative Court of 22 April 2016, the High Administrative Court partially annulled the Competition Agency's decision with regard to a fine imposed on the undertaking V Grupa d.o.o.[1005] In this particular case, the Competition Agency accused six of the largest personal protection security service providers of participation in a cartel and imposed a fine. The fined undertakings filed a claim against that decision with the High Administrative Court which dismissed the complaints and fully accepted the explanation of the decision of the Competition Agency stating that this cartel agreement contained restrictions by object. The High Administrative Court also dismissed the complaints with respect to the level of imposed fines for all undertakings except for the fine imposed on the undertaking V Grupa d.o.o. Although in setting a fine for this particular undertaking the Competition Agency took into account as a mitigating circumstance the fact that this undertaking was undergoing pre-bankruptcy settlement proceedings, the High Administrative Court thought that the Competition Agency should reconsider the amount of the fine and further lower it or impose a symbolic fine only on this particular undertaking, because it thought that the imposed fine could additionally worsen the already bad financial situation of the undertaking concerned.[1006]

629. In another case, the *Marinas Cartel* case,[1007] the High Administrative court accepted the parties' claim and annulled the Competition Agency's decision. In this particular case, the Competition Agency also fined several undertakings for participating in a hardcore cartel by attending a meeting of the Council of the Croatian Association of Nautical Tourism where they exchanged information relating to

1003. D. Aksamovic, *Judicial review in competition cases in Croatia: Winning and losing arguments before the High Administrative Court of the Republic of Croatia*, YEARBOOK OF ANTITRUST AND REGULATORY STUDIES, VOL. 2020, 13(22), p. 19.

1004. Ibid., 20.

1005. Judgment of the High Administrative Court of the Republic of Croatia of 22 April 2016, UsII-45/15-12.

1006. *Ibid.*, 4.

1007. Judgment of the High Administrative Court of the Republic of Croatia of 17 March 2017, UsII-39/15-10. For more details *see* para. 373, *supra*.

future pricing policies for berthing services. The Competition Agency qualified their behaviour as a hard cartel restriction and imposed a fine. The High Administrative Court did not uphold the Competition Agency's decision which it annulled mostly because it found that the challenged decision had been based on the insufficiently established facts of the case.[1008]

630. In the *Orthodontists cartel* case,[1009] the Competition Agency imposed on the Croatian Orthodontic Society a symbolic fine for concluding a prohibited agreement through the adoption of a 'minimum price for orthodontist service' price list. This price list was in force from 1 October 2010 to 9 October 2013. In the proceedings initiated on 2 September 2013, the Competition Agency established beyond doubt that the price list adopted by the Croatian Orthodontic Society was a price-fixing agreement which is prohibited by object and therefore it considered that it was not necessary to provide evidence of the actual anticompetitive effects of the particular agreement on the market and consumers. The Croatian Orthodontic Society challenged the Competition Agency's decision by filing a lawsuit before the High Administrative Court. To the surprise of many, the High Administrative Court confirmed the claim and overturned the decision of the Competition Agency. In the statement of reasons of its ruling, the High Administrative Court challenged the very concept of a restrictive prohibited agreement, as stipulated by the CA. It stated that it could not accept the argument of the Competition Agency when it claimed that a 'minimum price list for orthodontist service' constitutes a prohibited agreement as regulated by Article 8(1)(1) of the CA since dental services in Croatia are regulated by the Dental Services Act, according to which the Croatian Orthodontic Society is, among other things, entitled to set minimum prices for dental service providers. Moreover, the High Administrative Court in its judgment also stated that in order to be illegal, a price-fixing agreement must be enforceable in practice, meaning that the Competition Agency should have proved that there was price-fixing or that there was an intention to fix prices. Since, in the court's opinion, the minimum price list did not have as its object or effect the distortion of competition in the relevant market, the court concluded that the minimum price list did not constitute a prohibited agreement as regulated by Article 8(1) of the CA.[1010]

631. The Competition Agency challenged this decision asking the State Attorney's Office of the Republic of Croatia to request a review of the legality of the High Administrative Court's judgment before the Supreme Court. In March 2021, the

1008. For a critical overview, *see* J. Pecotić Kaufman, *Some Remarks on Judicial Control Issues in Connection to Recent Cartel Cases in Croatia: Shifting Trends and Appropriate Legal Test* (Speech held at the Annual FTC South-East Europe Workshop on Economic Issues in Competition Law Hosted by Croatian Competition Agency Zagreb, 11 September 2017), available at http://www.aztn.hr/seminar-aztn-a-i-ftc-a-o-primjeni-ekonomskih-alata-u-pravu-trzisnog-natjecanja/ (accessed 25 Sep. 2018).

1009. *See* para 351 *supra*.

1010. Judgment of the High Administrative Court of the Republic of Croatia of 5 March 2015, UsII-70/14-6, 4 and 5.

Supreme Court of the Republic of Croatia decided in favour of the agency, reversing the High Administrative Court judgment.[1011] The Supreme Court stated that the Competition Agency properly found that the document called 'Minimum prices for orthodontists services' is a prohibited agreement under Article 8 of the CA. The Supreme Court also repeated the Competition Agency's statements where Competition Agency stated that the law does not empower any association of undertakings to fix prices of products and services of its members and that any fixing of maximum of fixed prices constitutes an infringement of competition law.

632. Regardless of the positive outcome of this particular case, it should be emphasized that the current model of judicial review against the High Administrative Court's decision seems troublesome. A party dissatisfied with a High Administrative Court judgment has only a limited right to further recourse.[1012] The only legal remedy against a High Administrative Court judgment is to request the extraordinary examination of the legality of the final decision of the administrative court, which is an extraordinary legal remedy regulated by the Administrative Disputes Act.[1013] However, even such a request cannot be lodged directly by the parties.[1014] A request for the extraordinary examination of the legality of final decisions may be filed only by the State Attorney's Office of the Republic of Croatia.[1015] This means that the parties in an administrative dispute must propose to the State Attorney's Office of the Republic of Croatia the filing of a request for the extraordinary examination of the legality of final decisions of the administrative court or of the High Administrative Court. The State Attorney's Office may decide to file the request with the Supreme Court of the Republic of Croatia, but it may also decide not to file the request.[1016] The State Attorney's Office of the Republic of Croatia may also file the request on its own initiative, without waiting for a request.[1017] If the Supreme Court of the Republic of Croatia adopts the request, it may annul the judgment and remand the case for a new decision or it may reverse the judgment.[1018]

I. Constitutional Court

633. The Constitutional Court does not have direct authority in the enforcement of various administrative court decisions.[1019] Hence, in the last fifteen years it has been in the position to decide in numerous cases involving competition law issues

1011. Judgment of the Supreme Court of the Republic of Croatia of 2 March 2021, *Hrvatsko društvo ortodonata v. Competition Agency*, U-zpz 16/2015-4.
1012. Aksamovic, *supra* n. 1004, at 84.
1013. Article 78 of the Administrative Disputes Act.
1014. Aksamovic, *supra* n. 1004, at 84.
1015. *Ibid.*
1016. *Ibid.*
1017. *Ibid.*
1018. Article 78(4) of the Administrative Disputes Act.
1019. M. Jelušić, D. Šarin, *Rule of Law and the Role of the Constitutional Court of the Republic of Croatia in Enforcing Administrative and Administrative Court Rulings*, Split, 52 Zbornik radova Pravnog fakulteta u Splitu 175 (2015).

upon a constitutional complaint raised by an undertaking affected by the Competition Agency's decisions and/or the High Administrative Court's judgments.[1020] Therefore, it seems important to reflect briefly on the role of the Constitutional Court and on the Constitutional Court's recent decisions in competition cases.

634. Until recently, the Constitutional Court's decisions mainly remained unnoticed, possibly because the Constitutional Court in most cases rejected the constitutional complaint and upheld the High Administrative Court's decision.[1021] However, the decision of the Constitutional Court in the *Presečki grupa* case,[1022] where the Competition Agency fined three bus operators for participating in a cartel agreement, received a great deal of attention. One of the fined undertakings raised a claim against that decision to the High Administrative Court who upheld the Competition Agency's decision. Dissatisfied with that outcome, the fined undertaking filed a constitutional complaint with the Croatian Constitutional Court who held that the Competition Agency was right to find an infringement. The Constitutional Court did not challenge the Competition Agency's finding on the existence of a cartel which was also confirmed by the High Administrative Court. However, it annulled the High Court's decision upholding the Competition Agency's decision because it considered that the High Administrative Court's judgment lacked a logical and sufficient explanation, particularly with regard to the claimant's statement that in this case the Act on the Carriage of Goods by Roads as *lex specialis* should be applied, instead of the CA. In the Constitutional Court's view, the lack of such an explanation constitutes a breach of constitutional rights as regulated by Article 29(1) and Article 19 of the Constitution of the Republic of Croatia and therefore the Constitutional Court annulled the High Administrative Court decision and remanded the case to that court.[1023] However, a Constitutional Court decision did not end the *Presecki case* 'saga'. The High Administrative Court adopted a new judgment in Presečki grupa case in January 2017. In its judgment High Administrative Court again confirmed the initial judgment of the Competition Agency and again uphold the Competition Agency findings that four undertakings concluded illegal horizontal agreement and thus violated Article 8 (1) of the CA. Against that decision Presecki grupa again filed a Constitutional claim in April 2018. Constitutional Court annulled the High Administrative Court judgment for the second time, with the main argumentation that the High Administrative Court in its recent decision again failed to

1020. See, D. Aksamovic, *(Re) definiranje uloge Visokog upravnog suda Republike Hrvatske i Vrhovnog suda Republike Hrvatske u sporovima za zaštitu tržišnog natjecanja,* in Pravo tržišnog natjecanja u Republici Hrvatskoj i Europskoj Uniji, Hrvatska akademija znanosti i umjetnosti, Zagreb, 2021., p 39 – 61.

1021. *See*, for example, J. Pecotić Kaufman, *The Croatian Constitutional Court Upholds the Judgment of the Administrative Court Confirming Its Previous Position on the Application of EU Competition Rules (Tisak),* e-Competition Bulletin, no. 36693, Case Comment (2011), available at http://www.concurrences.com/en/page/article?id_article=36693 (accessed 2 Jul. 2018).

1022. *See* para. 634, *supra*. For a detailed discussion, *see* S. Petrović, *Tržišno natjecanje u praksi Ustavnog suda Republike Hrvatske – osvrt na recentne odluke Ustavnog suda* (U-III-925/2017/ "Presečki"/U-III-2791/2016, U-III-6196, U-III-2826/2016/"zaštitari"/) (12 June 2018), available at https://hdpptn.hr/wp-content/uploads/2018/06/usud-tr%C5%BE-natj.pdf (accessed 2 Jul. 2018).

1023. *Ibid.*

provide answers to the questions raised by the Constitutional Courts first decision relating to the same claimant, Presecki grupa. So following to this Constitutional Court decision, the High Administrative Court ruled again on this case in September 2018. This time the High Administrative Court annulled the Competition Agency decision requesting retrial. In a retrial, Competition Agency in October 2021 adopted new decision again concluding that Presecki grupa and other accused undertakings have concluded an illegal horizontal agreement and fined them with the total amount of approximately HRK 1 million.[1024]

635. In another already mentioned case where six of the largest private security providers were accused and fined for participation in a cartel,[1025] the *Private Security Companies cartel* case, the Constitutional Court also upheld the constitutional complaint and annulled the High Administrative Court's judgment because, in brief, it held that a magazine article alone is not sufficient evidence in a cartel case. Although, in the view of many, the Competition Agency showed clear evidence that there was a meeting of competitors, that a meeting was organized by their association, that in the meeting they discussed minimum prices of services etc., 'it was relevant for the Constitutional Court that none of them received the minutes of the meeting, with the price-fixing content on the first page'.[1026] Since in earlier cartel cases even slight indications of such behaviour were typically sufficient for finding an infringement, many wonder whether this ruling of the Constitutional Court sheds new and unconventional light on the standard of proof that the Competition Agency has to meet in order to fine undertakings, and whether, as a result of this Constitutional Court decision, public enforcement of the Competition Agency will in future be harder and less efficient.[1027]

II. Commercial Courts

636. Claims for damages are decided before the competent commercial court. In these proceedings, the CPA applies.[1028] With regard to damage claims, the CA prescribes that when deciding on compensation for damages, the competent commercial court must take into account the decision of the Competition Agency or the decision of the European Commission.[1029] If such a decision has not been reached,

1024. *See* para. 634, *supra*.
1025. Judgment of the High Administrative Court of the Republic of Croatia of 22 April 2016, UsII-45/15-12.
1026. *See* Pecotić Kaufman, *supra* n. 1022.
1027. Wolf Theiss, *Croatian Constitutional Court Makes Proving Cartel Agreements More Difficult* (19 April 2018) https://www.lexology.com/library/detail.aspx?g=75963df2-a397-4e71-8107-bb3cf3141897 (accessed 2 Jul. 2018); *see also* J. Pecotić Kaufman, *The Croatian Constitutional Court Upholds the Judgment of the Administrative Court Confirming Its Previous Position on the Application of EU Competition Rules (Tisak)* e-Competition Bulletin no. 36693, Case Comment (2011) http://www.concurrences.com/en/page/article?id_article=36693 (accessed 2 Jul. 2018).
1028. Civil Procedure Act and Act on Amendments to the Civil Procedure Act (consolidated 2013).
1029. Article 69a(3) CA.

but the Competition Agency or the European Commission has opened the investigation, the commercial court may decide to proceed with its proceedings or to suspend the proceedings until the Competition Agency or the European Commission reach a valid decision.[1030] The commercial court also bears the obligation to inform the Competition Agency of any claim filed regarding the right to seek compensation for damages resulting from an infringement of competition law rules.[1031]

§2. Time Limits

637. The time limit to initiate an administrative dispute before the High Administrative Court against a Competition Agency's decision is thirty days from receipt of this decision.[1032]

638. A request for the extraordinary examination of the legality of final decisions may be filed by the State Attorney's Office of the Republic of Croatia within six months from the day the party receives notice of the final judgment from the High Administrative Court.[1033]

§3. Scope of Judicial Review

639. The extent of the review in competition cases before the High Administrative Court depends on two elements: (1) the contents of the claim; and (2) the legal boundaries prescribed by the CA.[1034] In connection with the first element, Article 31 of the Act of Administrative Disputes prescribes that '[t]he court shall decide within the boundaries of the claim, but is not bound by the grounds of the complaint'. This means that the court has authority to decide only on the issues the claimant has brought in its claim. In other words, the court is not entitled to address issues which the claimant has not raised in the claim. However, the court is not bound by the grounds of the lawsuit.[1035]

640. In an administrative procedure in Croatia, a claimant may ask the court: (1) to annul a contested Competition Agency decision because it is illegal; or (2) it may ask the court to decide on the merits. If the court establishes that a decision of the Competition Agency is null and void, the court must adopt the statement of claim

1030. Article 69a(4) CA.
1031. Article 69a(5) CA.
1032. Article 67(1) CA.
1033. Article 78(2) of the Administrative Disputes Act.
1034. Aksamovic, *supra* n. 1012, at 83.
1035. For example, if the ground for the claim is the misapplication or erroneous application of substantive provisions of competition law and the court finds that there have been no errors in the application of the substantive provisions of competition law, but, on the contrary, the court finds that during the procedure before the Competition Agency the procedural rights of the parties have been infringed, the court will annul the contested decision, but not for the reasons raised by the claimant, but for the reasons determined by the court during the proceeding. *See* D. Đerđa, M. Šikić, *Komentar Zakona o upravnim sporovima* 195 (Novi informator, 2012).

and declare the decision null and void.[1036] On the contrary, if the claimant requests that the court decide the claim on the merits, and if the court finds the claim justified, it must accept the claim, nullify the disputed decision and resolve the matter itself. This means that the court's decision will replace the Competition Agency's decision. Unlike in EU law, the court has authority to substitute its decision for the decision of the Competition Agency in all infringement actions, not just in those concerning fines, as is the case in EU law. However, so far the High Administrative Court in Croatia has never rendered such a decision.[1037]

641. Concerning the scope or intensity of judicial review, Article 68 of the CA provides that: '[t]he panel of judges of the High Administrative Court of the Republic of Croatia shall discuss and decide on the basis of the facts presented during the proceedings'. Therefore, the court is not entitled to determine new facts during the court proceeding. The plaintiff may not present new facts but it may propose new evidence relating to the facts which have been presented during the proceeding.[1038] New facts may be presented only under the condition that the plaintiff demonstrates that such evidence could not have been obtained or the facts could not have been known at the time of the proceedings.[1039] Such a regulatory model significantly limits the parties' rights to a fair trial. It certainly does not comply with the standard of full judicial review vis-à-vis the national competition authorities' decisions developed in the *Menarini* case'.[1040] Therefore, it may be expected that in the near or more distant future the compatibility of the standard of judicial review will be the subject of review in Croatian legislation.

1036. Aksamovic, *supra* n. 1004, at 83.
1037. *Ibid.*
1038. Article 68(2) CA.
1039. Article 68(3) CA.
1040. *See* M. Botta, A. Svetlicinii, *The Right of Fair Trial in Competition Law Proceedings: Quo vadis the Courts of the New EU Member States?* (9th ASCOLA Conference Warsaw 2014 on Procedural Fairness in Competition Proceedings, Centre for Antitrust and Regulatory Studies, University of Warsaw, 26–28 June 2014), available at http://www.ascola-conference-2014.wz.uw edu pl /conference_papers/BOTTA_SVETLICINII.pdf (accessed 2 Jul. 2018).

Selected Bibliography

Akšamović, D., 'Judicial Review in EU and Croatian Competition Cases: The Procedure and Intensity of Judicial Review'. In *EU Competition and State Aid Rules,* edited by V. Tomljenović et al. Springer, Berlin, Germany, 2018.

Aksamovic, D., Judicial review in competition cases in Croatia: Winning and losing arguments before the High Administrative Court of the Republic of Croatia, YEARBOOK OF ANTITRUST AND REGULATORY STUDIES, VOL. 2020, 13(22), p. 19.

Aksamovic, D., (Re) definiranje uloge Visokog upravnog suda Republike Hrvatske i Vrhovnog suda Republike Hrvatske u sporovima za zaštitu tržišnog natjecanja, in Pravo tržišnog natjecanja u Republici Hrvatskoj i Europskoj Uniji, Hrvatska akademija znanosti i umjetnosti, Zagreb, 2021., p 39 – 61.

Alonso, Juan B., 'Vertical Aspects of Mergers, Joint Ventures and Strategic Alliances'. In *Mergers & Acquisitions and Joint Ventures,* edited by B. Hawk. Fordham University School of Law, 2004.

Beherens, P., *The Extraterritorial Reach of EU Competition Law Revisited: The 'Effects Doctrine' Before the ECJ*, Discussion Paper No. 3/16 (Europa-Kolleg Hamburg, Institute for European Integration 2016).

Best Practices Cooperation Between EU National Competition Authorities in Merger Review (November 2001) available at http://ec.europa.eu/competition/ecn/nca_best_practices_merger_review_en.pdf.

Botta, M. & Svetlicinii, A., *The Right of Fair Trial in Competition Law Proceedings: Quo vadis the Courts of the New EU Member States?* 9th ASCOLA Conference Warsaw 2014 on Procedural Fairness in Competition Proceedings (Centre for Antitrust and Regulatory Studies, University of Warsaw, 26–28 June 2014) available at http://www.ascola-conference-2014.wz.uw.edu.pl/conference_papers/BOTTA_SVETLICINII.pdf.

Butorac Malnar V., 'Croatia'. In *Implementation of the EU Damages Directive in Central and Eastern European Countries*, edited by A. Piszcz. University of Warsaw: Faculty of Management Press, Warsaw, 2017.

Butorac Malnar, V., 'The Kone Case: A Missed Opportunity to Put the Standard of Causation under the Umbrella of the EU'. In *EU Competition and State Aid Rules Public and Private Enforcement,* edited by V. Tomljenovic et al. Series Europeanisation and Globalisation (3), Springer-Verlag, 2017.

Butorac Malnar V. & Kunda I., *EU Competition Law in the Digital Era: What to Tell About Intel.* 2 EU Law in Context – Adjustment to Membership and Challenges of the Enlargement, 2018.

Selected Bibliography

Butorac Malnar V., Mataija, M. & Petrović S., *National Report: Croatia, In Private Enforcement and Collective Redress in European Competition Law,* edited by G. Bándi et al. Wolters Kluwer, 2016.

Butorac Malnar, V. & Pecotić Kaufman, J. 'Ocjena koncentracija poduzetnika po kriteriju opadajućeg poslovanja u doba recesije'. *Zbornik Pravnog fakulteta u Zagrebu* 61, no. 4 (2011).

Butorac Malnar, V., Pecotić Kaufman, J. & Petrović, S. *Pravo tržišnog natjecanja, Manualia Universitas Studiorum Zagrabiensis.* Pravni fakultet Sveučilišta u Zagrebu, 2013.

Büyüksagis, E., 'Directive on Antitrust Damages Actions'. *Schweizerische Zeitschrift für Wirtschaftsrecht* 1 2015.

Cox, Arthur, *Austria Asphalt: ECJ Clarifies the Application of the EU Merger Regulation to Joint Ventures* (30 November 2017) available at https://www.lexology.com/library/detail.aspx?g=63c83009-81a5-4e78-9246-36da6ad08326.

Croatian Bureau of Statistics, *A Statistical Portrait of Croatia in the European Union* (1 July 2013).

Croatian Bureau of Statistics, *Census of Population, Households and Dwellings 2011, Population by Sex and Age,* Statistical Reports (Croatian Bureau of Statistics 2013).

Croatian Bureau of Statistics, *Census of Population, Households and Dwellings 2011, Population by Citizenship, Ethnicity, Religion and Mother Tongue*, Statistical Reports (Croatian Bureau of Statistics 2013).

Croatian Bureau of Statistics, *Census of Population, Households and Dwellings 2011, Population According to Education Features*, Statistical Reports (Croatian Bureau of Statistics 2016).

Croatian Bureau of Statistics, *Croatia in Figures* (Croatian Bureau of Statistics 2016) http://www.dzs.hr/Hrv_Eng/CroInFig/croinfig_2016.pdf.

Croatian Chamber of Economy, *Croatia Your Business Partner* (Croatian Chamber of Economy 2016) http://www.hgk.hr/croatia-your-business-partner-najava.

Croatian Competition Agency, *Annual Report for 2005*, http://www.aztn.hr/uploads/documents/eng/documents/AR/Annual_Report_of_the_Croatian_Competition_Agency_for_2005.pdf.

Croatian Competition Agency, *Annual Report for 2008*, http://www.aztn.hr/uploads/documents/eng/documents/AR/Annual_Report_of_the_Croatian_Competition_Agency_for_2008.pdf.

Croatian Competition Agency, *Summary Annual Report for 2014*, http://www.aztn.hr/ea/wp-content/uploads/2015/05/Annual-Report-of-the-Croatian-Competition-Agency-for-2014.pdf.

Croatian Competition Agency, *Summary Annual Report for 2015*, http://www.aztn.hr/ea/wp-content/uploads/2015/05/Summary-GI-2015-ENG.pdf.

Croatian Competition Agency, *Annual Report for 2016*, http://www.aztn.hr/ea/wp-content/uploads/2015/05/Summary-GI-2016-ENG.pdf.

Cseres, K. 'Comparing Laws in the Enforcement of EU and National Competition Laws'. *European Journal of Legal Studies* 3, no. 1 (2010).

Čuveljak, J. 'Zastoj i prekid zastare'. *Hrvatska pravna revija* 3, no. 4 (2003).

De La T. & Fournier E. *Evidence, Proof and Judicial Review in EU Competition Law.* Elgar Competition Law and Practice, Cheltenham, Uk, Northampton, USA, 2017.

Driessen-Reilly, M. *Private Damages in EU Competition Law and Arbitration – A Changing Landscape.* Arbitration International, 2015 available at http://dx.doi.org/10.1093/arbint/aiv007.

Đerđa, D. & Šikić, M. *Komentar Zakona o upravnim sporovima.* Novi informator, 2012.

ECN Working Group Cooperation Issues and Due Process Decision-Making Powers (Report, 31 October 2012) available at http://ec.europa.eu/competition/ecn/decision_making_powers_report_en.pdf.

Ernst, H. 'General Introduction'. In *Introduction to the Law of Croatia*, edited by T. Josipović. Wolters Kluwer, 2014.

European Commission, Press Release: *Commission Prohibits Heidelberg Cement and Schwenk's Proposed Takeover of Cemex Croatia*, (5 April 2017) available at http://europa.eu/rapid/press-release_IP-17-883_en.htm.

Fabijanić Gagro S. & Vukas B. 'The Path of the Former Yugoslav Countries to the European Union: From Integration to Disintegration and Back'. *Maastricht Journal of European and Comparative Law* 12, no. 2 (2012).

Galič, A. 'Disclosure of Documents in Private Antitrust Enforcement Litigation'. *Yearbook of Antitrust and Regulatory Studies* 8, no. 12 (2015).

Glossary of Competition Terms (Institute of Competition Law n.d.) available at https://www.concurrences.com/en/droit-de-la-concurrence/glossary-of-competition-terms/Effects-doctrine?lang=en

Gorenc, V. et al. *Komentar Zakona o obveznim odnosima.* Narodne novine, 2014.

Harašić Ž. 'Autoritet i sud'. *Zbornik radova Pravnog fakulteta u Splitu* 52, no. 2 (2015).

Howard, A. 'Too Little, Too Late? The European Commission's Legislative Proposals on Anti-trust Damages Actions'. *Journal of European Competition Law & Practice* 4, no. 6 (2013) available at http://www.aztn.hr/ea/wp-content/uploads/2015/05/Summary-GI-2016-ENG.pdf.

ICN, *Merger Guidelines Workbook* (2006) available at http://www.internationalcompetitionnetwork.org/uploads/library/doc321.pdf.

International Conference on the Occasion of the 20th Anniversary of the Croatian Competition Agency, Zagreb, Croatia (15 December 2017) available at http://www.aztn.hr/panel-o-sudskoj-zastiti-u-predmetima-zastite-trzisnog-natjecanja-dilema-o-izravnoj-nadleznosti-vus-a/

Jelinić, Z. 'Instrumenti zaštite kolektivnih interesa i prava u hrvatskom pravu – između stvarne potrebe za jačanjem vladavine prava i efikasnog pravosuđa te mogućih nesnalaženja'. *Godišnjak Akademije pravnih znanosti Hrvatske* 5, no. 1 (March 2014).

Jelušić, M. & Šarin, D. 'Rule of Law and the Role of the Constitutional Court of the Republic of Croatia in Enforcing Administrative and Administrative Court Rulings'. *Zbornik radova Pravnog fakulteta u Splitu* 52, no. 1 (2015).

Kocmut, M. *The Role of Efficiency Consideration under the EU Merger Control*, Working Paper (L) 09/05 (University of Oxford Centre for Competition Law and Policy 2005) available at https://www.law.ox.ac.uk/sites/files/oxlaw/cclp_l_09-05.pdf.

List, M. & Butorac Malnar, V. 'SGEI in Croatia: The Legal Framework for Economic Necessity'. *European State Aid Law Quarterly* 15, no. 4 (2016).

Merola, M. & Armati, L. 'The Binding Effect of NCA Decisions under the Damages Directive: Rationale and Practical Implications'. *Rivista Italiana di Antitrust* 1 (2016).

Ministry of Culture (Croatia), State Institute for Nature Protection, *Protected Areas in Croatia*, available at http://www.dzzp.hr/eng/protected-areas/protected-areas-in-croatia-68.html.

Mlikotin Tomić D. & Pecotić Kaufman J. 'Evolution of Cartel Practice in Croatia'. In *Economic Integration, Competition and Cooperation/Integrations Economiques, Concurrence et Cooperation, Research Monograph,* edited by V. Kandžija & A. Kumar. University of Rijeka, Faculty of Economics, 2010, available at http://bib.irb.hr/datoteka/390283.evolution_of_cartel_practice_in_Croatia.pdf.

Moisejevas, R. 'The Damages Directive and Consensual Approach to Antitrust Enforcement'. *Yearbook of Antitrust and Regulatory Studies* 8, no. 12 (2015).

Mosso, C.E. 'Non-horizontal Mergers: A European Perspective'. *Fordham International Law Journal* 31, no. 5 (2007).

Nourry, A., Harrison, D. & Clifford, C. *Transactions and Practices: EU Joint Ventures.* Practical Law UK, Thomson Reuters, 2018, available at https://uk.practicallaw.thomsonreuters.com/1-107-3702?transitionType=Default&contextData=(sc.Default)&firstPage=true&comp=pluk&bhcp=1.

Novoselec, P. & Vidlička Roksandić S. 'Gospodarska kaznena djela u novom Kaznenom Zakonu'. *Hrvatski ljetopis za kazneno pravo i praksu* 17, no. 2 (2010).

OECD, *Definition of Transaction for the Purpose of Merger Control Review*, DAF/COMP(2013)25 (2013) available at http://www.oecd.org/daf/competition/Merger-control-review-2013.pdf.

Pais, S.O. & Piszcz, A. 'Package on Actions for Damages Based on Breaches of EU Competition Rules: Can One Size Fit All?'. *Yearbook of Antitrust and Regulatory Studies* 7, no. 10 (2014).

Pavlović, M. 'Značaj tužbe za zaštitu kolektivnih interesa i prava'. *Zbornik radova Pravnog fakulteta u Splitu* 52, no. 3 (2015).

Pecotić, J., *Zajednički pothvat (joint venture) u pravu tržišnog natjecanja* (Sinergija 2005).

Pecotić Kaufman J. *Fight Against Cartels in Croatia: More Than a Decade of Enforcement Practice.* GCP: The Online Magazine for Global Competition Policy, June 2009, available at http://bib.irb.hr/datoteka/418374.Kaufman-JUNE-09_1_.pdf.

Pecotić Kaufman, J. *On the development of (not so) new competition systems—findings from an empirical study on Croatia, Journal of Antitrust Enforcement*, 2021; jnab018, https://doi.org/10.1093/jaenfo/jnab018

Pecotić Kaufman, J. *The Croatian Constitutional Court Upholds the Judgment of the Administrative Court Confirming Its Previous Position on the Application of*

EU Competition Rules (Tisak) e-Competition, No. 36693, Case Comment (2011) available at http://www.concurrences.com/en/page/article?id_article=36693.

Pecotić Kaufman, J. *Some Remarks on Judicial Control Issues in Connection to Recent Cartel Cases in Croatia: Shifting Trends and Appropriate Legal Test*, Speech held at the Annual FTC South-East Europe Workshop on Economic Issues in Competition Law, (11 September 2017) available at http://www.aztn.hr/seminar-aztn-a-i-ftc-a-o-primjeni-ekonomskih-alata-u-pravu-trzisnog-natjecanja/.

Pecotić Kaufman, J. 'Control of Mergers in the Grocery Retail Market in Croatia'. In *Challenges for the Trade in Central and Southeast Europe*, edited by S. Renko & B. Knežević, Emerald Group Publishing Limited, 2013.

Pecotić Kaufman, J. & Butorac Malnar, V. 'The Interaction Between EU Regulatory Implants and the Existing Croatian Legal Order in Competition Law'. In *Economic Evidence in EU Competition Law*, edited by M. Kovač & A. Vandenberghe, Intersentia, 2016.

Pecotić Kaufman, J. & Slijepčević S. 'Koncentracije poduzetnika i mjerodavno tržište: Pravni i ekonomski aspekti'. *Zbornik Pravnog fakulteta u Zagrebu* 60, no. 2 (2010).

Pecotić Kaufman, J. 'Sankcioniranje fizičkih osoba za povrede tržišnog natjecanja, pokajnički program i novi čl. 65.a ZZTN-a', *Zbornik Pravnog fakulteta u Zagrebu*, 2022, pp. 00-00.

Pecotić Kaufman, J. & Šimić Banović, R. 'The Role of (In)formal Governance and Culture in a National Competition System: A Case of a Post- Socialist Economy', (2021), 44, *World Competition,* Issue 1, pp. 81-108.

Petrasincu, A. 'The Treatment of Vertical and Conglomerate Mergers in the EU: The EU Guidelines on the Assessment of Non-horizontal Mergers'. *Georgetown Journal of International Law* 40 (2009).

Petrović, S., *Tržišno natjecanje u praksi Ustavnog suda Republike Hrvatske – osvrt na recentne odluke Ustavnog suda* (U-III-925/2017/'Presečki'/i U-III-2791/2016, U-III-6196, U-III-2826/2016/'Zaštitari'/) (12 June 2018) available at https://hdpptn.hr/wp-content/uploads/2018/06/usud-tr%C5%BE-natj.pdf.

Redfern, A. & Hunter, M. *The Law and Practice of International Commercial Arbitration.* 3rd ed. Sweet & Maxwell, 1999.

Reppo, M. *EU Private Competition Law Enforcement: Rethinking the Impact of the Passing-on Defence and Indirect Purchaser Standing.* JAEM01 Master Thesis, Faculty of Law, Lund University, 2015.

Robertson, C. *How the European Union Functions in 23 Languages Council of the EU.* Legal Service, Directorate for the Quality of Legislation, SYNAPS 28, 2013 available at https://brage.bibsys.no/xmlui/bitstream/handle/11250/2393842/Robertson_28.pdf?sequence=1.

Rostaš-Beroš, L. 'Nadležnost upravnih sudova u zaštiti tržišnog natjecanja'. *Zbornik Pravnog fakulteta Sveučilišta u Rijeci* 35, no. 1 (2014).

Slaughter and May, *The EU Merger Regulation: An Overview of the European Merger Control Rules* (January 2018) available at https://www.slaughterandmay.com/media/64572/the-eu-merger-regulation.pdf.

Staničić, M. *Dugo putovanje Hrvatske u Europsku uniju.* Naklada Ljevak, 2005.

Selected Bibliography

Šikić, M. 'Pravomoćnost, konačnost i izvršnost u upravnom postupku'. *Zbornik Pravnog fakulteta Sveučilišta u Rijeci* 33, no. 1 (2012).

Tot I., 'Kazna zatvora za kaznena djela protiv slobode tržišnog natjecanja u hrvatskom pravu de lege ferenda'. In *Pravo tržišnog natjecanja- novine u hrvatskom i europskom zakonodavstvu i praksi*, edited by J. Pecotić Kaufman ed. Ekonomski fakultet Zagreb, 2012.

Triva, S. et al. *Građansko parnično procesno pravo.* Narodne novine, 1986.

Triva, S. & M. Dika. *Građansko parnično procesno pravo.* 7th ed. Narodne novine, 2004.

UNCTAD, *Trade and Development Board, Challenges in Design of Merger Control Regime for Young and Small Competition Authorities,* TD/B/C.I/CLP/45 (26 April 2017) available at http://unctad.org/meetings/en/SessionalDocuments/ciclpd45_en.pdf.

Vukas, B. 'The Process of the Establishment of the Independence of the Republic of Croatia from the Perspective of International Law'. *Review of Croatian History* 7, no. 1 (2011).

Wolf Theiss, *Croatian Constitutional Court Makes Proving Cartel Agreements More Difficult* (19 April 2018) available at https://www.lexology.com/library/detail.aspx?g=75963df2-a397-4e71-8107-bb3cf3141897.

Index

The numbers here refer to paragraph numbers.

Abuse of dominant position, 192–194, 436
Access to the file, 554–557
Act on Antitrust Damages, 41, 268–308
Adjudicative power, 214–226
Administrative procedure, 529–641
Agency agreement, 154
Agreement, 43, 74–78, 180–183, 325–426
Anticompetitive effects, 64, 65, 125, 178, 345, 352, 373, 407, 468, 471, 508, 509, 512, 519, 630
Appeal, 57, 243, 539, 621, 622
Association of undertakings, 48, 64, 74, 144, 145, 147, 180, 189, 241, 272, 326, 327, 334, 351, 377, 387, 529, 536, 598, 631, *see also* Trade association

Balancing test, 112
Bid-rigging, 252, 317, 319, 320, 324, 327, 359, 360, 364, 369
Block Exemption, 42, 45, 76, 78, 215, 333, 344, 358, 363, 378–384, 386, 407, 412, 418, 420
Block Exemption Regulations (BERs), 42, 44, 69, 75, 386, 389, 402, 405, 410, 416, 420, 422–426

Cartel, 256, 325–371
Clearance, 606–616
Collective rights management, 90, 140, 444, 494
Collective bargaining agreements, 130
Collusion, 366–371
Commitment decision, 223–225
Competition Act, 29, 39, 335, 343, 385
Complaints, 532–535
Composition, 209–212
Concentrations, 93–108, 195–204, 507–528
Concerted practice, 180–183
Conditions and obligations, 223, 607–616
Conglomerate mergers, 519–521
Constitution, 38
Constitutional court, 20, 25, 26, 31, 38, 325, 352, 633–635
Consumer sales promotion, 471
Cooperation agreements, 378–385
Coordinated effects, 116, 119, 588
Criminal sanctions, 317–320
Croatian Competition Agency, 29, 209–214

Daily penalties, 254–255
Damages, 41, 268–308
Dawn raid, 213, 248, 254, 354, 376, 400, 415, 540–542, 544–549, 622
Decisions by associations of undertakings, 48, 64, 74
De minimis, 64–73, 77, 78, 110, 186, 329, 391–395
Derogations, 59, 62, 63
Discounts, *see* Rebates
Discrimination, 442–451
Distribution agreements, 54, 402–421
Disclosure of evidence, 290–295, 299–302
Dispute resolution, 306–308
Divestiture, 259, 608
Dominant position, 79–92, 173–179, 427–506
ECN+ Directive, 36, 209, 226, 241, 147, 251

Economic analysis, 339, 345, 481
Effect, 64–73
Effects doctrine, 51, 55
Effect on trade, 31, 39, 184

Index

Efficiency, 121–123, 125, 219, 223, 319, 435, 545, 557, 610, 613
European Merger Control Regulation, 42, 44, 205, 208, 209
Excessive pricing, 429
Exchange of information, 183, 353, 373, 550, 557
Exclusionary practices, 452–506
Exclusive distribution, 403– 405
Exclusive dealing agreements, 406
Exploitative practices, 427–451
Express direct collusion, 339
Extraterritoriality, 52

Failing firm defence, 107, 515, 610, 612
Fines, 231–256
Fining, 226
Fixed prices, 420, 631
Franchising, 421

General Sector Inquiry, 529–530
Group boycott, 365

Hard–core restraints, –340, 343
Hearing, 554–557, 562–566
High Administrative Court, 620–632
Horizontal agreement, 325—386
Horizontal effects, 396, 517
Horizontal mergers, 510–513

Individual exemption, 151, 412, 414, 426, 526, 527
Innovation limitation, 363–364
Interim measures
  administrative procedure, 260–263
  civil procedure, 309–316
International coordination, 619
Investigation, ex officio, 531
Investigative powers, 540–548

Joint bidding, 371
Joint dominance, 85, 445, 446
Joint production, 382
Joint purchasing, 383
Joint selling, 384–385
Joint ventures, 205–207, 522–528
Judicial review, 620, 639–641
Judiciary, 13, 19, 50

Know-how licensing, 425–426

Liability, joint and severable, 270, 277, 279–282
Limitation periods, 245, 269, 270, 275–278, 306, 308
Loyalty rebates, 477

Market allocation, 330, 337, 358–362
Market extension merger, 518
Market Investigation, *see* General Sector Inquiry
Market power, 173–179
Market share, 588–589
Measures and conditions, 107, 223, 257, 260, 511
Media, 98–103
Mergers, 113–125, 510–521, 567–619
Merger control, 567–619
Minimum prices, 348, 350, 351, 392, 393, 400, 630, 631, 635

Negligible effect, 66, 68, 72, 73
Network industries, 58, 617
Notification, 552–553, 567–619
Null and void, 74, 265–267
Nullity, 265–267

Object, 64, 74, 366–371
Oligopolistic market, 85, 349, 445

Parallel behaviour, 338
Parliament, 14–16
Passing-on, 285–288
Patent licensing, 423
Precedents, 49, 50
Predation, 452–463
Preliminary market investigation, 529, 530, 552
Price-fixing, 333–357
Price squeeze, 503 – 506
Product extension merger, 518
Production limitation, 363– 364
Prosecutors, 213, 322–323
Public tender, 359, 360, 369, 371, 462, 608
Public utilities, 60–63

Quantification of harm, 283–284
Quantitative rebates, 487

Rebates, 476–494
Recommended prices, 395, 410, 415

Recoupment, 454, 458
Referral, 581, 593, 619
Refusal to deal, 495–502
Relevant market, 155–172
Relevant geographic market, 169–171
Relevant product market, 159–168
Request for information, 234, 536–539
Resale price maintenance (RPM), 70, 391, 395, 398, 411, 420
Research and development, 379
Restriction of competition, 64, 74, 184–191, 340, 343, 344, 360, 368, 412, 426, 488

SAA, 28, 30, 31, 190
Sector rules, 97, 105, 187, 348, 437
Sector–specific regulation, 187
Selective distribution, 409–420
Services of general economic interest, 62, 63
Settlement, 256
SIEC, 95, 98, 113
Single branding, 386, 407, 413
Single economic entity, 129, 141, 148, 149, 151–153, 469
Specialization agreements, 380
Spill-over effects, 448
Standardization agreements, 381
Standing, 266, 289
Statement of objections, 223, 532, 539, 554–556, 558–561, 565, 602–605, 607, 616
State–owned enterprises, 60–63
Structural remedies, 259, 608
Substantive test, 95, 113

Tacit agreement, 181, 328, 344, 348, 397
Tacit collusion, 116
Technology licensing, 422
Temporal markets, 172
Trade association, 142, 143, 146, 189, 325, 336, 351–353, 359, 361, 368, 376, 589, *see also* Association of undertakings
Trademark licensing, 424
Trustee, 614
Turnover calculation, 582–587
Turnover thresholds, 56, 99, 581
Tying, 464–475

Undertaking, 79–92, 126–154, 427–506, 607–616

Vertical agreement, 53, 54, 67–69, 78, 267, 386–426
Vertical merger, 507, 514–517

Index

www.ingramcontent.com/pod-product-compliance
Lightning Source LLC
Chambersburg PA
CBHW071438230926
51846CB00001B/276
* 9 7 8 9 4 0 3 5 1 6 2 6 4 *